BOUNDARIES AND BOUNDARY VIOLATIONS IN PSYCHOANALYSIS

BOUNDARIES AND BOUNDARY VIOLATIONS IN PSYCHOANALYSIS

GLEN O. GABBARD, M.D.
EVA P. LESTER, M.D.

BasicBooks
A Division of HarperCollins*Publishers*

The authors gratefully acknowledge permission to reprint portions of the following material:

Gabbard, G. O. (1995). Countertransference: The emerging common ground. *International Journal of Psycho-Analysis, 76*, 475–485. Portions reprinted with permission in Chapter 7.

Gabbard, G. O. (1995). The early history of boundary violations in psychoanalysis. *Journal of the American Psychoanalytic Association, 43*. Portions reprinted with permission in Chapter 5.

Gabbard, G. O. (1995). Transference and countertransference in the psychotherapy of therapists charged with sexual misconduct. *Journal of Psychotherapy Practice and Research, 4*, 10–17. Portions reprinted with permission in Chapter 10.

Library of Congress Cataloging-in-Publication Data
Gabbard, Glen O.
    Boundaries and boundary violations in psychoanalysis / Glen O. Gabbard and
  Eva P. Lester.
      p.   cm.
    Includes bibliographical references and index.
    ISBN 0–465–09577–1
    1. Psychotherapist and patient.   2. Psychoanalysts—Professional ethics.
  3. Acting out (Psychology).   I. Lester, Eva P.   II. Title.
  RC480.8.G33   1996
  616.89'17—dc20   95-30407
                                                                              CIP

95 96 97 98 ❖/HC 9 8 7 6 5 4 3 2 1

Contents

Contents

Foreword

D RS. GABBARD AND LESTER herein offer what is truly an original piece of work; I know of no other book that addresses the long-standing, very real problem of boundaries in psychoanalysis.

It has been generally known that violations of boundaries in psychoanalysis, although much less frequent than in other psychotherapeutic encounters, are not uncommon. But to know about something and to attempt to deal with it are two very different matters. Drs. Gabbard and Lester do their profession proud by dealing with it.

Some may object that, in view of the criticism psychoanalysis is subjected to from outside its portals, to criticize it from within is injudicious. But shoving a problem under a rug is hardly in keeping with psychoanalytic principles! This book analyzes the problem and helps to move toward its improvement.

That the authors have been able to treat so sensational a subject without sensationalism is noteworthy. They approach boundaries and boundary violations historically, offering careful documentation from both the past and the present. The boundaries they have in mind are twofold: the boundary between the patient and analyst in the analytic

situation, and the boundary between the ego and the repressed unconscious in both patient and analyst.

The authors conceptualize these boundaries using a metaphor of
physical density: They write of thinness and thickness of such boundaries. This book is timely in that recent trends have been toward
regarding the analyst as participant observer in the analytic situation,
subject to countertransference much as the analysand is subject to
transference, rather than as an omniscient, detached tabula rasa. And
the book is a timely reminder of the power and ubiquity of the fantasies
and taboos of the oedipal situation.

Drs. Gabbard and Lester not only call attention to a serious problem,
they also suggest the dynamics responsible for transgressing boundaries. Furthermore, they emphasize the need for forestalling such
transgressions through psychoanalytic education. In their description
of the types of pathology most frequently encountered in analysts who
transgress sexual boundaries with their patients, Gabbard and Lester
differentiate the rare cases of psychotic illness in the analyst from the
more frequent cases of psychopathic and paraphilic enactments,
"lovesickness," and masochistic acting out. Their comprehensive
description of these conditions is convincing and points to the frequency, in cases of boundary violations, of narcissistic pathology in the
analyst. Their "lovesickness" category reflects narcissistic pathology,
perhaps not of the severity involved in the psychopathic and paraphilic
groups, and holds forth an intrinsically good prognosis.

Drs. Gabbard and Lester remind us of the unique characteristics of
the psychoanalytic frame, geared to facilitate the most complete and
uninhibited communication of intimate personal experiences on the
part of the patient. In the process, this frame recreates symbolically the
nature of the oedipal relationship. The analytic setting thus reproduces
the incest taboo, primal oedipal seduction, and the symbolic threat of
castration and death related to the violation of this taboo. Symbolically,
the oedipal relationship is reproduced within a frame conducive to the
full exploration of its unconscious fantasies, and the permanence of the
prohibition against direct gratification of oedipal longings is
reasserted.

The possibility of exploring these profound human conflicts within
the safe context of the analytic situation is the counterpart to the temp-

tation to enactment of oedipal fantasies on the part of the patient and as part of the analyst's countertransference as well. Adding to this temptation the potential gratification of narcissistic omnipotence in breaking the incest taboo—enacting the fantasy of an omnipotent invasion of and triumph over the intimacy of the parental couple—results in a severe threat to the situation posed by narcissistic pathology in patients as well as unresolved narcissistic pathology in analysts.

Gabbard and Lester skillfully describe how the isolation of the analyst, severe losses in his life, and acute crises involving narcissistic lesions may activate what they call the syndrome of "lovesickness."

The theoretical frame provided by Gabbard and Lester lends itself to further analysis of the preconditions for analytic work in terms of the "thickness" or "thinness" of both the analyst's internal boundaries (with her dynamic unconscious) and her external boundaries (within the intersubjectivity of the psychoanalytic situation). One might argue that the capacity for psychoanalytic empathy implies both "thickness" in the external boundary, in terms of a firm maintenance of the analyst in his therapeutic role, and an optimal "thinness" in the internal boundary, that is, the openness to his unconscious processes and the freedom to explore his countertransference. Or it might be argued that the "thickness" of the analyst's internal boundaries in terms of an appropriate control over her instinctual needs, matched with a particular external "thinness," that is, openness to the interplay of projective identifications in transference and countertransference, may facilitate an empathy with the patient without the temptations of regressive enactments. In any case, various characterological dispositions of the analyst may protect him from boundary violations by particular combinations of "thickness" and "thinness" in the sense in which Gabbard and Lester define these terms.

The authors' recommendations about prevention and management of boundary violations are particularly thought provoking and stimulating. They stress the importance of exploring the ethical dimension of the psychoanalytic profession as part of candidates' training experiences and the importance of facilitating an honest exploration of erotic countertransferences. I also have observed that, to the extent that an atmosphere of discouragement of open exploration of erotic countertransference prevails in the psychoanalytic institute, the danger for uncontrolled or uncontrollable boundary violations seems to increase.

Regarding the optimal management of rumored or actually confirmed boundary violations within the setting of a psychoanalytic institute or society, Drs. Gabbard and Lester thoughtfully point to the many
complications and difficulties involved. I would add to their discussion
the problems created by our particularly litigious culture—the temptation to exploit redress of grievances for financial gains—and how this
process may corrupt both victims and victimizers and contribute to
transforming honest efforts to deal with boundary violations into a
bureaucratic nightmare. I believe we have to protect our patients from
unethical practitioners and to protect our practitioners from the acting
out of psychopathic transferences. To do justice to individual cases
means to combine a clear set of ethical standards with an institutional
flexibility that avoids psychopathic exploitation as well as a paralyzing
bureaucratic entanglement of the institution. Above all, the preventive
measures contemplated by the authors, and the honest acknowledgment of this painful problem represented by their present work, should
help us to reduce if not eliminate this unfortunate by-product of psychoanalysis, which can turn this potentially highly effective treatment
into a "radioactive" one.

Otto F. Kernberg, M.D.*

*Director, Personality Disorders Institute, The New York Hospital-Cornell
Medical Center, Westchester Division; Professor of Psychiatry, Cornell
University Medical College; Training and Supervising Analyst, Columbia
University Center for Psychoanalytic Training and Research.

Introduction

THE NINETEENTH-CENTURY British poet Dinah Maria Craik (1859) once noted:

> Oh, the comfort, the inexpressible comfort of feeling safe with a person, having neither to weigh thoughts nor measure words, but pouring them all right out, just as they are, chaff and grain together; certain that a faithful hand will take and sift them, keep what is worth keeping, and then with the breath of kindness blow the rest away. (p. 169)

Craik seems unwittingly to have anticipated developments that took place shortly thereafter in a distant Continental city. Freud's "discovery" of free association and the analyst's attentiveness within a safe and accepting analytic setting eventually created the optimal conditions for that talking cure for which Craik was unconsciously longing.

This climate of safety, it is now understood, rests primarily on the specific "frame" agreed on by the two participants, a frame whose integrity guarantees the smooth flow of interactions within the analytic space. Although psychological interpenetration of the two subjectivities occurs in this space, there is little physical contact beyond an occasional handshake. As a result of this extraordinary arrangement, operating within a specific set of boundaries, a good deal of self-discovery is forged in the smithy of the psychoanalytic process.

In recent years, however, the psychoanalytic profession has become aware of a disconcerting set of problems. Not all analyses are safe; not all analytic boundaries are maintained. We do not know the exact scope of the problem, but in the greater Boston area alone, more than 400 women have joined a support group designed for patients who have been sexually exploited by their analyst or therapist. The boundary violations involving sexual relations between analyst and patient are among the most egregious, but many others are also cause for concern.

While violations of analytic boundaries are as old as the psychoanalytic profession, only recently has organized psychoanalysis begun to address these problems. This sea change in our attitude was influenced by the changing view of countertransference and by the increasing understanding of the analyst's contribution to the processes taking place in analysis. This book is in part an outgrowth of this shift in psychoanalytic thought.

The psychoanalytic concept of boundaries did not begin with the notion of boundary violations in clinical practice. From Freud's early work on the oceanic feeling to our current interest in the subject, the concept of boundaries has been the topic of much theorizing. Paul Federn, a prominent ego psychologist, struggled with the concepts of inner and outer boundaries: the former separating the ego from unconscious fantasy and the drives, and the latter seen as a kind of peripheral sense organ and tester of reality. Object relations theorists like Jacobson wrote of boundaries as the demarcation between self and object representations. Recently, modern researchers such as Ernest Hartmann, with the use of experimental tools and both psychoanalytic and neurophysiological tenets, have elaborated further on inner and outer boundaries in the mind as a specific dimension of the personality.

To some extent, then, conceptual issues about boundaries and the clinical aspects of boundary violations in psychoanalysis represent two somewhat separate but related levels of discourse: (1) a theoretical view of the nature of boundaries in the mind and their relevance to fundamental issues in the analytic process, such as free association and dream recall, and (2) the clinical assessment of specific enactments in analysis involving the crossing and transgression of both inner and interpersonal boundaries.

In this volume we examine both discourses in detail. Overlap occurs in some areas but not in others. Indeed, one of the contributions we hope to make in this collaborative effort is to identify useful intersections between the traditional use of the concept of boundaries in psychoanalysis and the more contemporary concerns about violations of interpersonal and specific analytic boundaries in clinical practice.

The book is organized in such a way that an examination of boundaries precedes our discussion of boundary violation. Chapters 1 and 2 summarize the psychoanalytic literature on boundaries, in terms of both structure and process. Chapter 3 is an attempt to conceptualize three related constructs: the analytic frame, analytic boundaries, and the analytic object. Chapter 4 reviews the literature on gender differences in boundaries.

Chapter 5 begins our formal discussion of boundary violations by tracing the early history of such behavior within the psychoanalytic profession. Chapters 6 and 7 focus on a psychoanalytic understanding of boundary violations, sexual and nonsexual, respectively. Chapter 8 discusses the murky area of posttermination boundaries, with particular emphasis on the fate of the transference. Chapter 9 looks at supervisory boundaries, and Chapter 10 presents institutional responses to boundary violations and possible preventive measures.

This project raised some formidable challenges in presenting clinical material. Writing about colleagues is always fraught with difficulties, but presenting data about colleagues with serious boundary transgressions is even more problematic. We have dealt with the problem of preserving confidentiality and anonymity in two ways. In some cases, we have chosen to disguise individual identities by creating composite cases that capture the major psychological themes relevant to our discussion. In other cases, we have obtained written permission from the therapists and analysts we have treated after they have carefully reviewed the disguised case material pertaining to them. We hope the reader will share our view that the expanded understanding of boundary transgressions provided by clinical data warrants the use of delicate material for presentation.

Many people have assisted us with the preparation of this book. We are grateful to Joyce Davidson Gabbard and Murray D. Lester for their patience and support throughout the hectic months of writing. We also appreciate the assistance of Stephen Francoeur and Jo Ann Miller at Basic Books for their guidance throughout the course of the project. John Kerr's and Peter Gruenberg's comments on portions of the book were helpful, and we are particularly indebted to Otto Kernberg for his gracious agreement to write a foreword and for his thoughtful critique. Finally, we owe a special acknowledgment to Faye Schoenfeld for her meticulous typing and editing of the manuscript and her careful checking of references.

GG

EL

BOUNDARIES AND BOUNDARY VIOLATIONS IN PSYCHOANALYSIS

CHAPTER 1

The Concept of Boundaries in Psychoanalysis

FROM PAUL FEDERN AND EDITH JACOBSON to Ernest Hartmann and the recent writers on boundary violations in interpersonal transactions, the concept of *ego boundaries* has remained a pivotal, albeit vaguely defined, idea. The theoretical elaborations and clinical applications of the concept have gone through periods of focused interest followed by periods of relative neglect in the psychoanalytic literature.

The *American Heritage Dictionary* defines *boundary* as "usually applied geographically to a precisely defined terminating line of a country, city or the like." The terms *limit* and *boundary* are interchangeable in the physicalistic sense indicating "an extent beyond which an activity or function cannot or should not take place." Beyond this concrete, physicalistic definition, the term *boundary* has been used in a figurative sense to denote abstract closeness or similarity but not identity between two ideas, concepts, theoretical positions, or other such formulations.

In his early writings, Sigmund Freud used the term *boundary* in the figurative sense. As quoted by William Grossman (1992), Freud wrote the following in a letter to Wilhelm Fliess discussing the function of memory:

> Our psychic mechanism has come into being by a process of stratification: the material present in the form of memory traces being subjected from time to time to a *rearrangement* . . . to a *retranscription*. . . . Memory is present not once but several times over . . . for the paths leading from the periphery . . . the successive registrations represent the psychic achievement of successive epochs of life. At the boundary of such epochs a translation of the psychic material [takes] place. I explain the peculiarities of the psychoneuroses by supposing that such a translation has not taken place. (p. 40)

As Grossman (1992) noted, throughout his work Freud thought of boundaries as existing between levels of a hierarchy. *Translation*, for Freud, was one of the relations that defined the concept of boundary: "That is, the boundary is a conceptual boundary characterized by the different organizations of the systems so that one must be translated into the other" (p. 41).

Freud understood the drives as concepts that relate to and define the boundary, or the frontier, between the mental and the somatic. In "Instincts and Their Vicissitudes" (1915a), he wrote the following:

> Considering mental life from a *biological* point of view, an "instinct" appears to us as a concept on the *frontier* [italics added] between the mental and the somatic, as a physical representative of the stimuli originating from within the organism and reaching the mind, as a measure of the demand made upon the mind for work in consequence of its connection with the body. (pp. 121–122)

Freud (1913a) also said, "We cannot help regarding the term 'instinct' as a concept on the frontier between the spheres of psychology and biology" (p. 182). As Grossman (1992) further observed, Freud saw psychoanalysis itself as a boundary science. Discussing its claim to scientific status, Freud (1913a) stated that "psycho-analysis acts as an intermediary between biology and psychology" (p. 182).

Following the elaboration of the structural theory, and probably reflecting Federn's (1952) work on ego boundaries, Freud (1930) used the concept in a more specific way by stating in "Civilization and Its Discontents" that

> pathology has made us acquainted with a great number of states in which the boundary lines between the ego and the external world are uncertain or in which they are actually drawn incorrectly. There are cases in which parts of a person's body, even portions of his own mental life—his perceptions, thoughts and feelings—appear alien to him and as not belonging to his ego. . . . Thus even the feeling of our own ego is subject to disturbances and the boundaries of the ego are not constant. (p. 66)

Here Freud seems to refer to Federn's external boundaries, but he makes no mention of Federn's work. Significantly, Freud alluded to projective and introjective processes, before these were proposed and elaborated by Melanie Klein.

In his paper "On the Origin of the 'Influencing Machine' in Schizophrenia," Victor Tausk (1918) was the first to introduce the term *ego boundaries*, defining it as one's own consciousness of uniqueness and separateness from other individuals. In this paper, Tausk ascribed the schizophrenic experience of major changes in the sense of self to a weakening or even the loss of ego boundaries. Tausk's use of the term *ego boundaries* may be understood more as a metaphor of one's awareness of separateness of the self from others than as a structure. Earlier, Josiah Royce (1901) had invoked the term *boundaries* to refer to such awareness of separateness of self from nonself. At this very early stage the term was used metaphorically, and no attempt was made to arrive at a precise definition.

FEDERN AND EGO BOUNDARIES

In the late 1920s, in his paper "The Ego as a Subject and Object in Narcissism," read before the Vienna Psychoanalytic Society, Federn (1952) reintroduced the concept of ego boundaries. He was the first to attempt a focused elaboration of the term, thus ushering in the first of three phases in the evolution of the concept. Each of the three phases roughly corresponds to major shifts in theory. In the first phase, and on the basis of the structural theory, Federn defined and conceived of boundaries as a function and attribute of the ego. Subsequently, with the shift from structural theory and ego psychology to object relations theories, boundaries were seen as representing the demarcation between the self and the object. Finally, in recent years Ernest Hartmann (1991) introduced the third phase with his study of more than 800 nonpsychiatric patients presenting evidence of what he called thick or thin boundaries in the mind. Without departing from a clinical, dynamic perspective, Hartmann (1991) took advantage of recent progress in the neurobiology of mental functions and attempted to understand boundaries on the basis of neurophysiological principles.

Federn (1952) conceived of the ego not as a static structure, but as the continuous experience of the psyche, using the term *ego feeling* to refer to that experience. Federn felt that a coherent ego unit could be subdivided into a bodily ego and a mental ego. In that sense, his notions of ego boundaries applied to both mental and physical boundaries. From a developmental perspective, Federn viewed the infant's original boundaryless state as superseded by the development of ego boundaries that delineate what is "me" from what is "not me." He viewed the ego boundary as a kind of peripheral sense organ that also discriminates what is real from what is unreal. When an element is outside the ego boundary, it is viewed as a real object. In that manner, the ego boundary is critical for the function of reality testing.

According to Eduardo Weiss (1952), in his introduction to Federn's *Ego Psychology and the Psychoses*, Federn described the ego "as an experience, as the sensation and knowledge of the individual of the lasting or recurring continuity, time, space and causality, of his bodily and mental life. This continuity is felt and apprehended as a unity" (p. 8). Federn (1952) understood the term *ego feeling* not as an affective experience but as the ever-present awareness of "how far the ego extends, or, more correctly, the point beyond which the ego does not extend" (p. 331). He saw the ego not as a structure but as a functioning, dynamic entity involved in experiencing and organizing. The experiencing ego assesses and integrates the flow of sensation from the outside and from the inside and, in this way, evaluates the separateness from the external world as well as the distance from inner, unconscious material. Ego boundaries, Federn believed, are changing continuously.

Federn (1952) used the metaphor of the amoeba to describe this continuous fluctuation between expansion and contraction of boundaries, changes that he saw as triggered by the fluctuating cathexes within the ego. For instance, in states of vigilance and active interaction with the environment, ego boundaries are strong and firm, whereas the opposite is true in states of fatigue, sleep, quiescence, and withdrawal. In a similar fashion, the feeling of distance and estrangement from the external world may be understood as caused by the weakening of ego boundaries, diminished narcissistic cathexis, or withdrawal of libido from ego boundaries. For Federn, the paradigm of weak boundaries was the schizophrenic experience, in which there is no demarcation between unconscious fantasies, memories, and other mental states and external reality. The experience of a fusional state could thus be understood as the extreme weakening of ego boundaries.

Federn (1952) conceived of two kinds of ego boundaries: (1) inner ego boundaries that separate the ego from what is nonego (i.e., from the id and the superego, in essence constituting a type of barrier against unconscious drives and fantasies) and (2) external ego boundaries separating the ego from the external world. Federn believed that both inner and outer boundaries are weakened in certain mental illnesses, such as schizophrenia, and in severe regressive states.

Throughout his writings, Federn maintained his understanding of boundaries as a *metaphor* for the distinction between internal and external as well as the separation of conscious ego feeling from unconscious fantasy. When he attempted to conceptualize one's sense of reality, hallucinations, and delusions as related to fluctuations in the ego boundaries, Federn (1952) viewed ego boundaries not as a concrete line of demarcation but as a function. Therefore, as Sarah Polster (1983) pointed out, Federn was dismayed by the concreteness other writers ascribed to his concept of boundaries, an attribute that was contrary to his intentions. He repeatedly stressed that the conception of boundary as "a strict linear, ribbonlike or ditchlike circumference of territory," should not be attributed to him because his own ideas were opposite to those implied by this "static conception of the mental processes" (p. 248). Federn (1952) repeatedly stated that the concept of a firm demarcation would be "contrary to the nature of the ego itself as a changing unit of components which are entering or leaving" (p. 222).

When structural concepts became entrenched in the psychoanalytic literature, however, and despite Federn's protestations against viewing boundaries as a physicalistic entity within the structural model, ego boundaries came close to being seen as concrete entities within the psychic apparatus. Ego boundaries, therefore, were described both as a sense organ perceiving and categorizing external input, and equally as ego states, static and prone to repression. It is probably correct to say that Federn himself contributed to this development by maintaining a degree of ambiguity throughout his writings on the subject. As Polster (1983) noted in her critique, Federn's basic theoretical position made it difficult for him to find "an appropriate language" to use in his elaborations about boundaries. Federn simply understood the ego as a structural entity. Polster stated that "such a model was not conducive to the theoretical leap that Federn wanted to make, a leap in which he proposed to examine not only the way structures develop, function and manifest themselves but also the effect of relationships on structures and how these relationships are mediated" (p. 249).

Psychoanalytic thinking about boundaries in the 1930s, 1940s, and early 1950s continued along the line of concretization of the concept. Wilhelm Reich's (1949) concept of *character armor* probably represents an extreme position in this direction. The following quotation from Reich (1949) illustrates well how the concept of boundaries became reified within the structural model:

> Popularly, people are referred to as hard and soft, proud and humble, cold and warm, etc. Analysis of these different characters shows that they are merely different forms of *armoring of the ego* against the dangers threatening from the outer world and from the repressed inner impulses. (p. 145)

In the 1950s and 1960s, the psychiatric literature focused attention on the concept of one's personal space (i.e., the space that surrounds individuals and protects them from intrusions in ordinary interpersonal transactions). Labeled the "body-buffer zone," this quasiphysical, quasipsychological concept reflected clinicians' awareness of the significance of developing and maintaining boundaries in normal interpersonal transactions. Mardi Horowitz and colleagues (1964) noted that "closeness and distance, as well as the relative position of the patient and therapist, are modulated in therapy" (p. 651), so that although space was rarely referred to in the literature, psychiatrists and therapists were aware of the concept and used it in their work. Horowitz and his associates (1964) proposed that personal space is what surrounds every individual and may be regarded as an immediate *"body-buffer zone* ... the size, shape, and penetrability of the buffer zone [is determined by the] immediate interpersonal events as well as by the current ego state and motivational state of the individual" (p. 655).

BOUNDARIES IN OBJECT RELATIONS THEORY

Influenced by Melanie Klein, members of the British School of Object Relations, such as D. W. Winnicott and W. R. D. Fairbairn, shifted the focus of theoretical discourse from the libido theory and the structural model to the nature of interpersonal relations and their contribution to the gradual buildup of mental representations of self and object. Fairbairn (1963), rejecting Heinz Hartmann's (and Freud's) biological underpinnings, saw psychoanalysis as a clinical science. Pushing Klein's ideas about internal objects to their logical conclusion, he reasoned that the ultimate goal of the libido is not pleasure but the object, thus introducing the *object-seeking principle*. The ego was conceptualized as the original apparatus, the further development of which reflects and incorporates the child's relations to objects. As Jay Greenberg and Stephen Mitchell (1983) pointed out, however,

> of all the drive/structure model theorists after Freud, Edith Jacobson has been the most willing to extend her probing to the heart of psychoanalytic metapsychology. Her purpose throughout her writings is to align the economic point of view with the phenomenology of human experience. (p. 305)

In *The Self and the Object World*, Jacobson (1964) turned our attention to *self boundaries*, understood and defined somewhat differently from ego boundaries. Concerned primarily with the processes of internalization and the structuralization of the self, Jacobson focused on the demarcation between self and object representations through which the person establishes the separateness between experience of the self and the simultaneous experience of the object. During development, according to Jacobson, self and object representations undergo repeated fusions and defusions, but a normal outcome "presupposes the constitution of

well-defined self representations separated by distinct, firm boundaries from the likewise realistic representations of the love objects" (pp.
51–52). Although this perspective somewhat restricts the concept of
boundaries by focusing on the self–object experience, it provides
greater precision to this aspect of boundaries. In addition, by implying
that such demarcation takes place through innumerable constellations
of self–object representations during early experience, it enriches our
understanding of the complex developmental processes involved.

Jacobson's views influenced the writings of several theorists, who
became interested in the buildup of intrapsychic representations of self
and object and their interactions through development. Margaret
Mahler (Mahler, Pine, & Bergman, 1975), basing her writings on observations of the infant–mother dyad through well-defined periods during the first 3 to 4 years of life, attempted to establish stages of the
child's separation–individuation process. She did not deal specifically
with the concept of boundaries, although their absence is implied at the
stage of symbiosis. For Mahler, the self–object demarcation constituted
part of the gradual buildup of an individuated self. Specifically, Mahler
et al. (1975) used the term *symbiosis* to describe a developmental phase
in infancy during which the infant experiences the sense of merger or
boundarylessness with the mother.

Daniel Stern (1985) argued that the concept of symbiosis, or "primary fusion" existing *before* differentiation, is an erroneous developmental notion. As Stern (1985) put it, such a concept is a "pathomor-
phic, retrospective, secondary conceptualization" (p. 105). Stern also
pointed out that the cognitive and perceptual functions at birth are
much more sophisticated than originally thought and that this new
knowledge permits clinicians to conceive of the existence of an early
differentiation between self and other.

Fred Pine (1990), defending Mahler's position, argued that although
the infant may be aware of self and other as separate entities during
alert, wakeful periods, there are moments of merger experiences, most
notably as the infant falls asleep and melts into the mother's body after
nursing. Pine believed such brief moments of merger may be of great
significance in accounting for the symbiotic phenomena seen in both
normal and pathological states in childhood.

Otto Kernberg (1984), reflecting on the work of Jacobson, was more
explicit when he stated that the differentiation of self and object com-

ponents determines, jointly with the general development of cognitive processes, the establishment of stable ego boundaries. There is not yet an integrated self or an integrated conception of other human beings, so that this is a stage of "part–object" relations. Generally speaking, a firm demarcation of self and object representations (i.e., the existence of firm boundaries between self and object) has been implicitly regarded as a developmental achievement. The presence of blurred and inconsistent interpersonal boundaries, allowing regressive merger phenomena, has been considered to characterize severe personality disorders and regression into a psychotic state, in which the self–object demarcation temporarily disappears. In transcendent, religious, or mystical experiences, the subjective feeling is that interpersonal boundaries dissolve and the individual merges with the cosmos in what has been called the "oceanic feeling." Such experiences are not necessarily considered pathological.

PSYCHOLOGICAL STUDIES AND SYSTEMIC CONCEPTS

In the psychological literature of the 1970s, several publications appeared that aimed not only at a more precise definition of the concept of boundaries but also at devising methods to measure such boundaries. Sidney Blatt and his associates (Blatt & Ritzler, 1974), using the Rorschach test, constructed a scoring system to measure boundary permeability, or what they designated as *boundary deficit*.

Bernard Landis is probably the best known among these investigators, specifically for his monograph entitled *Ego Boundaries* (1970). His stated goal was to clarify the meaning of the term *ego boundary*, which Landis felt was rather confusing at that moment in the evolution of the concept. In addition, he hoped to test and extend the concept by focusing on an important boundary dimension of permeability: impermeability within a normally functioning population. His final goal was "to develop one conceptual bridge between diverse theoretical positions (namely, psychoanalysis and Gestalt field theory) via a common boundary construct" (p. 131).

Using the Rorschach, Landis tested a large number of individuals for evidence of permeability and impermeability of ego boundaries. He understood permeability as a looseness of ego boundaries, whereas he perceived impermeability as the opposite (i.e., the firm demarcation of such boundaries). Landis (1970) identified two groups; he saw what he called the impermeability (I) group as radically different from what he named the permeability (P) group. The two groups were understood to be at the ends of the spectrum of "conscious strivings for external and internal control" (p. 118). He agreed with Federn (whose work Landis reviewed and incorporated into his thinking) that schizophrenic patients as a group show excessive permeability—what he termed *fluidity*—in their boundaries. Landis (1970) believed that in schizophrenia, "radical boundary changes occur that, at least some of the time, may be qualitatively so different from neurotic boundary states as to be incommensurable with them" (p. 130).

The two groups identified by Landis using the Rorschach, those with high permeability and those with high impermeability, were then studied through clinical interviews and other tests to determine, if possible, the factors responsible for, or coexisting with, high or low permeability of ego boundaries. Although in principle Landis accepted Federn's separation of internal from external boundaries, his instrument was not sensitive enough to clearly distinguish between the two. Most of his findings appear to refer to external, or interpersonal, boundaries. Landis (1970) made two rather modest statements about the concept of boundaries in general:

(1) Ego boundary quality does not have a powerful enough, isolatable impact on many areas of functioning (i.e., the power of the construct is limited), and (2) boundary properties may sometimes not be a sufficient basis for distinguishing groups that will consistently show marked behavior differences, especially within a normal population where relative boundary intactness, rather than substantial impairment, is the rule. (p. 131)

Looking at the subjects at the two ends of the spectrum, however, Landis observed the following:

The Rorschach protocols pointed to several significant contrasts. Chief of these was the I-dominant person's greater striving for control over both internal impulses and feelings and events compared with the P-dominant person's greater receptiveness and vulnerability to affective challenges. . . . The impermeable-bounded subjects showed more psychological distance and restraint in their environment and interpersonal transactions, whereas the permeably bounded subjects revealed more social motility and overall closeness. (p. 132)

Landis (1970) was somewhat vague in describing boundary structure as a progressive crystallization of the individual's developing mode or modes of adapting to life experiences. What probably reflects the limited power of the Rorschach test to identify and measure this important dimension of the personality is reflected in Landis' conclusion: "Two distinct personality types were not found: the contrasts between the I-dominant and the P-dominant persons are matters of degree and emphasis, not dichotomies" (p. 133). Also, he said that "speaking in the most general terms, the I-dominant person may be more task-oriented or impelled to persist at an activity until he reaches his original goals, whereas a P-dominant person may be viewed as more self-absorbed than task-oriented or as more flexible in accepting a substitute goal" (pp. 134–135).

Landis (1970) returned again to the limitations of the Rorschach:

Although . . . tapping unconscious as well as conscious aspects of personality, people are not equally responsive to it, so that occasionally scoring is based on relatively few responses and at other times on 60 or more. . . . In addition, when one considers that the self is not uniformly bounded, it is clear that the Rorschach can yield only a general estimate of boundary properties, which may not do justice to the complexity and flux of boundary structure. (pp. 135–136)

Anticipating future developments in this area, Landis (1970) concluded that "an instrument that could gauge the quality (and variability) of a person's boundaries, for each significant relationship, would be a desirable goal" (p. 136).

In addition to Landis, several other clinicians and researchers have used projective tests to measure differences in the fluidity of ego boundaries in psychotic and other severely disturbed individuals. Hospitalized paranoid schizophrenic patients showed consistent fluidity and high permeability of boundaries on a variety of such tests. Also, "body ego" boundaries were tested in psychosomatic patients (Blatt & Ritzler, 1974). Those with symptoms involving the skin, joints, or musculature showed thick boundaries (what were called "barrier" scores), whereas patients whose symptoms involved the inner body (colitis, stomach ulcers, and so on) showed "penetration boundary" scores. Both types of symptoms were found to indicate increased permeability of ego boundaries. These findings were not duplicated, and the issues raised remain open.

In his 1989 book, *The Skin Ego*, the French analyst Didier Anzieu described a complex theoretical construct that refers primarily to a psychological body envelope that separates self from object. The skin ego represents the permeable psychic boundaries between the subject and its objects, thus representing an elaboration in the same direction as Federn's conceptualization. Narcissistic personalities, according to Anzieu, possess an unusually thick skin ego; in contrast, masochistic and borderline personalities show remarkably thin skin ego. Anzieu maintained that the skin ego addresses the permeable psychic boundaries between the subject and his or her objects. Here we may recall Jean-Paul Sartre's (1956) aphorism that "the body is wholly 'psychic'" and not an anatomical thing (p. 305).

Concurrent with the development of psychoanalytic notions of boundaries, the concept of boundaries was actively discussed by gestalt psychologists and social scientists. Accepting boundaries as a structure necessary to maintain the cohesion of the self was viewed as eventually leading to the reification of the construct (Polster, 1983). Kurt Lewin (1936) attempted to understand the ego as a set of subsystems combined in specific ways. His mathematical model promoted, but at the same time hindered, further elaboration of the organization of the self. By expressing so clearly the concept of boundaries as a *function of content and relationship*, he forestalled development of the more frequently articulated view on this issue by the systems theorists. Anthony Wilden (1972) described boundary as the basis, or a condition, of all self–other communication.

The systemic point of view emerged largely as a reaction to the perceived concreteness (that of a barrier) of the concept of boundaries in the structural model. The psychoanalytic structural model was thought to place limitations on the concept of boundaries, and a new language was needed "to encompass and describe the vagaries and evanescence of relationships" (Polster, 1983, p. 247).

Although in the 1960s and 1970s, psychoanalytic theorists seemed to depart from the more classical ego psychological thinking, such as the concrete "barrier" view of boundaries, they continued to view boundaries as entities rather than processes. David Rapaport and Merton Gill (1959) and Polster (1983), among others, offered a new definition of structure that was closer to that of the systems theorist's understanding of the concept (i.e., representing a pattern of processes rather than something static and concrete). Although this view represented a departure from the structural concepts of ego psychology, boundaries were still seen as qualities rather than functions. It was Wilden (1972) who, in his book *System and Structure*, provided the definitive explication of systems theory. Wilden saw boundaries as basic to all communication, the metaphor that addresses the continuous changes between separateness and inclusion within a communicative matrix. For Wilden, as for all systems theorists, boundaries represent a process, not a structure.

The systemic view of boundaries is an abstraction that is widely used by those working with groups, families, or even social institutions. As Polster (1983) stated, it is "dialectical processes of separation and inclusion which mediate a person's complex relationship with the world" (p. 247). The systemic paradigm of boundaries evolved before the seminal work by E. Hartmann on the subject, as well as before the insights accrued through the research on infant development, which may help theorists to map the gradual separation of self from others (i.e., the gradual evolution of a quality or function we designate as boundary).

In his articles on love relations, Kernberg (1977) took a systems theory position when he wrote of "crossing boundaries" in love relationships. Sexual passion, which for Kernberg represents a complex emotional "disposition" integrating sexual excitement, tenderness, and a deep commitment to the love object, is seen as

an emotional state that expresses the crossing of boundaries . . . in contrast to regressive merger phenomena, which blur self, non-self differentiation, concurrent with crossing the boundaries of the self, as well as a step in the direction of identification with structures beyond the self. . . . Crossing the boundaries of self, thus defined, is the subjective experience of transcendence. (Kernberg, 1977, pp. 94–95)

HARTMANN: BOUNDARIES IN THE MIND

In the introduction to his book *Boundaries in the Mind*, Hartmann (1991) presented boundaries as "a new dimension of the personality" (p. 7). Considering the long history of psychoanalytic and psychological writings on the subject, however, one has the right to question Hartmann's assertion. What may be new and significant in the evolution of our understanding of the nature of boundaries is Hartmann's approach to the subject: On the basis of Federn's position that inner and outer boundaries exist, Hartmann defined four boundary dimensions in the personality (i.e., thin and thick inner and outer boundaries), which he then identified in a large number of experimental subjects. With the use of a specific tool, the Boundary Questionnaire, which was constructed primarily from psychoanalytic concepts of personality functioning and applied to a large number of individuals over a long period of time, Hartmann and his team examined and attempted to test a number of hypotheses on the nature of boundary dimensions.

By reintroducing Federn's (1952) distinction between inner and outer boundaries and, significantly, by basing his conclusions on clinical experimental findings for a large and diverse sample of individuals, Hartmann opened the concept of boundaries to a broader clinical application. At the same time, by freeing the concept from the anergic considerations inherent in the idea of *ego* boundaries and, instead, speaking of *boundaries in the mind*, Hartmann avoided the controversy concerning boundaries being seen either as a structure or as a process. For Hartmann, boundaries were neither; they were a *measurable quality or attribute of the mind, resting ultimately on a neurobiological basis.*

Hartmann's research began with the study of individuals suffering from frequent nightmares who were part of his extensive work on sleep and dreaming. In these nightmare subjects, all volunteers from a nonpsychiatrically ill sample, certain characteristics were observed to recur consistently: fluidity and lack of cohesion in self-identity, openness and vulnerability in social situations, and an overall lack of firm defenses. Hartmann conceived of these characteristics as relating to a personality trait that he understood as "thin boundaries." Their opposites (i.e., stability and coherence in self-identity, firmness in interpersonal transactions, and constancy in overall functioning) were related to the presence of "thick" boundaries. He proposed "thick and thin boundaries as a broad way of looking at individual differences, a new dimension of the personality" (p. 7) as well as an aspect of the overall organization of the mind.

Hartmann's definition of boundaries is both overinclusive and tied to the thin–thick dichotomy: "Whatever two entities in our mind or our worlds we are talking about, they can be conceptualized as relatively separate (having a thick boundary between them) or in closer communication (with a thinner boundary between them)" (p. 21). The boundary dimension, Hartmann maintained, is best understood within this juxtaposition of the two opposite configurations. We may observe here that this dichotomy, or juxtaposition of the two opposites, dominates all theorizing about boundaries. Whether one is speaking of firm or loose boundaries (Federn, 1952), attempting to measure permeability versus impermeability (i.e., factors of openness versus closeness of a demarcation) (Landis, 1970), or defining boundaries within a similar set of opposites (Hartmann, 1991), the definition of the concept appears to be elusive.

Hartmann administered the Boundary Questionnaire to more than 800 subjects, mostly college students from various facilities. On the basis of these findings, as well as those from a number of other personality scales and direct personal contact in unstructured interviews, the investigators were able to correlate the thin–thick dimension with other dimensions of the personality. Such extensive correlation led Hartmann to observe the following: "It is clear therefore that the Boundary Questionnaire is not a general measure of sickness or psychopathology. People with thin boundaries appear to be no more 'neurotic' or 'introverted' than those with thick boundaries" (p. 100).

Hartmann saw thin and thick boundaries as relating to both constitutional factors and early experience. Early trauma, whether sexual or caused by neglect, abuse, deprivation, or a chaotic early environment, may predispose (although not consistently so) to the development of thin boundaries. Hartmann believed that in infancy and early childhood, boundaries are relatively thin but that they begin to solidify in latency (ages 5 to 10 years). Such thickening of boundaries depends on both environmental and genetic factors. An interesting and consistent finding was the positive correlation between a strong identification with the same-sex parent and thickness of boundaries.

The underlying assumption, which the questionnaire sought to address, was that a certain thickness in inner boundaries is basic for normal psychological functioning and that, at the same time, relatively thin outer boundaries enhance social interactions, in that they facilitate the individual's sensitivity to the psychic reality of the other. In more extreme instances, thin inner boundaries may designate fluidity and a lack of inner cohesion. Equally, excessively thick outer boundaries often promote a defensive, rigid, or even paranoid attitude toward the other.

One of the questions the research team sought to answer was whether there is a correlation between nightmares and thinness of boundaries. Such a correlation was not established convincingly by Hartmann's team; however, a strong and consistently positive correlation between thinness of inner boundaries and *frequency of remembered dreaming* was identified. Such a correlation is not surprising because dreaming itself, according to Hartmann (1991), represents an "extremely thin boundary state of mind. Dreaming contains vivid imagery not very distinguished from reality; one image merges into another; past and present merge; images, thoughts and feelings from different times in one's life all come together" (p. 155).

Artistic creativity was another concern of the research team. Although several of the subjects presenting thin inner boundaries belonged to what was seen as an "artistic" group, high-order artistic creativity itself was not firmly correlated with thinness of boundaries. Hartmann suggested that the presence of creative talent is probably more essential to artistic production than the presence of openness, sensitivity, and fluidity (thinness of boundaries). According to Ross Levin, Jodi Galin, and Bill Zywiak (1991), the presence of thin boundaries facilitates those qualities considered central to the creative process, such as enhanced associational mobility, flexibility in ideational content, perceptual openness, and easy access to internal fantasy. Levin et al. (1991) wrote:

> While admittedly highly speculative, we propose that a pre-existing state of thin boundaries, perhaps linked to the incomplete or fragmented internalization of self- and object-representations . . . may facilitate heightened access to primary process mentation . . . in some individuals, or perhaps within the same individual at different times, these intrapsychic conditions . . . may lead to heightened creativity, most likely of the artistic kind. (p. 72)

Hartmann (1991) attempted to place his findings within a neurobiolog-ical–neuroendocrine frame of reference:

> We would have to postulate such differences chiefly in the forebrain, espe-
> cially the cerebral cortex, whose ten or more billion neurons subserve most
> of the processes we are interested in. And the boundaries we are looking
> for would be boundaries or connections between cell assemblies of some
> kind—probably between large distributed neuronal systems. (p. 233)

Hartmann further postulated that norepinephrine and serotonin, whose increased activity in the brain produces a state of alert wakeful-ness, relate to thickness of boundaries, whereas their decreased activ-ity, producing a state similar to rapid eye movement (REM) sleep (i.e., relative thinness of boundaries) may play a crucial role in the regula-tion of these important functions.

OBSERVATIONS FROM INFANT RESEARCH

Attempting to understand the nature of the developmental lines of inner and outer boundaries at this time presents us with considerable difficulties. We believe it might be justified at this junction of our knowledge to maintain a rather general sense about inner boundaries (i.e., as relating to neuronal connections, to fluid or impeded commu-nication among cell assemblies, and to rigid or flexible patterns of exchanges of excitation, information, and so on). Answers to further questions in these areas will probably come from neurobiological and neuroendocrine studies. In the case of interpersonal boundaries, how-ever, further understanding will probably be related to studies in the area of infant research.

As Beatrice Beebe, Frank Lachman, and Joseph Jaffe (1991) pointed out, an important paradigm shift in infant research took place in the early 1970s. Up to that time, infant research was focused on the influ-ence of the parents' activities on the child. These authors pointed out that given the "increasing appreciation of infant capacities . . . research began to investigate a bidirectional model of influence" (p. 4). Child development in the last 2 decades has been seen as a continuous inter-action between infant and caregiver, based on mutual transformation and restructuring.

Infant research has produced solid evidence that the infant is biologically equipped to engage the environment in active interaction (Emde, 1988); the infant is self-motivated and is able to detect regularities and form expectancies. Infants as young as 3 to 5 months are motivated to control their own perceptual activity. Such control rests, to some extent, on the fact that very early on infants discover contingencies between their own activity and the immediate response of their mother. This generates a sense of efficacy and effectiveness in the infant.

Fast-accumulating data from infant research have established that the infant possesses important representational capacities during the first year, before symbolic thought is established. The infant has the ability to perceive features, is able to transfer information from one modality to another, can perceive contingencies in the caregiver's responses, and can appreciate changes in these responses. In addition, the infant is capable of developing expectancies, which are then categorized and remembered. In this way, the infant develops presymbolic representations of the various interactions with the caregiver. Are we justified in proposing that interpersonal boundaries are first structured as such presymbolic representations? Beebe et al. (1991) pointed out the following:

> Toward the end of the first year, representations of expected interaction structures are abstracted into generalized prototypes. These prototypes will become the basis of symbolic forms of self- and object-representations after the first year. Experiences of the first year will be radically transformed with the onset of symbolic thought, which will not be fully constituted until the third year. (p. 23)

The significance of these presymbolic representations, and their possible contribution to the development of interpersonal boundaries, might be indicated by their predictive value with regard to the type of attachment the infant will develop months later. Experimenting with the "still-face situation" (i.e., presenting the infant with the expressionless face of the experimenter), Jeffrey Cohn, Susan Campbell, and Shelley Ross (1992) were able to show that by the age of 6 months the child's style of coping has become stable. What is more significant is that this style is a reliable predictor of the child's type of attachment at 1 year. Secure attachment is reliably predicted in infants who, despite the stress of the still-face situation, are able to solicit a response from the object. In contrast, the absence of such soliciting behavior is predictive of an anxious, avoidant, or angry attachment at 12 months. It may be possible to postulate that secure attachment by 12 months indicates flexible, relatively permeable interpersonal boundaries and that anxious attachment points to impermeable, rigid demarcation. Finally, one might posit that in particularly anxious types of attachment, the type often observed in the infants of depressed, withdrawn mothers, excessively thin, fluid, pathologically permeable boundaries could be the result.

SUMMARY

In this review of the evolution of the term *boundaries* in the psychoanalytic literature, we have sought to illustrate how protean the term has been. Federn (1952) conceptualized boundaries as a function and attribute of the ego that fluctuates continuously. The ego boundary was a peripheral sense organ that discriminates what is real from what is unreal. Encompassing both mental and physical dimensions, the ego boundary referred to both inner and outer boundaries (i.e., the inner ego boundary separated ego from nonego, and the outer ego boundary separated ego from the external world).

Following Federn's work, the distinction between inner and outer boundaries received little or no theoretical attention for a number of years. Jacobson (1964) introduced the self–object demarcation as a cardinal step in the integration of self and object representations and directed discussion predominantly to interpersonal outer boundaries and their internalized dimensions.

Accepting Federn's premise, Landis (1970) saw boundaries within a structural frame of reference as differentiating the "phenomenal self" both from aspects of the personality not represented in consciousness and from the world of external reality as it is psychologically experienced by the individual. Landis measured permeability (thinness) and impermeability (thickness) of boundaries, which were seen as internal functions of the ego. Boundaries in Landis' work were conceived of entirely in structural terms. As one reads his monograph 2 decades later, the impression gained is that his findings refer predominantly, although not exclusively, to outer interpersonal boundaries.

Hartmann (1991) spoke of boundaries "in the mind," eschewing structural and energic concepts. He reintroduced Federn's separation between inner and outer external boundaries, but he extended both categories well beyond the limits imposed by structural–energic concepts. Hartmann conceptualized the boundaries in the mind as a measurable dimension of the personality.

CHAPTER 2

Boundaries and the Psychoanalytic Process

THE CONCEPT OF THE psychoanalytic process, not unlike that of boundaries, has eluded a firm definition despite a great amount of theoretical discussion on the subject. Dale Boesky (1990), summarizing the work of a study group of the American Psychoanalytic Association's Committee on Psychoanalytic Education, commented that after long deliberation the members of the group agreed that any efforts to arrive at a broadly accepted, systematic definition should be abandoned:

> At this point in the evolution of our science we are more aware of what we do not know, and we include in what we do not know any coherent or systematic definition of the psychoanalytic process, in contrast to a loosely acceptable group of definitional consideration. (p. 583)

Sander Abend (1990), Alan Compton (1990), and Edward Weinshel (1990) made similar attempts to approach the complexities of the issues relating to the psychoanalytic process. Although most authors writing on the subject would agree that this is an interactive process, the nature and limits of this interaction are not clear. Freud's (1913b) original definition remains at the heart of our conceptualizations:

> The analyst is certainly able to do a great deal, but he cannot determine beforehand exactly what results he will effect. He sets in motion a process, that of the resolving of existing repressions. He can supervise this process, further it, remove obstacles in its way, and he can undoubtedly vitiate much of it. But on the whole, once begun, it goes its own way and does not allow either the direction it takes or the order in which it picks up its points to be prescribed for it. (p. 130)

Etymologically the word *process* implies a movement forward, the intention to reach a goal, or the advancement toward some end. Within this frame of reference, the term *psychoanalytic process* could be seen as referring to what takes place during analysis or, as Boesky (1990) put it, "the activities of the analyst, the activities of the analysand, and the elements of change" (p. 555).

Although they accept Freud's position that the process is initiated and fueled by the analysand's thrust to express unconscious wishes and fantasies, a number of analysts recognize the need to conceptualize and specify the analyst's participation. Patrick Casement (1994) distinguished between *process* (the patient's unconscious search for what he or she needs from psychoanalysis) and *procedure* (the analyst's facilitation of the analysand's reach). Focusing on procedure, Casement maintained, offers the analyst a greater sense of control of what to do and of proper steps to take and enables the analyst to distinguish between psychoanalysis and other forms of therapy. He warned, however, that if the procedural side of the dialectic is given too much priority, the most essential aspects of the psychoanalytic process can be overshadowed.

In this chapter we follow the overinclusive, but at the same time clinically relevant, definition of the psychoanalytic process as simply *being in analysis*. We therefore discuss boundaries under the headings of free association, dream recall, and the effects of analysis on boundaries.

BOUNDARIES AND FREE ASSOCIATION

Breuer's patient's talking cure evolved into free (i.e., nondirected) association only with the analysis of the Rat Man. The technique of nondirected associations, a major breakthrough for the budding science, was announced by Freud to the Vienna Society on November 6, 1907.

In a letter to Stefan Zweig dated February 7, 1931, Freud commented that free association may indeed be the most seminal contribution made by psychoanalysis. Charles Brenner (1994) believed that the method of free association, as applied in the analytic process, is what opened the way to Freud's major contributions to the science of psychoanalysis.

Despite its significance, however, the literature on this topic is limited. Patrick Mahony (1987) commented on the fact that Freud gave the subject of free association precious little attention; although he returned to the subject on several occasions, he simply repeated himself. We agree with Mahony that, with few exceptions, subsequent contributions are sparse and have often reiterated the original ideas with fresh elaborations.

The term *nondirected* is probably more appropriate than *free* with reference to the association elicited when the analysand is asked to follow the "fundamental rule." Freud's theorem posits that conscious, purposive ideas are replaced by concealed, purposive ones when the analysand enters the process. The ensuing associations, therefore, are not strictly speaking free but determined, because "the patient remains under the influence of the analytic situation even though he is not directing his mental activities on to a particular subject. We shall be justified in assuming that nothing will occur to him that has not some reference to the situation" (Freud, 1925, pp. 40–41).

Several analysts have raised the question of whether "true" free association is actually possible. Lawrence Kubie (1950), doubting the very existence of free associations, believed that if they are obtained, they usually make up only a small portion of any analytic session. Others (e.g., Meerloo, 1952) have maintained that only at the end of a successful analysis is the patient in a position to associate freely. This belief, popular among European analytic groups, extends to considering the ability to free associate as one of the most important achievements of a successful analysis. This point of view, of course, rests on the assumption that the inability to free associate is entirely, or predominantly, due to the resistance. We come back to this issue later in the chapter when we propose that the ability to free associate is only partially determined by forces such as resistances operating within the analytic process. In addition, we believe that such ability, or the lack of it, relates to other parameters within the patient.

In *Free Association: Method and Process,* Anton Kris (1982) defined free association as a joint venture between analyst and analysand. The patient expresses whatever crosses his awareness, and the listening analyst, "guided" by his own associations and formulations, contributes only to enhance and maintain the expression of the patient's free associations. Kris believed that the process itself is what constitutes the main therapeutic factor in analysis; as long as free association proceeds, therefore, no particular intervention by the analyst is called for. Fantasies, imagery, reverie, and sudden shifts in one's state of consciousness are crucial for the free flow of associations. Free association taps not only what is central to awareness (i.e., the precise lexical symbols) but also what lies in the periphery of such awareness, where symbols are usually ambiguous, more reflective, and body-related. As Kris (1982) pointed out, "Completion of one's associations, including thought, feeling, wish, image, sensation and memory, leads to a sense of satisfaction" (p. 2).

The psychoanalytic process develops within the matrix of complex interpersonal transactions. The inner and outer (interpersonal) boundaries of each participant influence and in turn are influenced by the process. Furthermore, the *interplay* between inner and outer boundaries may be useful in attempting to understand issues related to the development and function of free association during the analysis.

Looking at the analytic process itself, inner and outer boundaries are equally at play. As a general proposition, we can state that a certain fluidity in outer (interpersonal) boundaries in the analyst (indicating the ability to communicate affectively with the other) is necessary for the therapeutic process. Empathy might thus be understood as implying relatively permeable interpersonal boundaries on the part of the analyst. This proposition, however, does not extend to the analyst's inner boundaries. For the proper conduct of the analysis, a cohesion and stability of inner boundaries in the analyst seems to promote an optimal analyst–analysand exchange. Heinz Kohut, as quoted by Jack Freinhar (1986), made this distinction when he remarked, "The good analyst . . .

will have a personality that is characterized by central firmness and peripheral looseness" (p. 483). The analytic boundaries between analyst and patient are discussed in greater detail in Chapter 3.

With reference to the analysand, on the other hand, the function of inner boundaries seems to be particularly significant. Two clinical vignettes of patients clearly belonging to opposite ends of the spectrum (permeability–thinness vs. impermeability–thickness) of inner boundaries are presented to illustrate these points.

THE CASE OF MS. A

Ms. A, a 39-year-old unmarried academic, was a highly intelligent, anxious, moody, talented woman, creative in her academic area but also in her poetry. She sought analysis because she felt her personal life was "a mess." She had had many close, sexual relationships with men, but none lasted beyond a period of infatuation. After initial merger fantasies, she ultimately experienced dissatisfaction with the partner, leading to an abrupt breakup of the relationship.

Ms. A usually came to the sessions with several dreams (and an occasional nightmare) dreamt at night or during daytime naps. In her associations she related an equally large number of fantasies, reveries, and images, in addition to early and recent memories. The flow of her associations ran freely; she associated profusely to her dreams or to important past and current events. Equally, she was capable of remaining silent throughout the whole session. She often missed sessions without apparent reason.

Ms. A came from a very large family. Both parents died several years before the analysis began. Father was described as somewhat eccentric, unpredictable, and highly controlling. The mother, overcome by several pregnancies and the responsibilities of a large family, was depressed, disorganized, and largely ineffectual. Family life was remembered as chaotic, confusing, and lacking in structure.

Ms. A often referred to her relief and delight when she first started attending school, where she found things were orderly and predictable. In school she was precocious, brilliant, and often troublesome. Sexually, she had been equally precocious and had had several sexual attachments with men, who were usually somewhat less accomplished than she was. In a relationship, she was unpredictable, demanding, moody, and extremely sensitive to her partner's actions and reactions.

In the analysis, Ms. A was exquisitely tuned to the analyst's presence, reacting to her smallest moves or changes of position, to her use of words, and of course, to any changes in schedule. She remembered interpretations several sessions later, and from what she reported, one could safely presume that the sessions extended into her outside life. Despite Ms. A's ability to enter effortlessly into nondirected, free association, she did not lose contact with the analyst during the sessions.

The analyst sensed from the start that maintaining clear boundaries in analysis was crucial for the development and course of the analytic process. She understood Ms. A as having permeable inner and outer boundaries, a developmental "deficit" probably related to her early experiences in a chaotic environment in the presence of a depressive, confused, and unpredictable mother. In many respects, one may consider the patient's early experiences as traumatic, a factor partly responsible, as we noted in Chapter 1, for the development of thin inner and outer boundaries.

In addition to Hartmann (1991), Frances Tustin (1981) and Gail Yariv (1989) have pointed out the importance of stability, continuity, and a predictable rhythmicity in the relationship with the primary object for the development of a clear separation of self and other, or inside and outside. Yariv emphasized that a rigid or pathological barrier between the child and the primary object would be easier for the child to negotiate than a situation in which "child, mother, and physical objects stay merged in a confused and chaotic way" (p. 105). What has been stressed by many authors is that when no clear demarcation exists between child and mother, Winnicott's (1953) transitional area (the area where play develops) will not develop properly.

It is of interest here that Ms. A had no memory of any playful interaction with her mother: "My mother tried hard to do what she was supposed to, but she had no idea what it means to play with a child."

Ms. A had often stated that her biggest fear in life was not loneliness but chaos, the dissolution of all boundaries. In her interpersonal relations, her usual defense after a real or fantasized hurt was to distance herself from the object. A fantasy she had nurtured for several years was to emigrate to a distant and sparsely populated country, like Australia. No one would know her there, and she could live alone at the edge of a forgotten little suburb, taking care of her garden.

Maintaining clear outer boundaries in the analytic situation was seen as crucial for the analysis: not necessarily being aloof and unresponsive, but keeping a certain affective distance from the patient. The analyst usually made short comments, linking material within a transference context, and tried to avoid long, involved interpretations. Despite the temptation to enter into extensive dream analysis, the analyst felt that remaining in the here and now of the session was critical. Ms. A's dependency needs, coupled with her fluid inner and outer boundaries, dictated a careful handling of the patient in the transference. A dependent transference, necessary for the working through of her preoedipal pathology, could, unless carefully titrated, lead to serious merger phenomena and severe regression in the transference with a further weakening in her boundaries. Eventually such a transferential relationship would stir up anxiety, or even panic, and the patient would flee the analysis as she had fled all intimate relationships.

In the third year of analysis, and while the transference was becoming rather intense, Ms. A remarked, "In the last few weeks, my dreams have become even more strange. I can't even put words to them." The deepening regression in the analytic situation seemed to have a further weakening effect on the patient's inner boundaries, something analysts often refer to as the weakening of the patient's defenses.

THE CASE OF MS. B

A case example at the other end of the spectrum is Ms. B, a 41-year-old married professional woman who came to analysis depressed, dissatisfied with her marriage, angry at her husband, anxious about her children, and feeling her life was at a standstill. The oldest of four children in a very traditional family, Ms. B grew up feeling envious of and highly competitive with her siblings and classmates, never feeling satisfied with her lot in life. Both parents, religious and very conventional, had rather rigid rules, and Ms. B became compliant but resentful and angry.

From the beginning of the analysis, the total absence of remembered dreams and the patient's inability to free associate became important issues during the sessions. Ms. B was highly articulate and rarely remained silent during the session, but the material she brought up could best be summed up as the patient's descriptions of herself and of people next to her or the orderly accounting of present and past life events. She went into minute detail and was coherent and a good raconteur, but as the analyst finally came to understand, the patient seemed to stand outside of herself, observing and reporting but unable to loosen up some inner constrictions or boundaries to permit a different type of self-reflection.

Mahony (1987) commented on this type of "free" association, when the patient *tells about* rather than tells *as it is or as it is happening*. He stated that "telling about lacks immediacy and points to a certain self-awareness on the part of the speaker. In this connection we recall the postulate of medieval mystics: if one is aware that one is praying, it's not the perfect prayer" (p. 33).

In Ms. B, associations, fantasies, imagery or reverie, and sudden shifts in the state of consciousness were only rarely observed. To put it differently, what was entirely lacking was the ability to pass effortlessly from discursive or verbal to presentational (i.e., imagistic) symbols, from ordinary, prosaic talk to the rich articulation of imagery, affect, and fantasy. The presentational symbols—fleeting, impermanent, and imprecise—are made mostly by the eye and ear and are the primitive instruments of intelligence. As the individual's thinking and communications with others begin to rest mostly on the use of verbal rather than presentational symbols, the meaning of such communications becomes more precise, but at the same time, the information conveyed through verbal symbols inevitably becomes more restricted.

Theodore Jacobs (1994b) observed that bodily movements ("body language") may replace verbal free association. Crossing or uncrossing of the legs, folding of the arms, and shielding of the eyes all may speak volumes to the analyst. These movements can be observed, however, only in relatively short, isolated instances of bodily expression or bodily discharge. The narrative of the analysand always depends on verbal discourse. Body language may well replace a thought or express an affective state, but it cannot substitute for sustained communication through speech. Free association requires a certain degree of regression (i.e., regression in the service of the ego). Although communications using language and speech are based on secondary processes, in true nondirected associations, the flow of speech moves in the direction of primary process.

We are postulating that during the analytic hour, by approaching a mental state close to primary process mentation, a process of loosening of boundaries takes place. Patients like Ms. A enter free association without any particular conscious effort. Analysands like Ms. B, however, find it difficult to grasp exactly what is meant by free association. Analysts have conceptualized this difficulty as the patient's resistance to allowing unconscious material to surface close to awareness. Undoubtedly, resistance is in operation here, often reinforced by conscious reluctance to disclose personal information; however, the mere fact that Ms. B could not even *understand* what she was asked to do points to a limitation beyond resistance. As the analysis proceeded, Ms. B was better able to "go further," as she put it, but the discursive character of her associations was still pronounced.

BOUNDARIES AND DREAM RECALL

Freud's self-analysis, and particularly the analysis of his dreams, guided him through the major discoveries in the early years of theory building. For several decades following these formative years, dream analysis remained the focus of every clinical analysis, and reports of cases often centered predominantly, if not exclusively, on the analysis of the patient's dreams. Recalling one's dreams was considered by many to be a reliable indicator of analyzability. Bringing up dreams during the analytic session became the barometer that predicted a smooth course for the analytic process. Equally, lack of dream recall was viewed as a major resistance within the transference. The success of an analysis was often predicated on an increased ability to recall dreams and associate to such dreams during the session.

The study of sleep and dreams in the laboratory established that REM sleep, the physiologic state associated with dreaming, is a universal phenomenon, suspended only in certain pathological brain states. Despite the fact that REM dreaming occurs several times a night, only a small percentage of dreams (two to three dreams per week on the average) are usually recalled (Belicki, 1986).

In the analytic literature, many have argued that a number of dreams each night succumb to repression on awakening, a manifestation of the dreamer's need to erect a barrier against the conscious awareness of the forbidden wishes expressed in the dream. Repression was thus seen as operating universally as a defense against unconscious drive derivatives woven into the central wish fulfillment of the dream. It is generally accepted that, during analysis, dream recall is subject to additional resistances such as those related to the transference and those arising from the uncovering of hitherto largely unconscious material. Such resistances in analysis are expected to be gradually weakened and eventually worked through by the end of a successful analysis.

The question of what facilitates or, equally, what interferes with dream recall has aroused sustained interest *outside* the consulting room. To test a number of hypotheses pertaining to these questions, several research projects have been conducted in recent years. David Cohen (1974), himself an investigator, completed a thorough review of the literature on the subject before attempting to formulate a theory of dream recall. Summarizing the findings of these studies, he warned against labeling infrequent recallers simply as "repressors" and seeing frequent recallers merely as anxious individuals presenting some type of pathology. The results of a number of such studies indicated that anxiety scales, as well as scales measuring ego strength, are not particularly valid in explaining difficulty or ability in remembering dreams.

The salience hypothesis, proposing that dreams recognized as salient by the dreamer are more easily recalled, proved somewhat more difficult to test. Nevertheless, the general consensus according to Cohen (1974) was that dreams salient to the dreamer are more readily recalled than dreams without any particular importance. Research reported by Kathryn Belicki (1986) confirmed that individuals who frequently recall their dreams rate such dreams as more salient than do infrequent recallers when asked about their dreams. The reasons for this phenomenon are not entirely clear.

According to Cohen (1974), the correlation most supported by the experimental findings was between dream recall and the dreamer's "superiority for imagery" (p. 145). Fantasy, daydreaming, the use of imagery in reverie, and lack of task-oriented thinking were the most frequently identified personality characteristics of dream recallers. At the same time, the role of motivation (i.e., interest in one's dreams) was rated as significant for dream recall. Finally, the importance of "practice" (i.e., the conscious effort to remember and report dreams) was considered beneficial to dream recalling.

Kathryn Belicki (1986) also discussed additional research regarding salience, motivation, absence of competing preoccupation, and presence of factors increasing emotional intensity in the dreamer. She confirmed Cohen's (1974) positions and further underscored what Cohen called the "personality factor." Although they are not clearly articulated, the personality characteristics facilitating dream recall (as identified by psychoanalytically informed researchers) have always been known to analysts. The experimental findings we mention here confirm analysts' clinical intuition.

With reference to boundaries, these findings seem to indicate that dream recall is enhanced by the particular ability to use imagery and fantasy and to enter into divergent thinking and, possibly, by the lack of rigid defenses against unconscious material. In our discussion of free association, we have stressed that similar factors (i.e., fantasy, imagery, and reverie, as well as sudden shifts in the state of consciousness) enhance the free flow of associations during the session. We propose that these factors, long known to psychoanalysts from their clinical experience and now supported by findings in neighboring disciplines, may be related to the individual's permeability (thinness) of inner boundaries.

Ms. A's dreams were long, based mostly on visual imagery and bodily sensations. Language and thought elements played a secondary role. In the second year of analysis, she reported the following dreams:

> I dreamt of my father . . . he is terribly old. It is in my parents' house; there are many, many rooms and bathrooms. My father is sick . . . he has diarrhea . . . he is defecating all over the place. It is horrible. He can't restrain himself. I look at him, but I do nothing. I think to myself, he is an old man, let him die. [Several months later, she reported:] I was in a room like our kitchen, a round table . . . the door opens to the outside. Something pushes under the table . . . a combination of a spider, a scorpion, or a lobster. It is getting bigger and bigger. I was the only one who could see that. It had an enormous jaw, like an alligator. I screamed . . . I started running to the street. My brother gets a gun to kill the monster.

Although the anxiety in Ms. A's dreams only occasionally reached the level of that of a nightmare (according to Hartmann's [1991] definition, a nightmare is simply what the dreamer calls a nightmare), in many of her dreams anxiety and dysphoria were sufficiently intense to wake her up.

With reference to Ms. B, throughout the first 2 years of analysis, no dreams were reported except for the patient's awareness of having dreamt or, possibly, a fleeting thought related to a dream: "I was with my mother," or "I had to take an exam." In the third and fourth year, Ms. B recalled somewhat larger segments, but only at infrequent intervals. By the end of the fourth year, she recalled the following dream:

> It was explicitly about you. We were there with our husbands . . . lots of people around. We were walking downstairs . . . party atmosphere. Food was served. There was a terrific calmness about you . . . you were very easy and very comfortable socially. Not necessarily gregarious but comfortable . . . a kind of sophistication I very much admired. We said a few words to one another, and our husbands spoke to one another.

The two types of dreams, in terms of representability, affective discharge, and drive content, reflect quite well accessibility not only to primary process material but also, and especially, to the dreamer's need and capacity to contain and control the dream structure, as is shown in the case of Ms. B's dream.

THE EFFECT OF ANALYSIS ON BOUNDARIES

As we have mentioned, a widely held view, mostly among European analysts, has been that the analysis has exhausted itself and should be terminated when the analysand begins to free associate. It is tempting to assume that such a position might have originated with the analysis of patients similar to Ms. B. Analyzing the resistance and loosening up of internal controls, it was hoped, would allow ideas, images, fantasies, and sensations to flow into awareness and thus promote a "looser" associational pattern in the patient. It was also postulated that dream recall would be facilitated through the analytic process.

As indicated by the various studies mentioned earlier in the chapter, dream recall may be enhanced by "practice," but resting as it does on fundamental personality attributes (the dreamer's "superiority for imagery" [Belicki, 1986; Cohen, 1974]), enhanced recall depends primarily on the fate of the analysand's inner boundaries. If developing and thickening of inner boundaries is a developmental achievement (Hartmann, 1991; Sabbadini, 1989; Yariv 1989), it could be postulated that analytic work may have some influence on the dreamer's ability to contain anxiety and use displacement, condensation, and symbolization to construct a "tighter" and more "manageable" dream.

THE CASE OF MS. C

The case of Ms. C illustrates how recurring dreams and nightmares may be altered in analysis. An anxious, dependent, and depressive woman, Ms. C came to analysis at the age of 48. She had had some psychotherapy in her 30s, from which she derived relatively limited therapeutic results. She experienced her male therapist as unsympathetic and occasionally sadistic.

The only daughter in a medium-sized family, Ms. C was bullied and most likely molested by her brothers. She never admitted the molesting openly, but she alluded to it often, each time becoming angry, ashamed, and ultimately very depressed. Her parents, according to Ms. C, were religious, upright, and disciplinarian. Burdened by financial stresses, they seemed preoccupied and constantly worried about almost everything. Ms. C left home as soon as she could. She met and married a supportive and kind man. Under his protective presence, she was able to function relatively well as a wife and mother. Socially, however, she was shy and mistrustful.

From the beginning of the analysis, Ms. C was able to associate freely. She soon developed an intensely ambivalent transference, alternating between strong fusional urges and paranoid, angry outbursts against the "indifferent" and "cruel" analyst. She brought several dreams and a number of nightmares into the analysis. In one she reported: "I was hitting my son. I kept hitting him harder and harder. I couldn't stop myself. I felt frantic. He had a cold, contemptuous look on his face. I woke up in a panic." Another time she related the following dream:

I am in a train with my grandmother. She carries a bag full of jewelry. Then I see another bag with some food inside. I am hungry, but as I try to get some food, I see worms and bugs coming out of it. I close the bag in disgust, but then I tell myself there may be some good stuff there. I put my hand in the bag, but all I get is something sticky, gooey, and disgusting. It is like shit. I wake up nauseous and in total panic.

Several of Ms. C's dreams took place in the bathroom: images of overflowing toilets, of feces everywhere, of vomit she cannot clean up. The analyst's interpretations touched on the memories of terror, deep shame, and disgust around the physical abuse she was subjected to, probably quite often, in the family bathroom.

As the analysis was coming to a close, this type of dream became less frequent. What was probably more significant was that the dreams became more cohesive and more tightly symbolized, or mentalized. In the last week, she reported the following dream:

I come into a toilet, a kind of toilet in an institution. There is a sink on the right, and as I look more carefully, there is an alcove. A pregnant woman is lying there, her hand on her ass, as if to hold back her feces. I turn on the sink and I vomit and then I clean up the sink. I have the feeling I haven't vomited everything, but I wake up and I am not in a panic. *I can now stop my dream before it becomes a nightmare.*

The changes in the functioning of Ms. C's inner boundaries in the course of analytic work were readily observed through the structural changes brought about in the dreams.

In the following case, significant changes took place regarding the patient's awareness and experiencing of her body and its parts.

The Case of Ms. D

Ms. D, a 35-year-old single mother, was a freelance commercial designer who, despite her acknowledged talent, was unable to succeed in her field. The youngest of three children from a middle-class family, Ms. D developed severe bronchial asthma in infancy and thus became the object of her mother's obsessive, anxious, and resentful preoccupation. She was continually taken to doctors, hospitals, and dry climates.

In early puberty the attacks diminished and eventually disappeared altogether, although a respiratory vulnerability persisted.

The years between ages 14 and 22 could only be described as totally chaotic. Ms. D became highly promiscuous ("I slept with more than 100 men in those years"); took all the street drugs she could get from friends, lovers, or dealers; became severely anorexic; drank heavily; and at the age of 21, had an acute psychotic episode for which she was hospitalized. The psychosis cleared up shortly after admission and has never recurred. Ms. D returned to her studies and completed all the requirements for a master's degree in fine arts. She stopped being promiscuous and had some relatively long and stable relationships.

At the age of 28, Ms. D decided to have a child and became pregnant by a man she barely knew who showed no subsequent interest in the child. She had a difficult pregnancy and, at first, resented the burden of taking care of her infant daughter. However, the attachment to the child eventually produced an important transformation in Ms. D. The presence of the child "anchored" her in reality, as she put it. The child herself, with her repetitive and routine rhythms of caretaking needs, helped Ms. D to organize and center her life. She found freelance work, and her everyday life started revolving around her daughter's schedule.

Despite this external stability, however, Ms. D remained anxious, unsure of her future, and tormented by doubts about her talent. If she were really talented, as she believed and as everyone around her had always told her she was, she should strive to paint instead of wasting her time with commercial work. Ms. D had numerous physical complaints for which she was constantly visiting doctors and clinics, always discovering a new problem but never following through with any one treatment. She was obsessed with the fear of illness and death. When she came to analysis, she was in an intensely ambivalent and unstable relationship with a former alcoholic, himself a hypochondriac, an irritable and dissatisfied man who had been in therapy for 15 years.

In the first few months of the analysis, the patient would often sit up because of anxiety or coughing bouts. She would also complain of stomachaches and nausea and was afraid she had stomach cancer. She remained silent for long stretches of time, and on the analyst's gentle urging to speak, she would respond irritably that she saw no reason to say anything: "What's the use of all this after all?" She often mentioned having "strange, scary" dreams the previous night but refused to relate any of these in the session. It soon became clear that she was afraid to allow a process of free association, "open up the floodgates," as she put it, and possibly get close to the hopeless, defenseless state she had experienced during her brief psychotic episode. Equally, the transference revived old affective states of feeling like a helpless, passive infant, mired in illness and physical pain that only mother could relieve. This constant complaining, however, did not prevent Ms. D from coming regularly to the sessions. In contrast to Ms. B, the paucity of material with this patient did not arouse frustration in the analyst, who felt from the start that a fragile patient like Ms. D needed time to trust the analyst and trust the process itself before venturing into free association.

The analyst's interpretations focused mainly on Ms. D's ambivalence toward the primary object, wishing and, at the same time, fearing to be taken care of. In the transference repetition, she felt helpless and passive, resisting becoming responsible for her own health. All the analyst's interventions were brief and direct. The "message" conveyed through words and through the rules and structures of the analytic frame was that analysis was providing the background safety to begin feeling a sense of agency and responsibility over her body and her health. This highly intelligent and talented young woman seemed to lack internal cohesiveness and to have porous inner boundaries. When the external reality provided a specific focus, as was the case with taking care of her child, she would function relatively well. The analysis, by its repetition, empathic climate, and clear, stable analytic boundaries, provided another such structuring situation.

For several months Ms. D said little in the sessions beyond repeating her usual complaints about her health, money problems, and other miseries in her life. However, she was punctual and missed few sessions. Gradually, the physical "symptoms" diminished, and in one session she said, "I am through with illness; that chapter is now closed." Ms. D broke up with her companion when he went through a bout of heavy drinking and self-destructive behavior. She met a graduate student, and the relationship seemed stable and close.

Federn (1952), who was particularly interested in the fate of boundaries in the treatment of psychoses, believed that with these patients it is not a matter of lifting repressions but of creating them. The therapeutic goal (at least in the early stages of the treatment) is not that of uncovering (i.e., "loosening up" inner boundaries), but rather of providing a situation in which some firming of boundaries may be promoted.

Similar concerns were expressed by Maurice Bouvet (1958), a French analyst particularly interested in the oscillations of closeness and distance between analyst and analysand and the analysand's need to control such closeness and distance (analytic boundaries) during analysis. Bouvet posited that with severely disturbed patients, primitive, pregenital transferences usually emerge and the analyst is experienced ambivalently, either as a good object to gratify all instinctual yearnings or as the destructive, malevolent object threatening the integrity and cohesion of the patient's ego. Issues of distance and closeness become crucial, and the patient may develop serious problems of depersonalization if the analyst fails to maintain optimal distance from the patient. Although Bouvet was not referring explicitly to boundaries, the issues he raised addressed the function and fate of boundaries in analysis.

Provided the frame and the analytic boundaries are firmly established, porous inner boundaries in the analysand may firm up somewhat over time, as was observed with Ms. D. Whether these are permanent changes or simply transference-bound is a question that cannot be answered at this time.

The capacity to enter into free association and dream recall may not increase substantially, even with a successful analysis, as in the case of Ms. B. Excessively thick inner boundaries, as found by the Hartmann team in severe obsessive–compulsive individuals, may undergo some loosening through the analytic process, but such cases have not been reported in the literature, and as of now we do not have clinical material on this issue.

Finally, the fate of thin interpersonal (outer) boundaries would probably be best tested in the analysis of borderline patients. Controlled studies with a large number of patients, possibly using experimental tools as well, will be necessary to answer these fundamental questions.

CHAPTER 3

The Analytic Frame, Analytic Boundaries, and the Analytic Object

IN CHAPTER 1 WE REVIEWED the varied use of the term *boundaries* in psychoanalytic theory. In Chapter 2 we focused on boundaries within the psychoanalytic process with particular emphasis on inner boundaries or "boundaries in the mind." In this chapter we turn to boundaries in terms of the interpersonal dimensions of the analytic setting. The interpersonal, however, is inextricably linked to the intrapsychic, and we will illustrate how the boundaries within the mind may have significant influences on the external boundaries discussed in this chapter.

In recent years the most common use of the term *boundaries* has been related to the notion of "professional boundaries" between analyst and patient (Epstein, 1994; Gabbard, 1995b; Gutheil & Gabbard, 1993; Waldinger, 1994), reflecting an expansion of the concept. In the process of defining the concept to include boundaries within the analytic space between patient and analyst, the term has become intimately related to a number of the leading controversies in psychoanalysis, including issues of abstinence, neutrality, optimal gratification, enactments, and self-disclosure by the analyst, as well as the notion of transference itself.

Much of the recent concern about professional or analytic boundaries has emerged from the alarm at egregious cases of boundary violations that often receive wide-ranging coverage in the media and damage the reputation of psychoanalysis as a profession.

In defining the analytic frame and the analytic boundaries within the process, we are also attempting to define the optimal psychoanalytic situation. Moreover, considerations of the frame and boundary facilitate the emergence of the analytic object, a crucial but largely unexamined development in analytic discourse. We thus begin our discussion by defining the frame, and the boundaries that constitute the architecture of the frame, as a way of leading directly into a consideration of the nature of the analytic object.

THE ANALYTIC FRAME

The analytic frame is an envelope within which the treatment itself takes place. Although the term conjures up images of a picture frame, the concept is not nearly so rigid. Rather, it is a dynamic and flexible set of conditions that reflect the analyst's ongoing efforts to respond to the patient while also establishing an optimal ambience for the analytic work. Robert Langs (1977) defined the frame as

> a multifaceted human container and living institution which sets the boundaries of the analytic relationship, creates the rules of the interaction, establishes the nature of the realities and fantasies that occur within it, offers an effective hold and means of security for the participants, defines the therapeutic qualities of the field, contributes to the nature of the communicative network within its confines, and generates certain selected anxieties in the participants as well. (p. 28)

Langs further divided the frame into two sets of components. One set involves the details of the contractual understanding about the setting of analysis. These are relative constants that include such items as absence of physical contact, confidentiality, location of meetings in the analyst's office, position of the analysand on the couch and the analyst in the chair behind the couch, payment of a set fee, and an agreed-on length and frequency of sessions. The second component involves human elements defining the interaction, including nonjudgmental acceptance by the analyst, an attempt to understand the meaning of communications and behaviors, relative anonymity of the analyst, agreement by the patient to say whatever comes to mind, abstinence from inappropriate gratifications, offering of appropriate gratifications of concern and efforts to understand, interpretation of unconscious conflicts as they become apparent, and a particular focus on understanding the interaction between the analyst and analysand.

Vann Spruiell (1983) wrote about the analytic frame from a somewhat different perspective from Langs. He stressed that his use of the term relates to "frame theory" and applies to the psychoanalytic setting certain views of social interaction derived from other disciplines. Specifically, Spruiell emphasized the rules by which certain kinds of interaction are "framed," meaning how they are defined and delimited from other kinds of interactions between people. He defined the frame of the analytic situation as referring to "unchanging basic elements or principles of organization defining a specific social event and distinguishing it from other events" (p. 9).

Much of Spruiell's emphasis is on the deliberately unbalanced nature of the analytic dyad. To a large extent, the analytic frame is constructed and defined by the skewed nature of the interaction between the two participants. While the patient lies on a couch and attempts to say whatever comes to mind, the analyst listens silently much of the time without concentrating too intently but without drifting off to sleep either. The evenly suspended attunement of the analyst hovers above the process in such a way that attention is shifted back and forth between the analyst's own internal processes and the analysand's associations. The analyst must simultaneously be a participant in a relationship and achieve a dual state of consciousness in which the relationship and the participation are observed at a distance (Friedman, 1991).

Following the analyst's lead, the patient eventually joins with the analyst in elaborating and constructing the frame. The patient "learns the ropes" and starts to create a private and intimate relationship in which the past can be understood in its current-day repetition.

Among other things, the analytic frame creates an atmosphere of *safety*. Powerful affects can be mobilized without fear of impingement or humiliating criticism from the analyst. The patient is given "space" to regress and to allow unacceptable unconscious wishes and feelings to emerge. It is precisely because the rules of the game are different from all other social interactions that the patient is free to experience him- or herself in a new light.

ANALYTIC BOUNDARIES

The concept of analytic or professional boundaries is sometimes mis-construed to mean simply an arbitrary set of rules by which ethics committees and licensing boards determine whether or not disciplinary measures are needed. The concept is also often misunderstood to endorse an attitude on the part of the analyst that is rigid, robotic, and remote. A reification of Freud's admonitions regarding technique often haunts the beginning analyst. Such an extreme posture does not capture Freud's intent, which was conveyed in a 1927 letter to Sándor Ferenczi:

> I considered the most important thing was to emphasize what one should *not* do, and to point out the temptations in directions contrary to analy-sis. Almost everything positive that one *should* do I have left to "tact," the discussion of which you are introducing. The result was that the docile analysts did not perceive the elasticity of the rules I had laid down, and submitted to them as if they were taboos. Sometime all that must be revised, without, it is true, doing away with the obligations I had men-tioned. (Jones, 1955, p. 241)

When boundaries are caricatured, they can indeed lead to a counter-transference posture that is inflexible and cold. However, the intent is exactly the opposite. Boundaries define the parameters of the analytic relationship so that both patient and analyst can be safe while also being spontaneous. Indeed, Elizabeth Lloyd Mayer (1994a) argued that one source of increased risk for boundary violations is the tendency to regard the analyst's warm and caring feelings for the patient as an aber-ration of sorts. In other words, love for the patient may be at odds with a particular view of the analytic attitude internalized from years of supervision and didactic instruction about the analyst as objective "surgeon." Mayer suggested that if such feelings were viewed as expectable, acceptable, and within the parameters of psychoanalytic technique, they would not be sequestered in a secret, split-off sector of the analyst's psyche where they might escalate to devastating proportions.

An analogy may be useful. Visitors to the Grand Canyon note that they are protected from falling into the chasm by a guardrail placed strategically at the edge of the canyon. This safety measure allows children (and adults) to play and enjoy themselves while being at minimal risk for catastrophe. Although analytic boundaries in general are more flexible than a guardrail, in some areas, such as sexual contact, they are just as unyielding.

Analytic boundaries, of course, are more than a guardrail—more than a restraint device. They also reflect aspects of the intrapsychic concept of boundaries we have described in Chapters 1 and 2. Richard Epstein (1994), whose primary focus is on professional rather than analytic boundaries, suggested that, to a large extent, the analytic frame can be regarded as an extension of the analyst's own outer ego boundaries. Analysts are continuously attending to the difference between what is going on inside the patient and what is going on inside themselves. The analytic boundaries assist in this function by representing a type of interpersonal boundaries. Similarly, just as healthy ego boundaries must be flexible enough to open at times and close at other times, so must the analytic boundaries be sufficiently flexible that accommodations can be made, depending on the needs of the analytic process.

Epstein (1994) noted that therapists with overly thin interpersonal boundaries may be prone to confusing their own internal experiences with those of the patient, whereas those with overly thick interpersonal boundaries may be walled off from experiencing unconscious communications from the patient. The latter type of analyst may be less capable of empathy and active fantasy and therefore be more prone to seek solutions in concrete actions. The two participants' inner boundaries are also important, because their flexibility may enhance access to primary process in both individuals.

One of the central paradoxes of the analytic situation is that the professional boundaries must be maintained so that both participants have the freedom to cross them psychologically. In other words, processes such as empathy and projective identification oscillate back and forth across the semipermeable membrane constructed by the analytic dyad. The analyst expects a therapeutic regression to occur in both participants so that more primitive states of fusion and exchange are possible.

A developmental analogy illustrates the importance of a free-flowing exchange of affect states. As Andrew Meltzoff and Keith Moore (1992) suggested, young infants differentiate and develop an identity from early experiences of affect transmission between infant and caregiver. Some of these intermodal exchanges of affect, similar to those communicated in a developmental state from the pre-object-relatedness period, are eventually revived in analysis. Through the analytic regression, the patient may communicate without words or representations but through bodily transmission of affect.

Relevant to this discussion is Thomas Ogden's (1989) developmental framework involving the dialectical interplay of three different modes of generating experience. Two of these modes, the paranoid–schizoid and the depressive, derive from an extension of the work of Melanie Klein. The third, the autistic–contiguous mode, reflects Ogden's own synthesis and extension of the ideas of Esther Bick (1968), Donald Meltzer (1975), and Frances Tustin (1981, 1984). The autistic–contiguous mode is the most primitive of the three from a developmental perspective and involves the development of an early sense of boundary between self and other based on the rhythm of sensation at the skin surface. As Ogden (1989) described the autistic–contiguous mode of experience,

> it is a relationship of shape to the feeling of enclosure, of beat to the feeling of rhythm, of hardness to the feeling of edgedness. Sequences, symmetries, periodicity, skin-to-skin "molding" are all examples of contiguities that are the ingredients out of which the beginnings of rudimentary self-experience arise. (p. 32)

If the continuity of the experience in this mode breaks down, one may develop anxieties about one's insides leaking out and becoming an amorphous entity without definition or surface.

In the paranoid–schizoid mode, although a sensory boundedness between self and object has been established, object relatedness primarily takes the form of projective identification. Certain aspects of the individual, along with affective states, are split off and ejected into another person. This allows the projector to safeguard an endangered aspect of the self while also omnipotently controlling an object. The projector unconsciously induces feeling states in the recipient that are congruent with the projected affects or self and object constellations. Because a subjective sense of "I-ness" has not yet been fully developed in the paranoid–schizoid mode, projective identification is a direct communication from projector to recipient without benefit of interpretation by a mediating subject. In this mode, the boundaries between self and object are sufficiently permeable that the recipient can feel coerced or "bullied" into responding as though he or she is part of the projector's inner world. Moreover, symbol and symbolized are emotionally equivalent, so that perceptions are regarded as things in themselves, as often seen in delusional transferences in which the "as if" quality has been lost.

Full subjectivity with a subject that mediates between symbol and symbolized develops within the depressive mode of experience. Boundaries between self and other are more firmly established, so that one experiences oneself as a person capable of thinking one's own thoughts and feeling one's own feelings. This mode also enables one to experience and empathize with the subjectivity of another. Whereas in the paranoid–schizoid mode, both self and others are experienced as objects, in this mode self and other can be experienced as subjects.

Although these three modes of experience have been separated to describe the specific characteristics of each, Ogden (1989) stressed that all three are operative to varying degrees in every facet of human experience. From time to time one or another mode may predominate; psychopathology is regarded by Ogden as forms of collapse of the richness of experience generated by the three different modes into one predominant mode. Similarly, shifts from one mode to another in patient, analyst, or both may influence the permeability of analytic boundaries.

The analytic boundaries ensure that the analyst can contain and process communications without acting inappropriately on them. Hence the analytic boundaries may be the built-in structures within the frame that check, control, and eventually "upgrade" primitive affects communicated through projective identification into a verbal, symbolic realm stemming from a developmental phase characterized by more mature object relations. The analytic boundaries need to be reasonably firm to permit these primitive communications to go from analyst to patient as well as from patient to analyst.

In Chapter 1 we traced the evolution of Jacobson's thinking (1964), particularly with regard to her understanding of the demarcation of self and object representations. The developmental process of repeated fusions and defusions in these representations is often recapitulated in the analytic situation, and it is incumbent on the analyst to recognize these regressive experiences and use them therapeutically. The optimal analytic approach to these externalizations of internalized object relations involves a particular analytic attitude that can best be characterized as simultaneously participating and observing, a state that Richard Sterba (1934) described as *dissociation within the ego* and Harry Stack Sullivan (1954) termed *participant observation.* Analysts must allow themselves to be "sucked in" to these temporary disruptions of the barrier between self and object, while carefully noting the determinants and meanings of such disruptions.

This discussion of the analyst's response leads directly into a consideration of what is known as the *professional, or analytic, role* (Almond, 1994; Casement, 1990; Gutheil & Gabbard, 1993). The structural characteristics of the frame, such as the office setting, the fee, the duration of the session, the abstention from physical contact, the avoidance of gift giving, and the position of the patient on the couch and the analyst behind the couch, are important in and of themselves, but all contribute to defining the specificity of the analytic role. As Richard Almond (1994) suggested, the analytic role allows the analyst to be subjectively or personally involved while also maintaining some degree of objectivity as a participant in a professional relationship. Casement (1990) stressed that the analyst's role is not to gratify libidinal demands (such as the wish to be loved, sexually satisfied, or taken care of in the way a parent takes care of a child), but to respond to *growth needs* (such as the need for empathic understanding, caring, and concern) and, on an ongoing basis, to make sense of the patient's past experience. These elements are often invoked to describe Winnicott's (1960, 1963) notion of the *holding environment.* This distinction can also be conceptualized as the difference between environmental provisions and instinctual gratifications (Grotstein, 1994; Lindon, 1994).

James Grotstein (1994) noted that the psychoanalytic rule of abstinence has become automatic and ritualized, so that it has lost much of its meaning. He suggested that abstinence must be redefined in the context of what the analyst needs to provide to the patient to make the process viable. He observed that "the sine qua non of analysis is *the provision of the rule of abstinence as well as of the secure frame of the analytic setting so as to achieve a holding environment for containment/transformation/metamorphosis*" (p. 600).

Stephen Mitchell (1993) likened the distinction of Winnicott (1960, 1963) and Casement (1990) to the difference between wishes and needs. However, he cautioned that determining which is which is often a highly complex undertaking and entails an inevitable amount of trial and error. He shares our view that the analytic frame must be flexible, and he has stressed that the appropriate frame may vary from patient to patient. Even the basic elements of the frame can have entirely different meanings to different analysands. He cited an example of a patient for whom lying on the couch was reminiscent of a masochistic submission to a domineering mother who insisted that the patient be absolutely silent and immobile after going to bed so she would not disturb the mother. In this case, getting up from the couch and moving around the office became a necessary part of the analytic frame.

According to Mitchell (1993), the attitude of the analyst toward the patient's demands or requests is much more crucial than the direct content of the analyst's response. He also pointed out that the analytic frame is constructed by both analyst and patient conjointly, and each may view the dimensions of flexibility versus rigidity in entirely different ways:

> It is apparent that one person's "firmness" is another's rigidity, and that one person's flexibility is another's "caving in." Both firmness and flexibility are important and should be among the considerations of any clinician struggling with these situations. . . . The problem with the principle of standing firm is the assumption that it must mean to the patient what the analyst wants it to mean. Sometimes it does, and the patient feels encouraged by the analyst's ability to set limits, stand by his faith in the analytic process, resist allowing himself to be seduced into dangerous departures.
>
> However, while the analyst thinks she is standing firm, the patient may feel he is being brutalized in a very familiar fashion. Many patients are lost because they feel utterly abandoned or betrayed by analysts who

think they are maintaining the purity of the analytic frame. The frame is preserved; the operation is a success; but the patient leaves, climbing off the operating table in the middle of the procedure. (p. 194)

A flexible frame has long been recognized as necessary for patients who have more serious impairments in ego functioning and who need interventions that go "beyond interpretation" (Gedo, 1993). In the 1950s, interventions designed to address patients who could not work well within the classical analytic frame were often grouped together under the rubric of corrective emotional experience (Alexander, 1950). Some of these interventions involved actively playing a role that was consciously designed to be different from that of the actual parental figure in the patient's life, and therefore corrective.

Today most analysts would acknowledge that every good analysis contains corrective experiences and that insight and corrective experiences work synergistically to produce good analytic results (Jacobs, 1990; Loewald, 1980; Viederman, 1991). These corrective experiences, however, are not contrived with the intent of behaving in a way that is diametrically opposed to the behavior of the patient's parents. Rather, they occur as an inevitable by-product of new experience in the analytic setting. For example, Hans Loewald (1980) observed the following:

The re-experience by re-enactment of the past—the unconscious organization of the past implied in repetition—undergoes change during the course of treatment. In part these changes depend on the impact of current experiences with the analyst that do not fit the anticipatory set the patient brings to his experiencing another, mainly parental, person. In this manner the way of reliving the past is apt to be influenced by novel present experience. (p. 360)

Although Kohut (1984) acknowledged that some form of corrective emotional experience occurs in analysis, he also made it clear that the analyst should not actively soothe the patient in an effort to become the good mother that the patient never had as a child. Instead, he proposed that the analyst should interpret the patient's yearning to be soothed. Howard Bacal and Kenneth Newman (1990), who were influenced by both Kohut and the British School of Object Relations, suggested that the analyst provides corrective selfobject experiences for the patient that go well beyond interpreting the wish for such experiences. There is certainly a potential for boundary violations when the analyst embarks on a deliberate effort to provide such corrective experiences for the patient. Casement (1990) warned that

> what is therapeutic in analysis is not to be attained through any simple provision of "better" parenting. Analysts often find in their clinical work that their attempt (actively) to provide good experience for a patient almost invariably deflects the analytic process because it interferes with the patient's use of the analyst in the transference. A prime reason for this is that patients often need to use the analyst in order to work through feelings about earlier experiences *as they had been*: it is not enough simply to have experience in the analytic relationship that might seem to be "corrective." (pp. 342–343)

The issue of how much gratification is optimal within the analytic boundaries and frame is a thorny one that defies simple guidelines. For one thing, the concept of gratification in some ways implies an unambivalent wish on the part of the patient. Does the patient with sexual longings for the analyst *really* want those wishes concretely gratified? Maybe yes, maybe no, but the vast majority of analysands would be highly ambivalent about such gratification. If the patient is a victim of childhood incest and is unconsciously resurrecting the childhood situation in the analytic setting, it is difficult to imagine how consummating a sexual relationship could be construed as *gratifying*. Most of us would question whether a father is "gratifying" his daughter's sexual longings even though we acknowledge that little girls have erotic desires for their father.

The analytic situation has been aptly described by Leo Stone (1984) as one of "deprivation-in-intimacy" (p. 77). The intimacy is one in which there is an inherent gratification, that is, the highest priority is the therapeutic obligation to the patient. Yet the setting also symbolizes a basic experience of separateness. Stone argued that one of the basic differences between an analyst and a traditional physician is that the former represents the mother-of-separation as opposed to the mother involved with intimate bodily care (which is more closely aligned with the role of the typical physician). He also stressed, however, that principles such as abstinence must be implemented with a certain latitude and flexibility or they will defeat the very purpose of the psychoanalytic enterprise.

Certainly the analytic process entails a good deal of frustration, and both participants know that all the patient's desires will not be satisfied. To establish an engagement that is lively and spontaneous, the analyst will inevitably vary the frame from day to day and from patient to patient. Mitchell (1993) suggested that

> what is most crucial is neither gratification nor frustration, but the process of negotiation itself, in which the analyst finds his own particular way to confirm and participate in the patient's subjective experience yet, over time, establishes his own presence and perspective in a way that the patient can find enriching rather than demolishing. (p. 196)

The understanding of what transpires between analyst and analysand is, of course, the essence of the process. The key here is that the analyst must strive to act in the patient's best interests, even though those interests may be difficult to ascertain from moment to moment.

Mitchell's comments on how analysts find their own particular way to participate in the negotiation process with the patient reflect a growing awareness in the field that the analyst's participation is a variable that shifts from analyst to analyst and, for each analyst, across patients. Jay Greenberg (1995) observed that there is an *interactive matrix* that serves to define the precise nature of the frame and the "rules" in each analytic dyad. In this regard, we must acknowledge that the varying degrees of elasticity of the frame are a reflection not simply of the patient's specific needs but also of the analyst's subjectivity.

One patient agreed to an analytic process four times a week but insisted on sitting in a chair rather than using the couch. Her analyst explored the request with her, and the patient spoke at some length about how her mother "disappeared" into mental hospitals several times while the patient was a child. To lie on the couch was experienced as a repetition of this trauma because the analyst disappeared from view. The analyst, on the other hand, explained that she found it much more difficult to achieve the optimal state of attentiveness when a patient was looking directly at her. After a few sessions of discussion, they finally negotiated a compromise in which the patient would begin the analysis on the couch but could sit up when she felt particularly vulnerable to "losing" her analyst. This negotiated frame took into account both the patient's needs and the analyst's subjectivity.

The analytic role is in part defined by the analyst's dedication to the patient. Roy Schafer (1983) elaborated this point further in his definition of the analyst's role as involving a group of characteristics that define the analytic attitude. Included in these characteristics are forthrightness, the avoidance of either–or thinking, an emphasis on analyzing rather than reacting, a courteous and respectful effort to be helpful, an avoidance of acting on selfish motivations, and neutrality.

Clearly, the analyst cannot entirely avoid reacting spontaneously, thereby making strict neutrality in the classical sense impossible to achieve. Greenberg's (1986a) definition of neutrality as an attempt to remain equidistant between the old object and the new object may be more useful for the present purposes. In the course of the analytic work, the analyst is repeatedly drawn into countertransference enactments that depart from an entirely neutral or nonjudgmental stance. To some degree, these responses represent behavior and feelings that are similar to those of old objects from the patient's past as well as from the analyst's past. In other ways, they represent new contributions from the analyst as a new and different object. The concept of countertransference enactment is considered in some detail in Chapter 7. The critical factor we wish to stress here is that whatever the nature of the enactments brought about by the interaction, there must be an effort to analyze their meanings in collaboration with the patient (Gabbard, 1995a; Mitchell, 1993; Renik, 1993).

A recent major shift in psychoanalytic thinking is the widespread recognition that the participation and personal presence of the analyst are always influencing the process, often in ways that are largely unconscious. For example, the analyst may espouse a nonjudgmental neutrality as part of the analytic frame but nevertheless unwittingly convey to her patient that she is disapproving of the patient's current romantic object choice. She may be surprised to hear her patient say, "I can tell you don't like him." Recognizing that she was unconsciously communicating something of her feelings to the patient, the analyst would then explore the patient's perception further to see how the experience was recapitulating past experiences of disapproval. At the same time, she would look within herself to identify her own contribution, from her own past, to the enactment.

Self-disclosure is generally regarded as a breach of an analytic boundary, but as the preceding vignette illustrates, some degree of self-disclosure is inevitable. Irwin Hoffman (1991a) suggested that there are times when more direct self-disclosure may enhance the process. For example, when a patient asks the analyst a direct question, it may be useful for the analyst to reveal some aspects of his experience as well as of the conflict concerning whether or not to answer the question. Self-disclosing of one's personal problems or difficulties from childhood is rarely useful and should signal to the analyst that something is awry. Most helpful disclosures involve some version of clinical honesty in the here-and-now experience of the patient and the process (Gabbard & Wilkinson, 1994). We would, however, draw a clear line at self-disclosure of sexual feelings for the patient (Gabbard, 1994a). Disclosure of erotic countertransference usually has a different meaning for the patient from other feelings in the analyst. It may overwhelm and confuse the patient. It may threaten the patient with the inherent link between sexual feelings and action. And it frequently leads to a collapse of the analytic space because the concrete has replaced the symbolic.

THE ANALYTIC OBJECT

The consideration of the analytic role serves as a convenient segue to an examination of the analytic object. Freud (1915a) recognized the uniqueness of the analytic relationship when he noted that analysis represents a type of relationship "for which there is no model in real life" (p. 166). Indeed, the analytic object is created by careful attention to the analytic frame and the analytic boundaries. The frame and boundaries facilitate the emergence of a specific type of object that is constructed by the interaction of the patient and analyst and contains the interpretive material generated during analysis.

There is an increasing consensus within the psychoanalytic literature that the mutative process of psychoanalysis involves both the internalization of the relationship with the analyst and the achievement of insight through interpretation (Baker, 1993; Cooper, 1992; Gabbard, 1995a; Pulver, 1992). From this consensus, it follows that the analyst must be both a transference object, subject to interpretive work, and a new object, subject to internalization. As Greenberg (1986b) noted, "If the analyst cannot be experienced as a new object, analysis never gets underway; if he cannot be experienced as an old one, it never ends" (p. 98). Follow-up studies (Pfeffer, 1993) reflect the fact that the analyst remains mentally represented for the patient as both an old and a new object, so that this bimodal representation is an achievement of analytic work that persists.

The analytic frame and the analytic boundaries together provide an atmosphere that facilitates the emergence of the analyst as a transference object (Baker, 1993). The relative anonymity and at least partial abstinence in the analytic role serve as fertile soil for the displacement of past objects in the patient's life into the present relationship with the analyst. Ronald Baker (1993) argued that the new object will not emerge until the transference object is extensively analyzed and interpreted. Baker's point is important because of the frequent confusion between the analyst as an idealized transference object and the analyst as a new object.

Particularly in the analysis of patients who have experienced childhood trauma, the analyst may be regarded as an idealized rescuer who will make up for the bad experiences from the patient's past (Davies & Frawley, 1992; Gabbard, 1992, 1994b). Mitchell (1993) observed, however, that the desires of adult patients should not be viewed as simply replacements or compensations for deprivations of childhood (as the patients themselves often view them). Childhood trauma goes through various adult transformations and becomes angry revenge or overvalued suffering. Hence gratification of these desires is not likely to bring about the result for which the patient hopes.

Much of the confusion arises from a tradition within the analytic literature of equating the analyst's role with that of a parent. Loewald (1960) compared the analytic process to one involving reparenting. Although there are certainly elements of the analyst–patient relationship that recapitulate and parallel the parent–child relationship, the analogy can be misused to justify a folie à deux in which the patient desperately wants the analyst to become the "good parent" to make up for the "bad parent" of the past and the analyst colludes with this wish by attempting to become an idealized figure who will compensate the patient for past traumas.

Spruiell (1983) shares our concern:

Even within the frame we do not act like parents; we do not succor, ignore, reward, spank, cajole, argue with, instruct, bathe, forbid, etc. Nor do we act like lovers, enemies, friends, siblings, or the patient himself or some part of him. We act like analysts—a fact sometimes forgotten in the literature where one finds assertions that within the "alliance" the analyst is "really" being a better parent than the patient ever had. It is as disastrous for analysts to actually treat their patients like children as it is for analysts to treat their own children as patients. (p. 12)

Casement (1985) argued that taking the patient's transference wishes literally and attempting to gratify them blurs the distinction between symbolic holding and literal holding. The patient needs to experience past trauma and the old object relationship as they originally were, as well as have the experience of analyzing this transference wish with the analyst. Only then can old trauma be worked through.

Systematic analysis of the transference within the analytic frame ultimately provides the patient with a new object experience. Morris Eagle (1987) suggested that the safety of the analytic setting along with the analyst's survival of the patient's attacks send a powerful message to the patient. He even compares it to an unspoken interpretation that helps the patient understand that the analyst is a new object, different from the original traumatic object, and that the analysis itself is not the original traumatic situation.

The analytic object, therefore, is in one sense an amalgam of the transference object and the new object. In that regard, it is a joint creation of the interpenetrating subjectivities of the two participants (Gabbard, 1995a). Ogden (1994) argued that the core of the analytic process is the dialectical movement of subjectivity and intersubjectivity between analyst and patient: "There is no such thing as an analysand apart from the relationship with the analyst, and no such thing as an analyst apart from the relationship with the analysand" (p. 63). In this homage to the Winnicottian view of mother and child, Ogden is suggesting that transference and countertransference reflect a dialectic between the analyst as a separate entity and the analyst as a joint creation of the intersubjectivity of the analytic process. Ongoing projective identification between the two participants creates an interpersonally decentered subject that he refers to as "the analytic third." The analysis itself takes shape in the interpretive space between the analyst and the analysand.

One implication of Ogden's view is that three subjectivities can be identified in the psychoanalytic work: the subjectivity of the analyst, that of the patient, and that of the analytic third. Projective identification simultaneously negates and reappropriates both subjectivities to create a new "subject." From the patient's perspective, this subject is also the analytic object. In this sense, the object is indeed a new creation of the setting. It is jointly constructed by analyst and analysand (and their internal objects) through the long repetitions of the analytic process within well-prescribed frames and "rituals." The analytic object could thus be understood as resembling what David Black (1993) designated as religious or socially constructed objects that "have a function of 'containing' the feelings, thoughts and fantasies arising in individual practitioners" (p. 624).

In conclusion, each analytic dyad creates its own analytic object. To accomplish this task, an analytic frame with its own unique set of analytic boundaries is forged in the crucible of the analytic interaction. Despite the individual differences in these elements, certain overriding characteristics define the analyst's role as specifically psychoanalytic. These include relative restraint; an avoidance of excessive self-disclosure; a regularity and predictability of sessions; a devotion to understanding the patient; a generally nonjudgmental attitude; an acknowledgment of complexity in motives, wishes, and needs; a sense of courtesy and respect for the patient; and a willingness to put one's own desires aside in the service of a greater understanding of the patient.

CHAPTER 4

Boundaries and Gender

I N THE PREVIOUS CHAPTERS, we outlined the distinction between external–interpersonal boundaries (i.e., boundaries between the self and the external object or between the ego and the external world) and inner boundaries (i.e., boundaries within the self, or boundaries between the ego and the id, the superego, or both). In this chapter, we discuss boundaries and gender, following the same inner–outer distinction. As clinical and empirical data in this area accumulate, such distinctions may eventually be shown to be invalid. Given the present state of knowledge, however, the conceptual separation seems theoretically and clinically useful.

GENDER AND INTERPERSONAL BOUNDARIES

Clinicians have long observed that women generally show a degree of permeability in their interpersonal relations. Peter Blos (1980) reported this in his work with adolescent girls, but similar observations have been made regarding women of all ages. Women are said to approach and become emotionally available to others more readily than men; they are less defensive than men in allowing closeness with others and strive to maintain interpersonal ties with children, men, and other women. Women with less integrated personalities show more readily (possibly too readily) a wish for fusion with others. In analysis, female patients develop erotized transferences (regressive transferences with a strong wish for merger with the object [Blum, 1973]) more frequently and with more intensity than men (Lester, 1985; Lester, Jodoin, & Robertson, 1989). Such erotized transferences in female patients are addressed equally to male and female analysts. Their wishes for merger, nurturance, and succor (and their desperate attempt to appropriate and control the object) are evident in their dreams, their conscious fantasies, and their enactments in the analytic situation.

With female analysts, the erotic wish more commonly refers to a maternal erotism than to oedipal, genital sexuality, although both are often at play, as illustrated by the following:

THE CASE OF MS. E

Ms. E, a twice-divorced professional woman, entered analysis complaining of emptiness, recurring bouts of depression, and a sense of failure and aimlessness in her life. She described her mother as "specializing in stupidity," a puppet in the hands of a controlling and tyrannical father. In her youth she felt alienated from both parents and sought comfort in mildly dyssocial peer groups.

Despite the long distance Ms. E had to travel to come to analysis, she rarely missed sessions. Once on the couch, however, she would soon enter a regressed state, remaining silent for long periods. She described feelings of deadness and formlessness. Minute changes in the analytic schedule would provoke acute anxiety and rage at the "uncaring" analyst. In the second year of analysis, and as the regressive transference intensified, the patient reported a series of dreams in which the analyst appeared undisguised. In most of these dreams, Ms. E arrived at the session and the analyst was not there or was busy. Recalling one dream, she said the following: "Strange . . . all I could remember were your breasts." Soon after, Ms. E started having a recurring fantasy of putting her head on the analyst's lap while the analyst stroked her hair and she felt comforted. As the transference deepened even further, she started fantasizing about nursing on the breast.

Men in analysis, in the vast majority of cases, tend to resist such fusional urges, except in cases of extreme regressive states, when such desires may surface. Fusional wishes stir up what Robert Stoller (1985) called "symbiosis anxiety," the fear of entering a state of extreme dependence and developing the fantasy/wish of merging with the object. Characteristically, transference material or transference enactments are permeated by anality and an aggressive attack on the object in an effort to stave off further regression. An example follows:

THE CASE OF DR. F

Dr. F, a married physician, came to analysis complaining of a lack of vitality and pleasure in his professional and private life. "My life is flat, colorless, a series of routines." A middle child in a very large family, Dr. F missed both his father's encouragement ("He was the boss, hard and cruel; no one dared to disobey him") and his mother's warmth ("She was always so busy . . . her only pleasure was her garden"). Dr. F learned to repress any "weakness" and to develop efficiency and consistency in his studies and his family responsibilities.

In the first part of the analysis, the focus was his strong oedipal antagonism against the "boss," seeing the analyst as an ally. As the representation of the cruel "boss" began losing its hold on his fantasy life, Dr. F began regressing in the transference. Erotic themes appeared in his dreams of the type found in romantic adolescent "crushes" on older female teachers. Genital sexual impulses were displaced to females outside the analysis. As the transference intensified further, "rage and contempt" against women appeared, and long periods of silence marked the sessions. The patient's regressive urges and his reactive aggressive impulses against the analyst were expressed in the following dream: "You seem withdrawn and passive. I start hitting you. First it is rage, then it is all sexual. It was like a nightmare. I woke up. I stayed awake for a long time, wondering about this rage. It is not sadism . . . it is revenge: Who is going to dominate whom?"

•   •   •

In the analysis of females by females, stalemates occasionally occur when the analyst allows for too much weakening of the analytic boundaries. These stalemates can be described as transference–countertransference enactments in the form of enmeshments.

An important clinical and research observation, which may point to gender differences in interpersonal and probably inner boundaries as well, is that certain personality disorders show a gender-related preponderance. We are referring here to the increased incidence of borderline personality disorder in women and that of narcissistic personality disorder in men (Akhtar & Thompson, 1982; Stone, 1989).

Borderline personality disorder (BPD), or borderline personality organization, according to Kernberg (1977, 1993), is characterized by an ever-changing interpersonal scene, in addition to—or probably in relation to—a diffuse inner state, the lack of cohesion in the self system, and the use of primitive defenses (splitting, projective identification, and so on). Stone (1993) noted the "increased central nervous system irritability" and saw it as the basis of several of the clinical manifestations of BPD, such as anger, affective storminess, and self-destructive acts. These features may be related to an increased permeability, a lability of both inner and outer (interpersonal) boundaries.

In a recently published study (Burbiel, Finke, & Sanderman, 1994), a large number of borderline patients were tested with a specific instrument measuring narcissism and ego boundaries ("inner and outer demarcations"). Compared to nonborderline subjects, the borderline cohorts showed clearly "deficient" (thin) boundaries. "Basically, regulation of boundaries concerning the own world of unconscious fantasies is not possible. The borderline-patient is not able to draw a line between himself and other persons, groups and demands arising in interpersonal relations" (p. 9).

Extensive epidemiological and clinical studies (Paris & Zweig-Frank, 1993) have established that severe, prolonged, or repeated early trauma connected to parental brutality or incest, a compromised central nervous system through parental alcohol or drug abuse, and a familial incidence of affective disorders are all considered predisposing factors for the development of BPD. Similarly, severe early trauma has been found in the histories of individuals with thin inner boundaries. Incest, which is common in the personal history of patients with borderline pathology, seems to have a specifically noxious influence on the development of firm inner and outer boundaries. As Seymour Parker (1976) pointed out, to develop a distinct and separate concept of oneself, the individual needs to participate in progressively wider networks of relationships. The incest taboo, observed universally through historical times within all sociocultural groupings, functions to protect boundaries and to enhance identity formation, in the absence of which a cultural mode of life is not possible.

Within this context, as mentioned in Chapter 2, Tustin (1981), Yariv (1989), and others observed that rigid, inflexible boundaries within the family, acting as barriers between self and others, may not be as potentially harmful to the child's development as situations in which there are no distinctions. The emerging self is not differentiated from mother or father or from other animate or inanimate objects, usually intermingling in a chaotic way in the child's personal experience. It appears that in these cases the development of transitional objects and a transitional space, which facilitates the development of play and through which play is reinforced (Winnicott, 1953), is seriously compromised.

In contrast to the higher incidence of BPD among women, narcissistic personality disorder (NPD) seems to be more common among men. John Gunderson and Elsa Ronningstam (1991) recently established that the pathognomonic personality characteristic of patients with NPD is the grandiose self-experience (i.e., the unfounded and unrealistic overvaluation of one's talents, achievements, uniqueness, invincibility, and superiority). To develop and maintain such grandiose self-experience, a certain impermeability—a thickness of interpersonal boundaries—seems critical. Many patients with NPD seem impervious to the criticism or disapproval of others and are blind to the evaluation others make about them and their achievements. They also seem able to maintain a grandiose self-experience, despite lack of evidence from outside, through well-drawn (largely impermeable) interpersonal boundaries.

Here Landis's (1970) research may be relevant. Landis did not introduce gender as a variable in his study, but his findings may be of value in conceptualizing the gender-related preponderance of certain personality disorders. Landis remarked:

Speaking in the most general terms, the I-dominant [impermeable] person may be task-oriented or impelled to persist at an activity until he reaches his original goals, whereas a P-dominant [permeable] person may be viewed as either self-absorbed and task-oriented or as more flexible in accepting a substitute goal. (pp. 134–135)

It is, of course, true that borderline patients often control their environment and become the center of family turmoil, but such control is exercised through further abolishing interpersonal boundaries and recreating the chaos often described in the families of a patient with borderline personality organization, rather than through the mechanisms of distancing or controlling others.

Further clinical evidence supporting gender differences in interpersonal boundaries is provided by a rather surprising finding in a study of the countertransference dream (CTD) (Lester et al., 1989). A clinical survey of all members and candidates for membership in the Canadian Psychoanalytic Society was undertaken to test the following two hypotheses (as proposed by Zweibel, 1985): (1) CTDs signal a disturbance in the analytic relationship and (2) most such dreams act as indicators of the analyst's feared or denied loss of competence. On the basis of the responses (75 percent responded to the survey), the second hypothesis was not corroborated: No differences were found in the incidence of such dreams among analytic candidates, recently graduated analysts, and senior analysts. Some correlation was found to exist between the intensification of the transference and the frequency of CTDs, a finding that was more or less expected. The unexpected finding referred to gender differences in the *manifest content* of the specimen dreams that were reported. Male analysts reported a high number of CTDs in which the manifest content was clearly erotic–sexual. In the CTDs of female respondents, the manifest content centered predominantly on the intrusion by the analysand into the analyst's private space: the analyst's home, her office, her bedroom, and so on.

The clinically and experimentally supported findings of thin interpersonal boundaries among women seem to be corroborated by recent studies on gender-related psychosocial differences. Studies addressing such differences range from purely feminist texts (Jaggar, 1983), to work on the influence of gender in establishing parameters of science and of scientific knowledge (Keller, 1985), to psychological studies (Gilligan, 1982), and finally, to more recent observations of gender differences in cognitive functions (Bleier, 1991; Notman & Nadelson, 1991; Witelson, 1985).

In her book *Reflections on Gender and Science*, Evelyn Fox Keller (1985) traced and convincingly established the masculine character of scientific objectivity in Western science. Keller pointed out that whereas Plato used the metaphor of knowledge as a homoerotic union (i.e., knowledge seen as Eros), Bacon saw knowledge as a heterosexual conquest (knowledge equals power). Keller (1986) commented: "Instead of banishing the Furies underground, out of sight, as the Greeks, modern science has sought to expose female interiority, to bring it into the light and thus to dissolve its threat entirely" (p. 74).

Modern science, according to Keller, makes a clear distinction between subject (the scientist, mostly male) and object (Nature, the mother, female). The male's need to oppose and separate from mother is responsible, according to Keller, for rejecting any experience of merging and identification between subject and object, because it may weaken the boundaries between the two.

Carol Gilligan's (1982) well-known research was specifically designed to question and identify the masculine character of moral psychology. Her findings challenged previous findings (Kohlberg, 1981), which indicated that women do not reach the highest level of moral development and moral reasoning as had been measured in studies of males. In her well-known book *In a Different Voice*, Gilligan (1982) pointed out that Lawrence Kohlberg based his notions of moral development on abstract principles removed from concrete human situations, thus ignoring the importance of interpersonal ties. When such considerations are taken into account in the design of the tests administered, women show very similar strengths in moral judgment to men. What Gilligan's research clearly demonstrated is that for women, maintaining connections and improving interpersonal ties has a higher priority than understanding abstract principles of moral behavior. Gilligan's findings had an important effect on the reappraisal of psychoanalytic notions regarding the development of moral conscience (superego).

Anthropological studies, as reviewed by Robert LeVine (1991), indicate that gender dimorphism, on the basis of the interplay of biological and sociocultural factors, exists and has existed through historical times in all societies. In all cultures, women are expected to take care of infants and children and to provide the care that will ensure the children's adequate functioning in society. This division of labor inevitably shapes and restricts the gender roles assigned to women. Gender dimorphism, LeVine pointed out, becomes evident early in the individual's life. Boys 3 to 6 years old in all human environments show more aggressive, rough-and-tumble behavior, whereas girls of the same age show more touching and communicative behavior.

Documented gender-related behavioral differences confirm the female's greater need to maintain connection and communication within the specific relational network in which she functions. In general, females use a communicative mode of gathering information, are sensitive to sounds, and in infancy, are very responsive to mother's voice. In addition, they react more to faces, speech patterns, and tone of voice and are more attentive in social contexts than males. Males are found to have more ability in spatial tests, whereas females show early verbal ability. Witelson (1985) and others have proposed a kind of neural dimorphism, a greater hemispheric specialization (greater lateralization) in males, but this proposition has been seriously questioned (Bleier, 1991).

Reviewing recent infant research based on direct observations of infants by psychoanalytically informed investigators, Malkah Notman and Carol Nadelson (1991) stated the following: "In sum, two different patterns emerge for girls and boys. Female neonates with their stable state system, increased awareness of the outside world, and greater involvement in gazing and vocalization, show an increased potential for greater connectedness to the caregiver" (p. 32). With reference to bonding and attachment (important milestones during the first year), significant gender differences have been observed:

> The male's greater irritability and lessened responsiveness to calming and soothing make overstimulation a concern for the male neonate. The mother's animated face and her gazing, given the male's less stable state system, may be experienced as too arousing. . . . An increase in fussiness, crying, or gaze aversion may follow from this overarousal. (Notman & Nadelson, 1991, p. 32)

Bonding and attachment may, therefore, be somewhat delayed and, in some cases, severely impeded.

GENDER AND INNER BOUNDARIES

As we noted in Chapter 1, Federn (1952) probably came the closest to a simple and clear conceptualization of inner boundaries, despite the limited theoretical tools at his disposal. He described the inner boundary as the demarcations between the ego and unconscious fantasies, wishes, and so on (i.e., demarcations between the ego and the id) as well as between the ego and the unconscious aspects of the superego. On the basis of modern theoretical premises, however, such conceptualization would not be adequate to explain the nature and function of inner boundaries as analysts understand them today.

The decline of the structural model in psychoanalysis has produced a conceptual vacuum with regard to the "mental apparatus." Object relations theories, self psychology, and intersubjective–relational models all deal primarily with interactional issues. The focus of recent psychoanalytic writings has shifted to the scrutiny of interactive processes during analysis and to the specific entities of transference and countertransference. Scrutiny has also been extended to other interpersonal encounters and to early developmental processes and their relevance to pathology in cognitive, affective, and symbolic functions. In the present climate of high ferment in cognitive neurosciences, psychoanalysis is focusing on clinical and other interactive processes. It is in these areas that, through the application of the psychoanalytic method and through observation and research on the emerging question, psychoanalysis may contribute to theory building. At this moment, the understanding of the brain and specific neurophysiological functions cannot be entrusted to clinical observation alone.

As mentioned previously, Hartmann (1991) eschewed Federn's ego psychological concepts and wrote of boundaries "in the mind." In attempting to conceptualize boundaries, however, Hartmann became overinclusive, and in the end, a definition becomes elusive. When Hartmann stated that boundaries exist at the simple level of input to our senses, therefore, he was dealing with perceptual acuity or field dependence–independence (i.e., the ability to focus thinking or, more precisely, task-oriented thinking, and the ability to contain emotion from "contaminating" thinking). A similar orientation was evident when he referred to *synesthesia*, "the coming together of perceptions from different sense modalities, or more technically, the occurrence of imagery in one sense modality in response to sensations in another" (p. 23). He also touched on altered states of consciousness, the crossover from thinking to feeling states, fantasy, and reveries.

In elaborating his thoughts, Hartmann (1991) saw defense mechanisms as closely related to boundaries. For instance, repression involves the "walling off" of painful memories or disturbing impulses (keeping them away from awareness), isolation relates to the keeping of emotions "walled off" from thought, and intellectualization may reinforce isolation by "putting up a wall of words and abstractions to avoid dealing wholly and emotionally with an issue" (p. 39).

As Morton Reiser (1990) pointed out, sensory registration containing information from the environment is first broken up into various components (size, color, affective tone, and so on) to facilitate processing. Such components are subsequently reassembled for perceiving, for storage in the association cortex, and for remembering. During reassembly, fresh percepts are connected with related percepts already stored in the association cortex. Furthermore, connections are influenced by brain stem centers involved in arousal and alertness and by subcortical structures controlling affective functioning. "The reciprocally interconnected cortical and subcortical systems constitute complex neural nets containing multiple reentry paths, feedback, and loops within loops, arranged in overlapping progressions. The computations required in these cognitive functions are amazingly complex" (pp. 132–133).

Viewed within this conceptual framework, the development of thin or thick inner boundaries may be related to both biological and environmental influences. For instance, among Hartmann's subjects (1991), who were tested extensively with the Boundary Questionnaire, individuals with a certain artistic sensibility were commonly observed to score within the thin end of the spectrum of inner boundaries. Artistic sensibility may rest on an inborn complexity in the interconnection of synapses, although such "complexity" alone may not be sufficient for high-level artistic production.

Hartmann (1991) also was able to confirm the gender-related differences in boundaries. In applying the Boundary Questionnaire to a large number of individuals, Hartmann's team established that, on the whole, women scored "significantly thinner than men—thinner by about twenty points" (p. 131). The questionnaire was constructed carefully to avoid gender biases, and all items were gender-blind.

Other innate factors that are not identified as such may predispose to the development of thin or thick inner boundaries. Hartmann (1991) proposed that the two neurotransmitters norepinephrine and serotonin may play an important role in the "maturing" (thickening) of boundaries during development. He stated:

> I would suggest that increasing the overall activity of these two amines at the cortex, which in a rough sense produces a situation similar to that of alert wakefulness, is associated with a relative thickening of boundaries, whereas reducing their activity, which produces a situation more similar to that of REM sleep, is associated with a relative thinning of boundaries. (p. 240)

It has been documented that clinical depressive illness is associated with a disturbance in the metabolism of these amines in the brain and that antidepressants in the group of selective serotonin reuptake inhibitors (SSRIs) aim to correct such disturbance. Several epidemiological studies have indicated that depressive illness is more prevalent in females, but whether such predominance is related to innate factors or to sociocultural influences is not clear. Similarly, the reported higher incidence of nightmares in females may refer to innate as well as to environmental factors.

Levin et al. (1991) observed that "a number of recent surveys have established that while periodic nightmares are relatively common, only a small percentage of the general nonpsychiatric population experiences frequent attacks, with women consistently reporting more frequent nightmares than men" (p. 63). The authors, accepting that this finding might be highly speculative, offer the proposition that "a pre-existing state of thin boundaries, perhaps linked to the incomplete or fragmented internalization of self- and object-representations . . . may facilitate access to primary process mentation" (p. 72).

Turning more specifically to environmental influences that may relate to gender differences in the development of inner boundaries, no clinical observations or reported studies have established the existence of such factors, at least in Western societies. Early sexual trauma, the most violent and pernicious "impingement" of the environment on the child (Winnicott, 1960), plays a specific role in the development of thin boundaries; although females are by far the most frequent victims of such trauma, the effect on the growing male child may be equally deleterious.

Early sexual trauma (i.e., beginning at the prelatency or early latency years, before the child develops access and connections to the outside world) is considered incestuous in the majority of cases. The incestuous nature of early sexual trauma may be particularly damaging to the development of inner boundaries because the lack of limits and frame within the family, as well as the secrecy and denial of the events, creates in the child extreme states of early, profound confusion and doubt about the validity of his or her perceived reality.

There is extensive literature on the effects of early sexual trauma on the development of the child (Arvanitakis, Jodoin, Lester, Lussier, & Robertson, 1993; Browne & Finkelhor, 1986; LeVine, 1991). Two of the frequently described symptoms, in addition to the often-encountered connection between early sexual trauma and borderline personality disorder, may relate to a unique disturbance in the consolidation of inner boundaries. We refer here to the commonly described dissociative states in these patients (states of disturbances in the sense of self, space, and time) and to the increased incidence of nightmares.

Konstantinos Arvanitakis et al. (1993) reported that more than half of adult survivors of early sexual abuse suffer from frequent nightmares. The specific content of these nightmares is suggestive of profound disturbance in the development of inner boundaries (Arvanitakis et al., 1993; McCarthy, 1994).

In one type of nightmare, the terror of the dream is expressed by the disintegration of the body or total failure of bodily functions. A female patient reported the following dream:

> My mouth is full of pins. They are stuck in my gums, in my teeth. I lean forward to spit them out. The more I spit, the more they are there. The pins become safety pins and then paper clips connected with one another. I keep pulling them out and suddenly I realize it is my guts I am pulling out. If I keep doing it, I will die. I wake up in terror. (Arvanitakis et al., 1993, p. 578)

A male patient who had been repeatedly molested by his father dreamt the following:

My body is decaying. I can see my head. It is turning black, the color of decay. . . . In the dream there is a sense of loss; I despair, all I have is my mind . . . somebody without a body . . . no boundaries. I have to be carried around in a plastic bag. (p. 579)

In a well-documented case (McCarthy, 1994), a similar lack of boundaries and secure sense of inner reality was observed in the patient's nightmares:

In mid-latency [the patient] had many dreams of trains entering and emerging from tunnels in a vast station. The platforms had no numbers, the station clock had no numbers and no hands, the trains had no drivers, and there was no one at all in the station. (p. 6)

Another recurring dream associated with acute anxiety was that of "a moonscape with canals filled with urine and feces . . . no people, a total desolation" (p. 7).

The frequency and content of these nightmares may point to a degree of "inadequacy" (thinness) of inner boundaries. Disturbances in self-identity, dissociative phenomena, and pervasive anxiety—common symptoms of early sexual abuse—may be seen, partly as clinical manifestations of the same "boundary pathology." Symptoms connected to early sexual abuse are more prevalent in women, because female children are more often victims of incest; however, one cannot consider such symptoms primarily gender-related. On the other hand, the preponderance of nightmares in females, in general, may be pointing in that direction.

At this point in the understanding of the issues involved, we may conclude that with regard to interpersonal (outer) boundaries, gender-related differences (i.e., increased permeability in females) have been reported on the basis of reliable clinical and empirical studies. We believe that both biological and sociocultural factors are at work. With regard to inner boundaries, a less clearly defined category, evidence supporting gender-related differences is still not conclusive.

CHAPTER 5

The Early History of Boundary Violations in Psychoanalysis

I N A LETTER of December 31, 1911, Freud wrote to Carl Jung about a matter of concern:

Frau C_____ has told me all sorts of things about you and Pfister, if you can call the hints she drops "telling"; I gather that neither of you has yet acquired the necessary objectivity in your practice, that you still get involved, giving a good deal of yourselves and expecting the patient to give something in return. Permit me, speaking as the venerable old master, to say that this technique is invariably ill-advised and that it is best to remain reserved and purely receptive. We must never let our poor neurotics drive us crazy. I believe an article on "counter-transference" is sorely needed; of course we could not publish it, we should have to circulate copies among ourselves. (McGuire, 1974, pp. 475–476)

More than 80 years later, similar concerns about countertransference enactments and sexual boundary violations haunt the psychoanalytic profession. Unlike Freud, however, most contemporary analysts agree that discussions of countertransference no longer require a shroud of secrecy. Our journals regularly offer scientific contributions that feature frank disclosures of countertransference issues in the author's work. The analyst's countertransference enactments are widely regarded as both inevitable and useful to the process (Chused, 1991; Gabbard, 1994f; Jacobs, 1993a; Renik, 1993).

Much of the enthusiasm for the concept of enactment, however, stems from the assumption that enactments are *partial* and that the analyst catches himself before the enactment leads to a gross and unethical boundary violation. Indeed, enactments occur on a continuum from subtle changes in body posture to frank sexual involvement with the patient. More profound enactments that involve significant violations of the analytic frame are less likely to appear in the pages of our journals and in the public forums of our scientific meetings.

The notion of professional boundaries is a relatively recent addition to psychoanalytic practice. Freud and his early disciples indulged in a good deal of trial and error as they developed psychoanalytic technique. Most of Freud's circle persevered in their efforts to define technique and were sucked into the vortex of a host of major boundary transgressions. As Freud noted to Oscar Pfister in a 1910 letter, "the transference is indeed a cross" (Meng & Freud, 1963, p. 39). As Freud's 1911 letter to Jung quoted at the beginning of this chapter suggests, the concept of countertransference had not been systematically elaborated, so that many of the early analysts lacked a solid conceptual framework for understanding what was happening to them.

The study of boundary violations in the history of psychoanalysis is also the study of the evolution of the concepts of transference and countertransference. As Andre Haynal (1994) pointed out, issues of transference, countertransference, and the optimal level of emotional involvement by the analyst were all evolved in the context of triangles involving boundary violations. First, Freud was the third party in the Carl Jung–Sabina Spielrein relationship, and shortly thereafter he was enlisted to solve the problematic involvement between Sándor Ferenczi and Elma Palos. Finally, a similar triangle was created when Freud analyzed Loë Kann, Ernest Jones's common-law wife.

The recent publication of the correspondence between Freud and Jung, between Freud and Ferenczi, and between Freud and Jones has provided extraordinary insights into the underlying dynamics of boundary transgressions in psychoanalysis. Analysts read these transcripts not only because of their historical value or because they provide titillating gossip; we study them to attempt to understand the fundamental vulnerabilities of the psychoanalytic situation. To paraphrase Santayana, those who do not study the history of boundary violations may be condemned to reenact it with their own patients.

Early on in his work with hysterical patients, Freud learned that patients often fall in love with the analyst and expect reciprocal feelings:

> In not a few cases, especially with women and where it is a question of elucidating erotic trains of thought, the patient's cooperation becomes a personal sacrifice, which must be compensated by some substitute for love. The trouble taken by the physician and his friendliness have to suffice for such a substitute. (Breuer & Freud, 1893–1895, p. 301)

As Lawrence Friedman (1994) stressed, the psychoanalytic situation involves an element of seduction. The patient is misled by the analyst to expect love, whereas the analyst tends to provide an ill-defined substitute for love. Friedman acknowledged the fact that the exact nature of that substitute remains difficult to define.

The vicissitudes of love or substitutes thereof continued to haunt Freud throughout the development of psychoanalytic technique. Recognizing the power of transference love to keep the patient involved, he noted in a letter to Jung that "the cure is effected by love" (McGuire, 1974, pp. 12–13). A little more than a month later, a comment in the Vienna Psychoanalytic Society minutes seemed to confirm this view: "Our cures are cures of love" (quoted in Haynal, 1994, p. xxvi).

It should be noted that Freud's understanding of transference was rather rudimentary in the years before and after the turn of the century. In his description of a patient who developed a wish that Freud would kiss her, he noted that such wishes arise through the phenomenon of transference, which he attributed to a "false connection" (Breuer & Freud, 1895, p. 302). This was the first appearance of the term *transference* in Freud's writing. In an extensive footnote to his discussion of Frau Emmy Von N., Freud (Breuer & Freud, 1895) elaborated on this notion. His meaning clearly reflected a rather restricted view of transference, namely, that when an unconscious connection is not apparent to the patient, the patient manufactures a conscious or false connection to explain his or her behavior. This idea that transference love was inherently "false" or "unreal" was revisited at some length 20 years later in "Observations on Transference Love" (Freud, 1915b). A careful reading of that paper suggests that Freud had shifted his view a bit to acknowledge that there were "real" aspects of transference love in addition to those that stemmed from unconscious connections with significant figures in the patient's past.

In his struggle to clarify whether transference love was similar to or different from love outside the analytic setting, Freud appeared somewhat equivocal (Gabbard, 1994b; Schafer, 1993), lending an air of ambiguity to the issue that persists to this day. In a postscript to the Dora case, Freud (1905a) recognized that transference involved an erotic reenactment of a drama from the past. If the past experiences were of a positive nature, the patient would be suggestible and compliant in the transference. If they were negative, the patient would be resistant (Kerr, 1993).

Because Freud was influenced by figures such as Bernheim, many observers have assumed that he regarded persuasion and suggestion as the active ingredients in psychoanalytic treatment. His position was actually a bit more complex. Freud regarded erotic attraction as the true vehicle of cure, whether the cure was by hypnotic suggestion or psychoanalysis. In his correspondence with Jung, he explained that the patient's erotic attraction to the analyst accounts for the patient's efforts to understand and listen to the analyst's interpretations.

FREUD, JUNG, AND SPIELREIN

Much of Freud's conceptual struggles with transference, countertransference, and the concept of love can be glimpsed in his correspondence with Jung. In 1904 Jung analyzed Sabina Spielrein, his first analytic case, in a period of approximately 2 months (Kerr, 1993). Following termination, Jung and Spielrein developed a working relationship in Jung's psychology lab. When Spielrein became a beginning medical student, the friendship between the two intensified. In the midst of this friendship, there were intermittent interviews that revived aspects of the analyst–patient relationship. Four years after the original 2-month treatment, Jung and Spielrein engaged in a tempestuous love affair that culminated in Spielrein's attacking Jung and drawing blood when he attempted to end the relationship. Her reaction to Jung's efforts to end the relationship is a common development in such affairs and has been described as "cessation trauma" (Gutheil & Gabbard, 1992).

The relationship between Jung and Spielrein is a cogent illustration of why so many "posttermination" romantic relationships present the same difficulties as those that are concurrent with analysis. Although the treatment had officially ended, the transference and countertransference dimensions of the relationship continued with a life of their own outside the formal confines of treatment. These phenomena are discussed extensively in Chapter 8.

Whether or not Jung and Spielrein actually engaged in sexual intercourse cannot be established with certainty from the written correspondence and other documents remaining. However, the details of "did they or didn't they" are relatively unimportant in light of the pervasively boundaryless relationship that characterized the years following the analysis. The scholarship of John Kerr (1993) and Aldo Carotenuto (1982) has reconstructed the Jung–Spielrein relationship in sufficient detail that much can be gleaned from the data about the development of such relationships.

As Jung's first patient, Spielrein was extraordinarily special. Infatuated with Jung, Spielrein went on to attend medical school and move into the role of student and friend. The two of them soon began to view each other as soul mates who were connected through mystical, telepathic bonds. Jung, who was prone to an interest in the occult and parapsychology, became convinced that Spielrein and he could know what the other was thinking without verbalizing their thoughts.

It is noteworthy that Jung pointedly avoided using the term *transference*, even after the appearance of Freud's Dora case in 1905 (Freud, 1905a; Kerr, 1993). He eventually used the term *transposition* instead. There is something inherently humbling in the psychoanalytic notion of transference. The analyst must reluctantly acknowledge that forces are at work that transcend his or her irresistible magnetism. If any other analyst were sitting in the chair, similar feelings would appear. Analysts who fall in love with their patients and become sexually involved with them often long to believe in the exclusivity of the patient's feelings toward them and cannot bear the pain of thinking that feelings of such intensity could be transferred to someone else (Gabbard, 1994f).

Another dimension to the Jung–Spielrein relationship was brought to light by Kerr's (1993) analysis of the psychological themes in their scientific writings of the time. Jung was preoccupied with the image of mothers as terrible and destructive. Apparently because of his intense resentment of his own mother, Jung dwelled on an image of a malevolent, incestuous mother who was responsible for man's mythological descent into hellish nether regions. At the same time, Spielrein's writings were concerned with the inevitability of destruction as a necessary accompaniment of love. As Kerr notes, "the two texts, his and hers, adjoin each other like severed halves of a forgotten conversation" (1993, p. 333).

Spielrein's long-neglected thesis deserves further study. Sexuality, in her view, always harbors an implicit threat of dissolution of the self. From a Darwinian perspective, the survival of the species is superordinate to the narcissistic investment of the individual. Part of her notion that sexuality involved dissolution was based on her view that fusion rather than pleasure might be the aim of the sexual act (a hypothesis that psychoanalytic clinicians often confirm in the exploration of patients' sexual fantasies). The ego must always resist sexuality at some level, therefore, and Spielrein suggested that the defenses against disintegration of the self most often took the form of inner images of death and destruction.

Connections between sexuality and death had been observed for centuries in legend (Tristan and Isolde), in colloquial phrases (the French term for orgasm, *la petite mort*), and in verse (the poetry of John Donne). However, the particular connection forged by Spielrein seems to have had specific significance for the relationship she was involved in with her former analyst. Indeed, the relationship nearly destroyed Jung's career and brought Spielrein to the edge of despair. Jung tried to rationalize his way out of his unethical behavior by explaining to Spielrein's mother in a lengthy letter that he had never charged her a fee for his services:

> I could drop my role as doctor the more easily because I did not feel professionally obligated, for I never charged a fee. . . . But the doctor knows

his limits and will never cross them, for he is *paid* for his troubles. That imposes the necessary restraints on him. (Carotenuto, 1982, p. 94)

In another letter, he stated to Spielrein's mother that "I have always told your daughter that a sexual relationship was out of the question and that my actions were intended to express my feelings of friendship" (Kerr, 1993, p. 207). He later described his correspondence with Frau Spielrein to Freud as a bit of "knavery."

Many modern cases of sexual boundary transgressions by analysts in some ways confirm Spielrein's thesis. One of the most striking aspects is the self-destructiveness in the analyst's behavior that is obvious to everyone but the analyst. It appears that the analyst unconsciously enacts a masochistic scenario that relates to childhood wishes of self-sacrifice. Often the details of this fantasy involve a wish to "go out in a blaze of glory" by acting on incestuous wishes for a parent and experiencing the retaliation and punishment for a forbidden act of pleasure. Sexual consummation with the patient offers a special means of actualizing such motives. Jung ultimately enlisted Freud's help in extricating himself from the situation, but Spielrein continued to feel that she had been used and was deeply hurt by the relationship.

FREUD, FERENCZI, AND PALOS

Freud later observed a similar turn of events in Ferenczi's treatment of Elma Palos. Ferenczi had previously analyzed Elma's mother, Gizella, a married woman, whom he had had as his mistress. Ferenczi fell in love with Elma in the course of his analyzing her and finally persuaded Freud to take over the case (Dupont, 1988; Haynal, 1994). What ensued was a rather remarkable series of boundary violations. Freud made regular reports to Ferenczi regarding the content of the psychoanalytic treatment of Elma and specifically kept Ferenczi informed of whether or not Elma continued to love him. He also sent confidential letters to Gizella about Ferenczi. Ultimately, Ferenczi took Elma back into analysis, but she ended up marrying an American suitor, and Ferenczi married Gizella in 1919.

It is clear from the Freud–Ferenczi correspondence that Freud found the situation messy and highly disconcerting (Brabant, Falzeder, &

Giampieri-Deutsch, 1994). In a letter to Gizella Palos in 1911, he made the following observation:

> The main difficulty is this: Does one want to build this alliance for life on concealing the fact that the man has been her mother's lover in the fullest sense of the word? And can one rely on the fact that she will take it well and overcome it in a superior manner when she knows it? (pp. 320–321)

Freud did not try to disguise his feeling that Gizella should be the preferred choice for Ferenczi. In his correspondence with Ferenczi, Freud made a number of disparaging comments about Elma, including that she had been spoiled by her father's lavish attention and was incapable and unworthy of love. Judith Dupont (1994) explained this departure from neutrality as a reflection of Freud's concern that a young wife and children might have distracted Ferenczi from his devotion to the psychoanalytic "cause."

Ferenczi appeared to gain some perspective on the situation when he interrupted the treatment of Elma and sent her to Freud. On New Year's Day of 1912, he noted to Freud that "I had to recognize that the issue here should be one not of marriage but of the treatment of an illness" (Brabant et al., 1994, p. 324). Later, on January 20 of the same year, he wrote the following to Freud:

> I know, of course, that by far the greatest part of her love for me was father transference, which easily takes another as an object. You will hardly be surprised that under these circumstances I, too, can hardly consider myself a bridegroom any longer. (Brabant et al., 1994, p. 331)

The relationship between inner boundaries (i.e., self and object representations) and the erotized countertransference of Ferenczi appears to have been pertinent. Ferenczi viewed Elma as psychotic or near-psychotic and was fascinated by the apparent fusion of self and object and by her openness to him. A similar phenomenon occurred later in Jung's career with Toni Wolff, but the chapter in Jung's memoirs describing this episode was expurgated (Kerr, 1994).

Despite this messy situation, Freud subsequently took Ferenczi into analysis, a process that occurred in a series of three meetings (some of which occurred during 2- to 3-week holidays) between 1914 and 1916. A more informal analysis took place in the summers of 1908 and 1911. Freud appeared to have some misgivings about jeopardizing the friendship by introducing an analytic relationship but nevertheless proceeded (Haynal, 1994). The ensuing analysis (we use the term advisedly) took place after Freud and Ferenczi had voyaged to America together for the Clark University lectures. On the ship they did a bit of mutual analysis. Harold Blum (1994) suggested that their subsequent periods of analytic work should be thought of as "analytic encounters." Freud would write Ferenczi letters addressed "Dear Son," in which he would suggest that they would have two analytic sessions a day while also having a meal together. Hence the analytic relationship occurred in parallel with other relationships, including mentor–student, close friend, and traveling companion (Blum, 1994). Moreover, Freud apparently wished that Ferenczi would marry his daughter (Haynal, 1994).

To be fair to Freud, this blurring of the roles of friend and analysand caused him to undertake Ferenczi's analysis with some trepidation. Indeed, the correspondence between the two of them suggests that Ferenczi placed a great deal of pressure on Freud to analyze him and that Freud finally capitulated after expressing considerable reluctance. On the other hand, Freud had analyzed Max Eitingon during strolls through the streets of Vienna and Kata Levy during summer holidays at her brother's house (Dupont, 1994). Ferenczi apparently entered the analytic process with bitterness that was masked by obsequious loyalty. In a letter of May 23, 1919, he made the following comment to Freud:

> From the moment you advised me against Elma, I developed a resistance against your person, that even psychoanalysis could not overcome, and which was responsible for all my sensitivities. With this unconscious grudge in my heart, I followed, as a faithful "son," all your advice, left Elma, came back to my present wife, and stayed with her in spite of innumerable attempts in other directions. (quoted in Dupont, 1994, p. 314)

After the analysis, Ferenczi continued to have resentment toward Freud because Freud had not analyzed his negative transference. Freud defended himself in a letter of January 20, 1930:

But you forget that this analysis took place 15 years ago, and at that time we were not at all sure that this kind of reaction must happen in all cases. At least, I was not. Just think, taking our excellent relationship in account, how long this analysis would have had to go on to allow the manifestation of hostile feelings to appear. (quoted in Dupont, 1994, p. 314)

In that same letter, Freud seems to have come to the recognition that analyzing someone with whom one has a preexisting friendship is ill-advised: "I notice that, in connecting things with our analysis you have pushed me back into the role of the analyst, a role I never would have taken up again toward a proven friend (quoted in Dupont, 1994, p. 314).

Although Ferenczi renounced his wish to marry Elma, he went on to engage in other forms of boundary violations that were also problematic. After his break with Freud, deeply bitter about his "training" analysis, he began to experiment with mutual analysis. With four female American patients, he tried analyzing them for an hour followed by an hour in which he would let the patient analyze him. Entries in his diary at this time demonstrated his confusion of his own need to be healed with that of his patients: "Our psyche, too, is more or less fragmented and in pieces, and, especially after expending so much libido without any libido-income, it needs such repayment now and again from well-disposed patients who are cured or on the point of being cured" (quoted in Dupont, 1988, p. 13). A few months after this entry of January 17, 1932, he abandoned mutual analysis, apparently because of the obvious problems with confidentiality. If he stuck to the basic rule of saying whatever came to his mind, he would be telling one of his patients about the personal disclosures of other patients.

Another form that Ferenczi's wish to be loved and healed took was an effort to provide his patients with the love their parents had failed to provide them (Gabbard, 1992). He saw his patients as victims of actual sexual trauma and abuse, and he sought to repair that damage. His technique included kissing and hugging the patient like "an affectionate mother" who "gives up all consideration of one's own convenience, and indulges the patient's wishes and impulses as far as in any way possible" (Grubrich-Simitis, 1986, p. 272). He had grown up in a family with many siblings and never felt he received the love that he wished to have from his mother (Blum, 1994; Grubrich-Simitis, 1986).

She was harsh and cold, in Ferenczi's view, and he thus tried to give to his patients what he did not receive as a child (Gabbard, 1992).

On December 13, 1931, Freud expressed his growing concern about Ferenczi's technique in a famous letter:

> We have hitherto in our technique held to the conclusion that patients are to be refused erotic gratifications . . . where more extensive gratifications are not to be had, milder caresses very easily take over their role. A number of independent thinkers in matters of technique, will say to themselves: "why stop at a kiss?" Certainly one gets further when one adopts "pawing" as well, which after all doesn't make a baby. And then bolder ones will come along, will go further to peeping and showing and soon we have accepted in the technique of psychoanalysis the whole repertoire of demiviergerie and petting parties, resulting in an enormous increase of interest in psychoanalysis among both analysts and patients. . . . Father Ferenczi gazing at the lively scene he has created will perhaps say to himself: maybe after all I should have halted my technique of motherly affection *before* the kiss. (Jones, 1957, p. 164)

Clearly, Freud was already aware of the well-known "slippery slope" phenomenon in which boundary violations that begin as minor and apparently harmless gradually escalate to major violations that are damaging to the patient.

FREUD, JONES, AND KANN

Freud was involved in another boundaryless ménage à trois when he undertook the analysis of Loë Kann. Ernest Jones and Kann had been living as husband and wife (although not technically married) since shortly after they met in London in approximately 1905. Kann apparently came to him as a patient, suggested by Jones's comment in a letter to Freud: "Now I have always been conscious of sexual attractions to patients; my wife was a patient of mine," (Freud–Jones correspondence, June 28, 1910, Paskauskas, 1993). In 1908, when Jones moved to Canada, Kann joined him there.

Jones's reputation in Canada was marred by rumors that he was recommending masturbation to patients, sending young men to prostitutes, and even showing obscene postcards to patients to stimulate their sexual feelings. A former patient threatened to charge him with having had sexual relations with her, so Jones paid her $500 worth of blackmail money to prevent a scandal. He explained this situation in some detail to James Jackson Putnam in a letter of January 13, 1911 (Hale, 1971). He clarified that he had seen this patient four times for medical purposes and that there was no truth to her claim that she had had intercourse with him. Because she also attempted to shoot him, he retained the protection of an armed detective. Jones described the patient as a hysterical homosexual woman who, after leaving his care, went to a woman doctor of strict moralistic views with whom she fell in love. Jones implied that his female colleague encouraged the former patient to bring charges against him. He felt he was foolish to pay the blackmail money and that the situation would be harmful to him whether he did or not. In a footnote to the Freud–Jones correspondence, Andrew Paskauskas (1993) suggested that the female doctor was Emma Leila Gordon, an extremely religious member of the Women's Christian Temperance Union, who frowned on alcohol consumption and loose living.

Concerned that he would lose Kann, Jones asked Freud if he would analyze her. She was afflicted with a number of somatic symptoms as well as morphine addiction. In 1912, Kann and Jones moved to Vienna so Freud could begin his treatment of her. Freud was evidently quite taken by her; he told Ferenczi in a letter of June 23, 1912, that "I will be pleased to be able to expend much Libido on her" (Haynal, 1994). The bond between Freud and Kann grew stronger as the treatment continued, even to the point that he invited her to spend Christmas Eve with his family (Appignanesi & Forrester, 1992). Freud made regular reports to Jones, apparently without regard for confidentiality, just as he had done with Ferenczi when he analyzed Elma. In fact, a major topic of the Freud–Ferenczi correspondence was their parallel observations about Jones, whom Ferenczi was analyzing, and Kann.

When Jones felt increasingly excluded from the process (more by Kann than by Freud), he became sexually involved with his maid, Lina. Meanwhile, Freud steered Kann in the direction of Herbert Jones, a young American to whom she was drawn (Appignanesi & Forrester, 1992).

Freud clearly saw Ernest Jones as sexually impulsive, and the correspondence during this time reflects his disapproval of Jones's behavior. In a letter of January 14, 1912, he said to Jones, "I pity it very much that you should not master such dangerous cravings, well aware at the same time of the source from which all these evils spring, taking away from you nearly all the blame but nothing of the dangers" (Paskauskas, 1993, p. 124). Paskauskas suggested that the reference to Jones's cravings as "dangerous" might have reflected Freud's concern about Jones's sexual boundary violations with patients. Paskauskas also quoted Jones's letter of April 1, 1922, regarding his analysis of Joan Riviere: "It is over twelve years since I experienced any [sexual] temptation in such ways, and then in special circumstances" (Paskauskas, 1993, p. 466). It is also significant that Freud's technique papers were written during the same time frame, which suggests that their emphasis on abstinence and objectivity may have grown out of concern for the boundaryless behavior of his disciples (Barron & Hoffer, 1994).

FREUD'S VIEWS ON ETHICS

Freud's need to place himself in the role of consultant to his male protégés regarding their women was clearly an overdetermined role that he found himself repeating again and again. Adam Phillips (1994) noted that Freud appeared to experience considerable glee in his ability to handle women whom Jones found unmanageable, like Loë Kann and Joan Riviere. He also was patronizing to the point of condescension in his attitude toward Jones on these matters.

Freud's attitude about sexual relations between analyst and patient, however, was not nearly as cut and dried as implied by his correspondence with Jones and by his 1931 letter to Ferenczi. Although Jung expected a severe rebuke for his dalliance with Spielrein, Freud was surprisingly understanding and empathic. He wrote to Jung:

Such experiences, though painful, are necessary and hard to avoid. Without them we cannot really know life and what we are dealing with. I myself have never been taken in quite so badly, but I have come very close to it a number of times and had a *narrow escape*. I believe that only grim necessities weighing on my work, and the fact that I was ten years older than yourself when I came to [psychoanalysis], have saved me from similar experiences. But no lasting harm is done. They help us to develop the thick skin we need to dominate "counter-transference," which is after all a permanent problem for us; they teach us to displace our own affects to best advantage. They are a *"blessing in disguise."* (McGuire, 1974, pp. 230–231)

Freud took a similar attitude of tolerance when a sexual transgression by Victor Tausk came to light (Eissler, 1983). Kurt Eissler noted that in contrast to the high ethical standards we have today in psychoanalysis, Freud quite possibly felt less puritanical about sexual boundary transgressions. Freud, like Jung, appeared to blame female patients for the transgressions of analysts: "The way these women manage to charm us with every conceivable psychic perfection until they have attained their purpose is one of nature's greatest spectacles" (McGuire, 1974, p. 231). Freud's view of the female superego as more lax than the male counterpart is a clear subtext in this remark. Despite this censure of women, however, Freud expected the male analyst to be skilled enough to avoid the seduction (Eissler, 1983).

It is possible that Freud did not view ethics as a paramount concern to his new science. In a letter to the Protestant minister Pfister, who was a practicing analyst, Freud made the following comment:

Ethics are remote from me. . . . I do not break my head very much about good and evil, but I have found little that is "good" about human beings on the whole. In my experience most of them are trash, no matter whether they publicly subscribe to this or that ethical doctrine or to none at all. . . . If we are to talk of ethics, I subscribe to a high ideal from which most of the human beings I have come across depart most lamentably. (Quoted in Roazen, 1975, p. 146)

There is no doubt that Freud was skeptical about the capacity to harness and sublimate the power of the drives. His letter to Pfister addressed boundary transgressions as inevitable miscues in the development of a new science. In another effort to reassure Jung about his fiasco with Spielrein, Freud drew an analogy in a letter of June 18, 1909:

In view of the kind of matter we work with, it will never be possible to avoid little laboratory explosions. Maybe we didn't slant the test tube enough, or we heated it too quickly. In this way we learn what part of the danger lies in the matter and what part in our way of handling it. (McGuire, 1974, p. 235)

Kerr (1993) frankly doubts that the revelation of Jung's relationship with Spielrein would have caused Freud much concern. Kerr pointed out that sexual transgressions between analyst and patient were veritably ubiquitous among Freud's early disciples. Wilhelm Stekel was well known as a "seducer." Otto Gross, who believed that the healthy solution to neurosis was sexual promiscuity, was engaged in group orgies to help others relieve themselves of their inhibitions (Eissler, 1983). Jones married a former patient. Even the clergyman Pfister was infatuated with one of his patients. Kerr (1993) emphasized that disagreements with Freud's theories were much more troubling to Freud than sexual transgressions.

A more cynical view of Freud's attitude was that the advancement of psychoanalysis as a clinical and scientific endeavor was of such paramount importance in his hierarchy of values that it superseded considerations of ethics. Recent discussions of the Frink case have made it clear that Freud was willing to lift his proscription against analyst–patient sexual relations if the cause of analysis might be advanced as a result (Edmunds, 1988; Gabbard, 1994b; Mahony, 1993; Warner, 1994). When Horace Frink, a young American analyst, came to Freud for analysis in 1921, he told Freud that he was madly in love with one of his former patients, Angelica Bijur. Freud encouraged Frink to divorce his wife and marry Bijur. He also told Bijur that she should divorce her husband and marry Frink to avoid a nervous breakdown. Bijur was the heiress of a wealthy banking family, and clearly Freud saw the marriage between Frink and Bijur as potentially leading to a large donation to further the cause of psychoanalysis. In November 1921, he made the following comment in a letter to Frink:

> May I still suggest to you that your idea Mrs. B[ijur] had lost part of her beauty may be turned into her having lost part of her money. . . . Your complaint that you cannot grasp your homosexuality implies that you are not yet aware of your fantasy of making me a rich man. If matters turn out all right, let us change this imaginary gift into a real contribution to the Psychoanalytic Funds. (Quoted in Mahony, 1993, p. 1031)

The results of this marriage were, of course, disastrous, and Freud's behavior can only be viewed as reprehensible. Mahony (1993) commented on the historical double standard applied to Freud and argued that Freud's way of comporting himself must be judged by the same set of standards used for other analysts. When a patient achieved insight, Freud seemed willing to modify his principle of abstinence (Hoffer, in press). For example, in a letter to Ferenczi dated February 17, 1918, Freud noted: "The day before yesterday a patient left behind a bonus of 10,000 crowns for the cure of his masochism, with which I am now playing the rich man with regard to children and relatives" (quoted by Brabant & Falzeder, in press). He also allowed Anton von Freund, a former analysand, to endow the International Psychoanalytic Press.

A RETROSPECTIVE ASSESSMENT

Looking back at these historical events, one way to understand them is as inevitable labor pains accompanying the birth of a new field. Personal and professional lives were intertwined in almost every conceivable way. Freud melded friendship and analysis in the treatment of Marie Bonaparte, during which he disclosed a good deal of personal information about himself. Bonaparte later was in treatment with Rudolf Loewenstein, only to ultimately become his lover (Appignanesi & Forrester, 1992). Jones sent the Stracheys to Freud for analysis as well as to be future translators of his work. Jung analyzed Trigant Burrow aboard a sailboat on several occasions. Leo Rangell's (in press) view is that many of these early boundary violations must be viewed in a historical context of a new science struggling to define its parameters and should not be regarded as indications of lax technique or immoral character. Although this perspective undoubtedly has some validity, the psychoanalytic pioneers had some knowledge of the inadvisability of the transgressions. Both Freud and Klein knew they should not be analyzing their children and went to considerable lengths to conceal those treatments. The early analysts may have felt that they had suffered greatly in the development of the new science and considered themselves "exceptions" to the rules that applied to others.

Whatever the reasons for this pervasive pattern of boundary violations, damage was done; complications surrounding a mother's labor may indelibly scar the child. The early boundary transgressions of the psychoanalytic pioneers shaped the dimensions of the new profession and must be viewed as a legacy inherited by future generations.

One of the main aspects of the legacy is a lack of clarity about the boundaries of the analytic situation. Certainly nonsexual boundary violations are far more pervasive than frank sexual relations between analyst and patient. Anna Freud acknowledged in later life that she felt exploited by many aspects of her father's analysis of her, including her father's publishing accounts of her daydreams (Young-Bruehl, 1988). Klein encouraged analysands to follow her to the Black Forest for her holiday, where she would analyze her patients while they reclined on her bed in her hotel room (Grosskurth, 1986). Winnicott held Margaret Little's hands through many hours as she lay on the couch and, on at least one occasion, broke confidentiality by telling her about another patient he was treating and about his countertransference reactions toward that patient (Little, 1990). Judy Cooper (1993) reported that when she was in analysis with Masud Kahn, he continued to give her papers he had written and asked her to read them. Indeed, the training analysts' expectation of loyalty from the candidate being analyzed has been a major boundary problem throughout the history of psycho-analysis, even to the point that in some cases former analysands have taken care of their former training analysts in old age.

Both sexual and nonsexual boundary violations were common among analysts who were highly influential in the development of psychoanalysis in the United States. Margaret Mahler had a sexual relationship with August Aichhorn, who was analyzing her (Stepan-sky, 1988). Frieda Fromm-Reichmann (1989) fell in love with her patient and married him. Karen Horney allegedly had an affair with a younger male candidate she was analyzing (Quinn, 1987). Stephen Farber and Marc Green (1993) chronicled the history of a number of starstruck ana-lysts in southern California, who conducted boundaryless analyses with their celebrity patients. Analysts served as technical advisors for films produced by their patients. Others collaborated on screenplays with their patients. Still others encouraged donations from their patients to various foundations with which the analyst was connected. Most of all, there was general blurring of the boundary between an analytic and a social relationship.

The historical response of psychoanalytic organizations within the United States to boundary violations has been variable. In many cases the solution to any transgression of professional boundaries was to prescribe more analysis. When disciplinary actions were taken, there was often such a backlash that whistle blowers and ethics committee members felt they were under attack for enforcing ethical standards.

One such case occurred in 1941, when Gregory Zilboorg, a prominent member of the New York Psychoanalytic Association, was accused of unethical conduct by a writer who was in treatment with him. According to the charges, Zilboorg had entered into a dual relationship with his patient in which he advised him on job-related issues in addition to conducting his analysis. For his business consultation, Zilboorg expected to be paid an honorarium of $1,000 a month on top of what he was receiving for his analytic fees (Farber & Green, 1993).

After an investigation of the charges, 9 members of a 12-member panel voted to censure Zilboorg. Presenting himself as a victim of vicious and predatory behavior by his colleagues, Zilboorg stirred considerable sympathy. When the issue came up before the full membership of the New York Psychoanalytic Association, Zilboorg threatened to sue every member of the organization who voted for his censure. In an impassioned letter of support to Zilboorg, Karl Menninger, then president of the American Psychoanalytic Association, proclaimed:

> Of course you have made mistakes; so has every other analyst. . . . But when, on the other hand, a patient feels you have made a mistake and persuades one or two or half a dozen colleagues that you have made a mistake and then one or two of these colleagues pursue the matter by complaining to an organized scientific society about your mistakes and charge you with fraudulent intentions, which is to say criminal intentions, and when this scientific body takes such complaints seriously and listens to them and debates them over a period of months, I think an extremely serious miscarriage of good taste, public policy, scientific principle and common decency has occurred. A number of very bad precedents were set by what occurred in New York, and whatever mistakes you may have made (I do not believe anymore that you even made any mistakes, but I am putting this subjective clause in here because I don't think it matters whether you did or not) it is a resounding shame and disgrace

that these alleged mistakes should have been exploited and capitalized upon by colleagues with personal grudges against you. The bringing of a patient to a scientific organization to give evidence against a physician is one of the most dangerous and vicious precedents that I can think of and violates all medical precedents. (Faulkner & Pruitt, 1988, p. 357)

In the face of threats of lawsuits and protests from colleagues, the charges were soon dropped. The meaning of "ethics" in those days often involved protection of one's colleagues. Moreover, other analysts were concerned that they might have to face charges by their patients, and no one wanted to deal with that prospect.

Another reason to stress the importance of historical developments in the area of analytic boundaries is that the intergenerational transmission of attitudes about the concept of boundaries can be extraordinarily powerful. In the mid-1960s, a training analyst in an institute was charged with sexual misconduct. Two decades later, two analysts he had analyzed were also charged with sexual misconduct in the same city. Blind spots in one analytic generation may well become blind spots in the next. Our emphasis on the historical legacy can be problematic, however, if we misuse it to blame our analytic parents rather than address basic challenges of the analytic situation that transcend time and place.

If analysts are to prevent destructive enactments of boundary violations, we must begin with a psychoanalytic understanding of how such enactments evolve. In addition, we must enrich our understanding of the impact these violations have on our patients. For too long, institutes and societies showed greater concern for the protection of the transgressing analyst than for the patient who was deprived of an analytic treatment. This legacy of the "old-boy system" is now being corrected by greater attention to the patient's suffering and appropriate reparation.

The history chronicled in this chapter is certainly not exhaustive. An attempt to be encyclopedic would fill an entire volume. Rather, our intent has been to describe a powerful historical context that has influenced generations of analysts. In the chapters that follow, the relevance of these historical incidents will be clear as we note the tendency of history to repeat itself.

CHAPTER 6

Sexual Boundary Violations

THE TRANSGRESSION OF professional boundaries in the form of analyst–analysand sexual involvement is a particularly disturbing illustration of how difficult it is for analysts to keep their own needs out of the analytic situation. As we noted in the discussion of Ferenczi in Chapter 5, many individuals who choose careers as psychoanalysts or psychotherapists feel they were insufficiently loved as children, and they may unconsciously hope that providing love for their patients will result in their being idealized and loved in return. In this manner, analysts may regulate their self-esteem through their work with patients (Finell, 1985; Gabbard, 1995d). In attempting to meet their patients' needs, analysts may in fact be meeting their own needs. As Robert Winer (1994) observed, the desire to cure and the desire to be cured are "two sides of a very thin coin" (p. 186).

Sexual passion, even outside the realm of analyst–patient involvement, is by its nature associated with the crossing of boundaries. As

Kernberg (1977) stressed, the basis for the subjective experience of transcendence in the act of making love is essentially a crossing of the self-boundaries. For Kernberg, the paradox of sexual love is the experience of transcending the boundaries of the self in identification with one's love object while simultaneously maintaining a discrete sense of the self.

In the case of analyst–patient sexual involvement, an additional boundary is transgressed. In the transference–countertransference dimensions of the analytic process, both members of the analytic dyad represent forbidden objects, so that sexual relations between analyst and analysand are symbolically incestuous. In other words, the boundary transgressed is that between the self and a forbidden incestuous object. As Freud noted in 1905, "the finding of an object is in fact a refinding of it" (1905b, p. 222). This formulation is, of course, equally true for both patient and analyst.

It is well known that one group of high-risk patients for exploitation by psychotherapists is composed of patients who have a history of incest (Feldman-Summers & Jones, 1984; Gabbard, 1994a; Kluft, 1989; Pope & Bouhoutsos, 1986). With such patients the boundaryless situation of childhood is reenacted in the analytic setting. Often these patients have always experienced caring as a phenomenon that is inextricably tied to sexuality. Many can be characterized as having "thin" boundaries, as described by Hartmann (1991) and discussed in Chapter 3. They fit Hartmann's conceptual framework of fluidity and lack of self-cohesion (many have borderline personality disorder or a dissociative disorder), openness and vulnerability in social situations, and an overall lack of firm defenses. Internal distinctions between self and other, as well as between fantasy and reality, may be difficult for them. They have been treated as an extension of someone else's body for the purpose of that caretaker's pleasure. Although one can never blame the patient for the unethical transgressions of the analyst, these patients often consciously or unconsciously convey to the analyst that nothing short of a repetition of the original incestuous relationship will be helpful.

Although discussions of sexual boundary transgressions generally imply that interpersonal boundaries are being crossed, earlier in the progression down the "slippery slope," inner boundaries between self and object representations are eroded. Long before the first physical contact between analyst and patient occurs, the analyst generally begins to feel a special kinship with the patient. Often the patient may be regarded as a "soul mate" who is either remarkably like the analyst or is capable of perfectly understanding the analyst. As in the case of Jung and Spielrein noted in Chapter 5, both analyst and patient may come to believe that they can even know each other's thoughts without giving voice to them. This fantasy of telepathic communication reflects the early erosion of intrapsychic self–object boundaries that occurs before the transgression of the professional or interpersonal boundaries.

Organized psychoanalysis has long struggled to develop an effective response to sexual involvement between analysts and their patients. Institutes and societies have often been paralyzed because one of the leading figures in the psychoanalytic community is the subject of the charges, and those conducting the investigation have a variety of residual transferences to a figure who may have been their analyst, supervisor, or teacher. In some cases, resistance to examining the problem takes the form of assuming that such transgressions are only problematic for a small handful of "impaired professionals," who are often written off as substance abusing or psychopathic. In this manner, analysts can reassure themselves that those who have sex with patients have nothing in common with them, creating a convenient "us–them" scenario that temporarily relieves their own anxiety about their potential for such enactments. Psychoanalysts, who endorse the complexity and overdetermined nature of human interaction, suddenly become shockingly reductionistic when confronted with a colleague who has developed a sexual relationship with a patient.

Anyone who has studied this phenomenon in any detail soon learns the disconcerting truth: We are all potentially vulnerable to various kinds of boundary transgressions, including sexual ones, with our patients (Gabbard, 1994a, 1994b; Margolis, 1994; Schoener, Milgrom, Gonsiorek, Luepker, & Conroe, 1989). A personal analysis and years of psychoanalytic training do not constitute an insurance policy against such disasters. Many of the most prominent analysts in the profession, both historically and contemporaneously, have become sexually involved with patients, and some have married those patients. No institute or society is spared these embarrassments, and most have various "family secrets" about such activity among prominent members. The closets of our psychoanalytic institutions are filled with skeletons (Gabbard, 1994c).

Sex between analyst and patient is a complex phenomenon that deserves serious study. Evaluation and treatment of analysts who have had sexual relations with their patients reveal a variety of psychody-namic themes intrinsic to such acts. Similarly, different clinicians become enthralled with patients at different times in their lives for a myriad of reasons. Although most instances involve severe counter-transference problems, some of the most egregious examples have lit-tle to do with countertransference at all. A predatory and exploitative male analyst with severe narcissistic pathology may simply see any attractive female patient as a potential sexual partner and proceed accordingly. Similarly, although many of the patients are incest victims, many more are not. In one study, only 32 percent of patients who had had sexual relations with their therapist had a history of childhood sex-ual abuse (Pope & Vetter, 1991). Sexual involvement between analyst and patient, like all other symptomatic behavior, is governed by a plu-rality of determinants.

The psychoanalytic profession has shown a remarkable ability to minimize the harm inflicted on patients by a sexual liaison with their analyst. Despite Freud's (1915a) admonition that "it would be a great triumph for [the patient] but a complete defeat for the treatment" (p. 166), many analysts over the years have interpreted his comment to mean that if one falls in love with a patient, the analysis should be ter-minated so the two can embark on a love affair. Colleagues who are aware of such outcomes have often tolerated these developments with a remarkable lack of concern. Freud was correct in asserting that such patients have extraordinary difficulties in subsequent analytic treat-ment. Their capacity to trust that a subsequent analyst will maintain the analytic frame and create a safe environment for exploration of wishes and fantasies is severely jeopardized. Nevertheless, colleagues who hear of such relationships often merely shake their heads and make such terse observations as "the flesh is weak." Many others reflect Freud's (1930) somber pessimism of "Civilization and Its Dis-contents" and speak of the awesome power of the drives (Gabbard, 1994c).

Love, of course, is irrelevant to ethical considerations in analyst–patient sex, but some analysts have excused such behavior on the basis of the notion that "true love" is at work. Margaret Mahler, for example, reported that she and her analyst, August Aichhorn were "in love with one another, making impossible the classical relationship between analyst and analysand" (Stepansky, 1988, p. 68). Frieda Fromm-Reichmann (1989) wrote about being swept off her feet by her analysand: "You see, I began to analyze Erich. And then we fell in love and so we stopped. That much sense we had!" (p. 480).

Although such sentiments undoubtedly describe the subjective feelings of the participants accurately, the implication is that "real love" can somehow be differentiated from transference and countertransference love (Gabbard, 1994d). Charles Brenner (1982) stressed that transference love does not differ in any substantial way from romantic love outside the analytic setting (except, of course, that the former is analyzed).

The situation is complicated because the patient who is the recipient of his or her analyst's love may feel extraordinarily special. Indeed, Mahler's statement in her memoirs illustrates this outcome:

> In taking me under his wing and vowing to see me restored to the good graces of the Viennese psychoanalytic establishment, Aichhorn only buttressed my self-image as an "exception"—now in an entirely positive sense as opposed to the negative sense inculcated by Mrs. Deutsch. Under Aichhorn's analytic care, I became a sort of Cinderella, the love object of a beautiful Prince (Aichhorn) who would win me the favor of a beautiful stepmother (Mrs. Deutsch). At the same time, my analytic treatment with him simply recapitulated my oedipal situation all over again. (Stepansky, 1988, p. 68)

As poignantly noted in this observation by Mahler, the feeling of being special, of being an exception, is ultimately a Pyrrhic victory for the patient because it represents a fulfillment of oedipal wishes that bypasses the analytic understanding and working through of such longings. Often patients who have had sex with their analyst do not allow themselves to acknowledge their feelings of being hurt and betrayed until the relationship dissolves, at which point the rage may be extraordinary, and outcomes ranging from suicide to lawsuits are common. Much like incest victims, they frequently blame themselves for corrupting their analyst and hence suffer a profound sense of guilt or shame.

Ethical standards are created to prevent situations in which there is a *potential* for harm. Even if there are occasional situations in which the harm is difficult to demonstrate, the accumulated data on therapist-patient sexual involvement strongly suggest that it is associated with harm. In a comprehensive review of the subject, Martin Williams (1992) concluded that although the studies are not without flaws, there is certainly sufficient evidence to create ethical standards prohibiting such involvement.

Under the rubric of sexual boundary violations, there is a diverse group of behaviors in which analysts may engage. At one end of the continuum are forcible rapes, with the patient either anesthetized or fully awake, and highly perverse sex acts involving humiliation of the patient. At the other end of the continuum are verbal forms of sexual misconduct. One male therapist told his female patient that she was so sexy that he could not help getting an erection in her presence. Another analyst told a female patient explicit details of his masturbatory fantasies about her. In between these two ends of the continuum are a variety of transgressions, including such phenomena as oral sex, fondling of breasts or genitals, passionate full-body embraces, various states of undress, and insertion of objects into body orifices, with varying degrees of mutual consent. Although the majority of cases involve a male analyst and female patient, all four gender constellations are common. In a series of 2,000 cases of therapist–patient sex, Gary Schoener et al. (1989) observed that approximately 20 percent involved female therapists and 20 percent were same-sex dyads.

A TYPOLOGY OF ANALYSTS

Because analyst–analysand sexual involvement is a highly complex phenomenon, we present a heuristically useful psychodynamically based typology of analysts who have transgressed sexual boundaries to aid in understanding the major psychological issues that emerge in such situations. The observations and formulations in this chapter are largely based on the experience of one of the authors (Gabbard) in evaluating and treating more than 70 cases of therapists who have had sex with their patients. We also believe that careful study of such clinicians may hold the key to developing methods of prevention. Most analysts and other psychotherapists who have had sex with patients fall into one of four categories of disorder: (1) psychotic disorders, (2) predatory psychopathy and paraphilias, (3) lovesickness, or (4) masochistic surrender (Gabbard, 1994a, 1994b).

In developing these categories, we wish to stress that they should not be excessively reified or viewed as having rigid demarcations. Some practitioners have features of more than one category, and occasionally an idiosyncratic clinician may defy inclusion in any of the categories. We also emphasize the need to *understand* our colleagues and help them rather than write them off as criminals who need to be locked up and stripped of their licenses. As more and more states criminalize therapist–patient sex, the message appears to be that treatment and understanding should take a backseat to condemnation and incarceration. We are not implying that disciplinary measures should be avoided, only that humane rehabilitation based on an understanding of the individual practitioner should go hand in hand with whatever disciplinary measures are deemed appropriate. We return to this issue in Chapter 10.

Psychotic Disorders

It is rare for practitioners to become sexually involved with their patients as a result of a bona fide psychotic disorder. Occasionally, a manic episode of a bipolar affective disorder is involved in the practitioner's feelings of omnipotence regarding his or her powers to cure others through love or sexual relations. Psychotic organic brain syndromes, often related to frontal lobe involvement, have occasionally been involved in cases of sexual misconduct. When these severe disorders play a role in sexual boundary violations, the disturbed practitioner has usually been acting psychotic in other ways, causing considerable alarm in colleagues and family members. These cases are sufficiently rare, however, that we have not accumulated systematic data on such patients, and they are not the principal focus of our study.

Predatory Psychopathy and Paraphilias

Within the category of predatory psychopathy, we include not only true antisocial personality disorders but also severe narcissistic personality disorders with prominent antisocial features. In other words, it is the sexual *behavior* that is predatory and psychopathic. Although all clinicians suffering from paraphilias or perversions are not necessarily psychopathic predators, those who act on their perverse impulses with *patients* usually are found to have a severely compromised superego associated with character pathology on the narcissistic-to-antisocial continuum.

These practitioners are generally male and usually have manifested predatory sexual behavior throughout their lives. Although we would like to think that the mental health professions and psychoanalytic institutes screen out such practitioners from their ranks, the disconcerting truth is that these predatory clinicians are not rare. Indeed, because their transgressions often involve multiple victims and a variety of bizarre and sadistic behaviors, they are disproportionately represented in media reports of sexual boundary violations. These analysts frequently have histories of having been identified in a training program to be dishonest or unethical in a variety of ways. In many cases, someone attempted to blow the whistle on them and expel them from the training program, but the trainee aborted the process by hiring a lawyer who threatened to sue if the plans for expulsion were implemented. Many of these individuals are masters at manipulating the legal system and often manage to escape severe legal or ethical sanctions. Training committees, intimidated by the threat of litigation, may decide the path of least resistance is simply to graduate the practitioner and hope that he practices in a different state.

Another variant of the predator is the profoundly narcissistic analyst who has risen to the top of his profession. He may be in a position of major responsibility in local, national, or international organizations. He may be internationally renowned for his writing, and he may be revered as a teacher. The adulation he receives is intoxicating to the point that he begins to believe that he is different from and superior to others. His grandiosity is fueled, and he begins to rationalize his boundaryless behavior as acceptable simply because of who he is. Ordinary standards of ethics do not apply to him. He can get away with things that others cannot because of his stature in the field. He lacks remorse about his sexual involvement with patients because he believes they are lucky to have had sexual favors from him.

After the sexual transgressions are revealed, many colleagues recall other incidents that should have raised concern but were ignored. Colleagues had frequently colluded with the analyst's omnipotence by admiring his "unorthodox" flexibility when he boasted about his creative use of actions or interventions that are outside the realm of usual analytic technique. The idealization of senior colleagues may create situations reminiscent of the fairy tale "The Emperor's New Clothes," in which otherwise intelligent analysts disbelieve or rationalize what they see in plain view.

Analysts or therapists in this category regard patients as objects to be used for their own gratification. Because they lack empathy or concern for the victim, they are largely incapable of feeling remorse or guilt about any harm that might have been done to the patient. In many cases of narcissistic character pathology, the analyst appears charming and capable of functioning professionally in a variety of spheres, but significant superego lacunae allow for corrupt behavior without pangs of conscience. In more severe forms of psychopathy, there is massive failure of superego development related to profound impairment of internalization during childhood development. Some of these clinicians have a childhood history of profound neglect or abuse, and the only form of object relatedness they appear to know is sadistic bonding with others through the exercise of destructiveness and power (Meloy, 1988).

The Case of Dr. G

Dr. G was a 48-year-old analyst who was charged with sexual misconduct after six different patients came forward alleging that he had sex with them. Each of them described the same pattern. He was initially warm and understanding with these women, all of whom described extensive problems in their interpersonal relationships. After a few weeks of therapy or analysis, Dr. G would tell them that their principal problem was their inability to trust men. He would say, "You probably don't even trust me enough to take your blouse off." When the patients responded indignantly that of course they would not undress in front of him, he would reply, "See what I mean?"

With considerable charm and persuasiveness, he continued to pursue his patients sexually by saying to them one variation or another of the following speech: "If you cannot trust *me* enough to have sex with me, how do you ever expect to be able to trust men outside of therapy? This relationship is a safe place to explore your sexuality and your trust problems. You have to start somewhere." In this manner, he eventually chipped away at the reluctance of his patients to engage in a sexual relationship with him. When they finally went along with his overtures, he asked them to confide their most terrifying sexual fantasies to him. He would then act them out with the patients to help them "work through" their fears.

Although he initially denied the charges, after he lost his license to practice, he acknowledged that there had been truth in the complaints but adamantly denied any wrongdoing. He maintained that in every case the sex had been consensual and that the women had benefited from having sex with him. He had no remorse whatsoever and flatly scoffed at any implication that harm had been done.

Investigation of his background revealed that he had come close to being expelled from the psychoanalytic institute where he trained, but one of his supervisors had come forward in his defense and argued for his retention within the program. As is often the case in such situations, more analysis was recommended, with which Dr. G complied.

The vast majority of these cases appear to involve a male practitioner and a female patient. However, there are a small number of cases in which female therapists systematically seduced female patients and involved them in degrading and sadistically humiliating sexual activities (Benowitz, 1995). Predatory male therapists who are homosexual or bisexual may also seduce patients of the same sex (Gonsiorek, 1989).

LOVESICKNESS

The majority of analysts who become sexually involved with their patients appear to fall into this category. A number of characteristic features are commonly found in the lovesick analyst, including significant narcissistic vulnerability but with greater superego integration than is found in the typical predator (Gabbard, 1991a, 1994d, 1994g; Twemlow & Gabbard, 1989). When the analyst is male, the typical scenario is that a middle-aged practitioner falls madly in love with a much younger female patient. This infatuation usually occurs in the context of extreme stress in the analyst's life. The stressors may include divorce, separation, illness in a child or spouse, death of a family member, or disillusionment with his own marriage or career.

These practitioners may also be professionally isolated. They may be in a solo practice situation in which virtually all of their contacts with other people from early in the morning until late into the evening are with patients. If the analyst's emotional and sexual needs are not being met at home with a nurturant and loving partner, he may begin to look to patients for these needs to be gratified. The sexual boundary violation may be the end point on a slippery slope that begins with sharing his own problems in sessions with his patients. His presentation of himself as needy and vulnerable may appeal to caretaking needs in his patient.

Narcissistic themes are prominent in lovesick analysts, although their narcissistic vulnerability is sometimes masked by reasonably good functioning and social supports until a serious crisis enters their lives. In other cases, the narcissistic vulnerability is worn on the analyst's sleeve and has been evident to colleagues and friends for many years. The narcissistic themes in the lovesick therapist generally involve a desperate need for validation by his patients, a hunger to be loved and idealized, and a tendency to use patients to regulate his own self-esteem. Some may even have borderline features characterized by a tendency to rapidly idealize patients and impulsively act on their feelings of infatuation. Arnold Goldberg (1994), in discussing lovesickness outside the realm of sexual boundary violations, suggested that the term *lovesickness* may be a misnomer because the core of the problem is a narcissistic imbalance rather than an issue of love.

Indeed, *lovesickness* is a term that reflects the *manifest content* of the intoxicating experience that these analysts and therapists describe. Although lovesickness accurately captures that experience at a phenomenological level, the state can be deconstructed into a variety of latent contents. These include structural characteristics, developmental and object relations issues, narcissistic problems, and psychodynamic themes. In this section of the chapter, we systematically examine these deconstructed components of lovesickness, recognizing that different combinations of these elements apply to different analysts or therapists who have fallen in love with their patient.

Much is made of superego lacunae in discussions of unethical therapists, but in the case of lovesick practitioners, we might well speak of "ego lacunae." As poets have known for centuries, intense passion may override rational thinking. Two ego functions in particular are frequently impaired: judgment (i.e., the ability to anticipate consequences of one's actions) and reality testing. The latter is sufficiently circumscribed to designate it as a "nonpsychotic loss of reality testing"

(Twemlow & Gabbard, 1989, p. 83). The impairment involves a loss of the "as-if" quality characteristic of the analyst's ordinary experience of countertransference. In other words, there is an inability to distinguish a countertransference wish from the reality of the situation, so that the analyst cannot appreciate that something from the past is being repeated and that feelings for significant persons from the analyst's past are displaced onto the patient. The countertransference has become erotized in the same way that some incest victims and border-line patients develop erotized *transference* (Blum, 1973; Gabbard, 1991a, 1994b; Lester, 1985). The loss of insight accompanying this folie à deux does not necessarily generalize to other therapeutic relationships. It is commonplace to discover that while a lovesick analyst was having sex with a particular patient, the other treatments were conducted within a reasonable analytic or therapeutic frame and that the patients involved were satisfied with their treatment.

The loss of judgment often involves the analyst's inability to appreciate the self-destructive nature of the behavior as well as the potential for harm to the patient. For example, a young female analytic candidate sought consultation with a senior colleague to discuss her feelings of infatuation for a male patient. She explained that the love was mutual and that she could not see how harm could be done to either of them. The consultant confronted her with one concrete form of harm that would befall her if she acted on her feelings, namely, that she would lose her medical license. The candidate responded, somewhat naively, that she had not thought of that.

This obliviousness to the consequences of one's actions is generally accompanied by feelings of euphoria. A lovesick analyst may feel like he is walking on air or intoxicated in the presence of his beloved. The increase in the libidinal investment in the self as a result of sexual passion and love has been observed by several authors (Chasseguet-Smirgel, 1973; Kernberg, 1977; Van der Waals, 1965). Freud (1914a) observed that not only the parent but also the self could be taken as a love object through projection of the ego ideal. It is often the case that an analyst who has fallen madly in love with his patient has obscured the patient's real qualities by seeing an idealized image of himself in the face of the patient, just as Narcissus fell in love with his own image in the water. This enhanced self-esteem is tenuously balanced, however, in that it depends on the continued impairment of the boundary between self and object.

Much of the confusion between self and object can be understood in terms of the level of symbolic thinking characteristic of the analyst's mental functioning. Hanna Segal (1957, 1994) distinguished concrete symbolism—a situation in which misperception and false beliefs are based on the fact that there is a direct equation between the symbol and what is symbolized—from a higher form of symbolic thinking, in which the difference between the symbol and the object it represents is apparent. Perceptual processes in the concrete form of symbolism are highly influenced by projective identification. Many analysts who fall madly in love with their patient as an externalization of an aspect of themselves are functioning in a paranoid–schizoid mode (Ogden, 1986), as we described in Chapter 3; in this mode, the object is concretely identified as a projected part of the subject, and the analyst relates to the patient as though the patient is part of the self.

A number of recurrent psychodynamic themes emerge in the analysis of clinicians who have had sex with their patients. As noted in the beginning of this chapter, many analysts are attempting to elicit from their patients the love they did not receive from their parents. These longings for love are defended against by giving to others, one unconscious determinant of their career choice. Analysts may be gratifying their own needs while consciously believing they are altruistic in attending to the needs of others.

Another common theme is the reenactment of incestuous longings or of an actual incestuous relationship from the past of either member of the dyad. The social and ethical proscription of sex between analyst and patient may merely intensify the lovesickness in the same way that the forbidden nature of the oedipal object intensifies longings. When a lovesick male analyst begins to disclose his personal problems to a younger female patient, interlocking enactments of rescue fantasies may emerge. The female patient may have harbored a childhood fantasy that she was somehow ministering to the father who was despairing over his marriage. This rescue fantasy of the little girl may have developed into overt incest or quasi-incestuous emotional interactions with the father. The analyst, on the other hand, may be unconsciously rescuing his depressed mother in his efforts to heal his patient (Apfel &

Simon, 1985). Rescue fantasies in both male and female analysts appear to be closely linked to sexual excitement and, ultimately, sexual boundary violations in the analytic setting (Gabbard, 1994a, 1994f).

Female patients who have suffered abuse and neglect in childhood may be particularly appealing to the lovesick analyst who is intent on rescue. They may implicitly or explicitly demand to be cared for in a way that transcends the analytic frame. Male analysts may misconstrue a longing for maternal nurturance as a genital–sexual overture and respond accordingly (Lester, 1990, 1993). Patients may reluctantly go along with the analyst's sexual overtures because, as incest victims, they are accustomed to expecting a sexual relationship in association with the caring they receive.

Most individuals who seek out a career in psychotherapy or psychoanalysis harbor a conscious or unconscious fantasy that love is healing (Gabbard, 1994d, 1995d). Hollywood portrayals of psychotherapy reinforce the notion that love is curative, so that many patients harbor that fantasy when they enter into analysis or therapy. In fact, a common fantasy of patients entering analysis is that their problems are based on having received insufficient parental love during their childhood and that the mechanism of cure is that the analyst will love them better and more completely than their parents did. This paradigm of cure is precisely the countertransference trap in which many analysts find themselves ensnared. Patients with borderline personality and dissociative disorders in particular often insist that love is the only thing that will help them and that words are useless.

A particular variant of this fantasy is frequently involved in the cases of female analysts or therapists who become sexually involved with male patients. In this scenario, the patient tends to be a young man with a personality disorder diagnosis characterized by impulsivity, action orientation, and substance abuse (Gabbard, 1992, 1994d, 1994g). Despite the fact that he may have a history that involves antisocial activity or narcissistic exploitation of others, the female clinician begins to think that she can "settle him down" with her love. The young male patient may have considerable interpersonal charm and behave in such a way with the female therapist that she begins to think of him as "just a baby." The female analyst harbors the fantasy that if this young man had just had good mothering in childhood, he would have turned out differently. With that reparative mode operating at full throttle, the female then undertakes a reparenting process that turns into a sexual relationship.

In American literature and film, there is a ubiquitous cultural myth that a "rowdy" young man simply needs a "good woman" to settle him down. In Barbra Streisand's 1991 film, *The Prince of Tides*, the audience is left with the impression that Tom Wingo's treatment success is primarily related to his love affair with his therapist, rather than to any insight or understanding related to the therapist's professional expertise. A victim of childhood trauma and a cold, distant mother, Tom is finally given the love and nurturance he deserves in a reparative therapy with Dr. Loewenstein. At the beginning of Clint Eastwood's 1992 film, *Unforgiven*, the protagonist repeatedly comments on how he was a cold-blooded murderer and a drunk until the right woman transformed him into a decent husband, father, and breadwinner. Another theme in these female therapist–male patient dyads relates to the woman's vicarious enjoyment of the danger and risk typified by her male patient's lifestyle.

The Case of Dr. H

Dr. H was a 34-year-old female therapist to whom a 29-year-old heroin addict was referred for treatment; the therapy was court-ordered because of a run-in with the law. Dr. H's initial reaction to the patient was that he was a "sociopathic heroin addict." As she began psychotherapy with him, however, her view started to change. He seemed depressed about the way his life had gone and seemed ready to reform his lifestyle. She began to think of him as a baby who had missed out on a nurturing mothering experience as a child and needed a woman's love and concern.

Dr. H soon became infatuated with her "bad boy," who seemed to her to have a soft and tender side that no one else had noticed. She had been living with a man for 5 years but had been growing progressively disenchanted with him. In fact, at the time she began seeing her handsome and charming heroin addict, she and her significant other had almost completely ceased sexual relations. In her daydreams she imagined that her patient was a spectacular lover who could unabashedly enjoy women without the usual "emotional baggage."

In one session, the patient expressed considerable concern that he was broke and would be evicted from his apartment. Dr. H offered to loan him some money for his rent, and he expressed intense gratitude and hugged her at the end of the session. Dr. H felt as though she would melt in his strong embrace. She knew her feelings were out of control, and she terminated the professional relationship. She actively pursued further involvement with him, however, by visiting him in his apartment and becoming sexually involved with him.

She kept the relationship secret from her live-in boyfriend but speculated that she might have been hoping the relationship with the patient would cause her boyfriend to leave her. In fact, he *did* soon discover that she was involved with a patient and walked out on her as a result. Meanwhile, her patient made increasing financial demands on her to the point that she felt it would be best to let him have one of her credit cards. She loved to hear about her patient's misadventures and recognized that they tapped into a "wild side" within her that she had never been able to express in action before. She got a vicarious thrill out of hearing of his life of impulsivity and run-ins with the law. The sexual aspect of the relationship was highly stimulating and brought her to orgasm for the first time in many years.

Nevertheless, she began to grow worried about being part of a long-standing pattern. She learned from her patient that he had had sexual relationships with two previous health care professionals. She also started to feel that she was being taken advantage of financially. When she tried to put limits on his expenditures, her former patient became violent, threw her against the wall, and threatened to beat her up if she did not do what he said.

Dr. H was so terrified for her life that she resigned from her position at the clinic where she worked and moved to another city without telling her ex-patient where she was going. For several months, she lived in fear that he would track her down and hurt her. At about this time she came for analysis, recognizing that she had made a dreadful mistake and needing to understand what was going on with her.

Dr. H told her analyst that sex had not been the real issue in the relationship. She felt that her patient was an abandoned baby and that nobody would take care of him unless she did. She felt that she was the only hope the patient had. In the course of her analysis, she recognized that she herself had felt like an abandoned baby and was overidentified with the patient. In trying to rescue the patient, she was trying to rescue herself. Her mother had not been a good caretaker, and Dr. H had felt throughout her life that she had to take care of her three siblings because her mother could not. Dr. H firmly believed that her love would cure her patient. She felt that love could cure a drug problem, temper outbursts, and other forms of abusive behavior.

Dr. H had the following dream early in the analysis: She came into her analyst's office and found him looking exhausted and jaundiced. Soon he fell asleep while she associated on the couch. Dr. H let him sleep but eventually woke him up when it was time for the session to end so he would not miss his next appointment.

In her associations to the dream, Dr. H noted that she would rather think of herself as helping her analyst than getting help from him. Her analyst commented that a similar phenomenon had happened with *her* patient: She wanted to take care of him rather than look out for herself. Dr. H said she was much more comfortable giving than taking and therefore was vulnerable to people who had no compunction about taking from others. She went on to say that either she or her analyst had to be sick, and she would feel better if it were the analyst who was sick so she could take care of him. She imagined that if the analysis terminated because the analyst were sick, she would continue to take care of him.

Dr. H spent a good deal of time in her treatment analyzing her attraction to sociopaths. She noted that she could never work in law enforcement because she was so easily manipulated and conned by men with this type of pathology. She noted that she allowed herself to be conned because of her admiration of their rule breaking. She said she had a shaky understanding of ethical principles and felt that she maintained some semblance of moral behavior based on a knowledge of externally applied rules rather than an internalized sense of what was clearly right and what was clearly wrong. Particularly in the area of emotional intimacy, she said that she was confused about appropriate boundaries. She said she could not separate intimacy from sex and assumed that if she were close to someone, she would become sexual with that person. This same pattern emerged in the transference, when she said she was not clear why she and her analyst could not become sexually involved.

Dr. H associated this pattern with her childhood, in which her mother had been highly authoritarian about any behavior that could remotely be regarded as sexual. Dr. H's father, who was generally emotionally aloof, would occasionally massage his daughter's legs when they were sore. Even though there was no incestuous involvement between Dr. H and her father, her mother constantly said things to suggest that there was. Her mother also said to Dr. H when she was 12 that she was becoming a prostitute, even though she was in no way sexually active. She reflected that her affair with her patient had been a self-fulfilling prophecy, enacting the very prediction made by her mother.

Throughout her childhood and adolescence, Dr. H noted a strong wish to assert her autonomy by rebelling against her mother. She experienced her mother's control over her as though her mother were a tyrant who would not allow her to have her own separate identity. She deliberately chose boyfriends when she was in college who would outrage her mother. Similar patterns developed in the transference to her analyst: She saw him as controlling and wanted to defy him.

Although the case of Dr. H is somewhat extreme because of the overt criminal behavior of the patient with whom she chose to fall in love, the lovesick pattern is quite typical of female therapists who have transgressed sexual boundaries. The familiar pattern of projecting one's own need for love onto the patient and attempting to rescue the patient from a harsh childhood is clear in Dr. H's case. Perhaps of most interest, however, is the nature of her superego pathology. Dr. H clearly did not have an internalized sense of moral or ethical standards and relied on external rules to govern her behavior. Her mother had been internalized as a harsh and archaic superego that would overreact to the slightest hint of sexualized behavior.

In many ways, Dr. H's impulsive behavior with her patient resembled the psychodynamic pattern that Leon Wurmser (1987) described in drug users. He reported that an impulsive act of drug use may represent a defiance or temporary overthrow of a particularly harsh and exaggerated archaic superego structure. In Dr. H's excitement about her patient's antisocial behavior and her secret sexual relationship with him, she was enacting a powerful fantasy of overthrowing her tyrannical and controlling mother, who had been introjected as a key component of her superego. She did have the capacity for guilt and shame and had experienced an unusual burden of shaming from her mother throughout her childhood and adolescence, to the point that it became a stifling internalized affect.

Her guilt feelings were partially dealt with through a self-destructive tendency to sacrifice herself for her patient. The sexual involvement was a compromise formation in which she both defended against her stifling superego pressures as well as gratified them by punishing herself. The punishment could have led to death or the loss of her state license, but she had sufficient judgment to extricate herself from the relationship before disaster occurred.

As Dr. H continued the analytic exploration of her unconscious motivations for the disastrous relationship, she came to recognize that she was fending off a state of psychological deadness. She felt alive and energized through her relationship with her dangerous lover. Through much of her early childhood, she had experienced her mother as a distant figure who was inaccessible to her. She unconsciously identified with this "dead" mother, in the manner described by Andre Green (1986), and felt a desperate need for someone else to bring her to life. Her relationship with her live-in boyfriend was similarly lifeless, and her patient represented an escape route from her unbearable psychological deadness. The emotional unavailability of her father exacerbated this internal lifelessness.

Dr. H had imagined that she was an exception to the usual ethical standards because her intense love for her patient transcended such mundane codes. Other therapists rationalize their behavior by saying that they did not actually have genital intercourse, so they were not truly involved in sexual exploitation. Even though oral sex or genital fondling have occurred, these clinicians assuage their consciences by reassuring themselves that they have maintained a limit in the relationship.

A number of years ago, Harold Searles (1979) made the following observation:

> It has long been my impression that a major reason for therapists' becoming actually sexually involved with patients is that the therapist's own therapeutic striving, desublimated to the level on which it was at work early in his childhood, has impelled him into this form of involvement with the patient. He has succumbed to the illusion that a magically curative copulation will resolve the patient's illness which tenaciously has

resisted all the more sophisticated psychotherapeutic techniques learned in his adult-life training and practice. (p. 431)

Professions of love and caring often mask unconscious feelings of despair and rage at the patient's tendency to thwart the analyst's omnipotent strivings to heal. Andrea Celenza (1991) reported a case of a therapist who began a seduction of the patient when the treatment was at an impasse. The therapist could not tolerate countertransference feelings of a negative valence, nor could he tolerate the patient's negative transference. The seduction was viewed by Celenza as an unconscious attempt to bypass negative feelings in the patient (as well as in himself) and to foster an idealizing transference that both patient and therapist could bear. Rage and resentment toward the patient are often just underneath the surface in the lovesick analyst, who defends against such feelings with an escalating reaction formation so that the sadistic underpinnings of the acts of sexual transgression are maintained outside of conscious awareness.

The fantasy that sex will magically cure the patient is one that dates back to the origins of psychoanalysis. Writing about the early days of his medical career in Vienna, Freud (1914b) described receiving a patient from Chrobak who had attacks of anxiety. Chrobak explained that the patient's anxiety was related to the fact that her husband was impotent and they had never had sex in their 18 years of marriage. Chrobak indicated to Freud that the only prescription for the patient's problem was "penis normalis dosim repetatur!" (p. 15). Roughly translated, the prescription was for repeated doses of a normal penis. Freud expressed reservations about this means of cure.

The sadistic origins of the therapeutic copulation fantasy are so split off or repressed that analysts are frequently astonished to hear that their patient felt harmed or betrayed by the sexual relationship. In these cases, the analyst maintains that he was in love with the patient and only doing what she wanted. He appears incapable of seeing the inherent hostility and exploitation in the behavior. In this regard, the sexual relationship between analyst and patient resembles the common dynamics of perversions such as fetishism, in which the truth of an aspect of experience is known by one part of the personality but denied and split off by the other part. Ferenczi viewed incestuous relations with children as a form of "hate impregnated" love. The same can be said of therapist–patient sex.

Some severely narcissistic therapists literally believe that their sexual prowess is such that patients will be healed of their sexual anxieties by having sex with them. This cultural myth of sex being therapeutic is so widespread that many women also believe it. In a case reported by James Eyman and Glen Gabbard (1991), a middle-aged female patient insisted that the only thing that would help her was an orgasm induced by sexual activity with her therapist. Two male therapists had tried this method with her without any change in her condition, but she firmly maintained her conviction. Even in the feminist film *Thelma and Louise*, the suggestion is that all Thelma needed to transform her from an unhappy housewife to a fulfilled woman was sex with the right man, that is, a hitchhiker she picked up on the road who later robbed her.

This compartmentalization of experience along fetishistic lines also applies to the lovesick analyst's way of handling superego pressures. Kernberg (1977) emphasized that almost by definition, the intrinsic quality of sexual passion overrides the mature functioning of the superego. What one sees in some lovesick therapists who are ordinarily ethical in their conduct is the capacity to compartmentalize the superego prohibitions and handle them in a way that renders them irrelevant to the specific circumscribed relationship with the patient. Other therapists, like Dr. H, are actively rebellious against such rules stemming from childhood experiences of controlling parents whom they felt they needed to fend off to maintain autonomy.

Another psychodynamic theme common to the lovesick analyst revolves around mourning and grief. The sexual relationship with a patient may in and of itself represent a manic defense against painful feelings of loss (Gabbard, 1994d). The clinician may be undergoing losses in his or her personal life and feel that dealing with further losses in the office is unbearable. In this regard, termination may be a particularly problematic time. Every analyst must deal with an inevitable loss at the time of termination of treatment. Both analyst and patient may collude in warding off feelings of grief by embarking on a new relationship, in which they may meet for lunch, attempt to socialize, and pursue common interests. They may ultimately descend the slippery slope to a fully sexual relationship. Both analyst and patient deny the ending by embarking on a new beginning. As Stanley Coen (1992) stressed, sexualization may transform painful feelings into more positive, exciting ones.

Judith Viorst (1982) interviewed 20 analysts regarding their feelings about termination of patients. These analysts used the same defenses as their patients to deal with the pain of the loss. Postanalytic contact fantasies were prominent in the service of denying the permanence of the loss. In fact, one analyst acknowledged that he dealt with his feelings about termination by imagining that he would marry each of his female patients.

Another variant of this defense against loss is seen when the analyst cannot allow the patient to get better because it represents an intolerable loss of connection for him with the patient. Winer (1994) viewed therapist–patient sex as an extreme instance of this failure to let the patient improve and let him or her go. It is also, of course, a dramatic instance of the analyst's needs superseding those of the patient.

Another disillusionment may be at work in the lovesick analyst. Commonly, one finds that these analysts are intensely resentful toward their institutes or their own training analysts, whom they feel did not treat them in the way that they deserved to be treated. There may be anger at not being promoted to training analyst or an administrative post to which they felt entitled; regarding their training analysis, they may feel that certain aspects of their psyche were left unexplored or unanalyzed in the treatment. Ferenczi, for example, was bitter toward Freud for never analyzing his negative transference and said so in a letter to Freud (Dupont, 1988). He expressed his anger by rejecting Freud's technique and developing his own, more indulgent methods, in which he would give the patients the maternal love (and physical affection) they did not receive as children.

When the analyst or therapist is employed by an institution, one also sees resentment or anger at the institution as a frequent determinant in sexual transgressions with patients. The therapist may unconsciously wish to embarrass the institution in the same manner that adolescents attempt to embarrass their parents with delinquent behavior. Hence, the revenge motive is also at work in many of these cases.

Conflicts about gender identity and sexual orientation may be significant issues in analyst–patient sexual liaisons. Some male analysts, insecure about their masculinity, have a strong need for female patients to validate their appeal as men. Sexual enactments with a patient may be one way the analyst attempts to convince himself that he is truly male and sexually desired by females.

The Case of Dr. I

Dr. I entered analysis after he was charged with sexual misconduct by one of his colleagues, who saw him in another city with a patient. He acknowledged that he had exercised poor judgment, but he said the love he and his patient felt for each other was a "love that knows no bounds." He said he had never felt this kind of love in any relationship before. At the time the relationship started, he was 48 and the patient was 34.

He described how the relationship started. At the end of an analytic hour, the patient got off the couch and, in an uncharacteristic way, turned and looked directly at him. She said to him, "You look like you're in pain." He was deeply touched by her comment and felt she cared about him in a way that his wife never could. She touched his shoulder for a moment and looked at him. In that glance, Dr. I felt she affirmed him as a man.

Dr. I and his wife had been living lives of quiet desperation for years. He became obsessed with thoughts about his patient that occupied him throughout the day and into the night. He had the sense that if only he could reciprocate her love, his pain, which she had perceptively noted, would be healed. He found himself driving by her home in the evenings, and he wrote notes to her that he never mailed. He worked out extensively at a gym where he hoped she would appear. As he lifted weights, he would look at women passing him and try to catch the same look in their eye that he had experienced with his patient.

Ever since the episode when his patient touched him, Dr. I was convinced that she would receive his interest with open arms. He finally told her during a session that he could no longer contain himself, that he was passionately in love with her. She responded, "I know." She got up and embraced him, and they sat on the couch together. She said that she would leave her husband for him. Dr. I responded that it would be unethical for them to have a sexual relationship. He went on to say that although he could contain himself physically, he could no longer contain his feelings.

From that time on, there were numerous sessions in which they would embrace on the couch. Eventually, embraces turned to deep, passionate kisses and genital fondling. Dr. I was concerned that he would not be potent and was afraid to take the relationship beyond the stage of fondling and kissing.

They started meeting outside the office in other cities when Dr. I traveled to professional meetings. During these times, they would often share a hotel room, but he tried to abstain from sexual relations to reassure himself that he was being ethical. His patient would massage his genitals until he attained an erection, but he would discourage her from going further. Finally, she began to fellate him until he ejaculated. At this point, he felt that she had "cured" him of his problems with potency, and they began engaging in genital intercourse.

In his analysis, Dr. I frequently talked about his victimization at the hands of women from his past. His mother paid no attention to him and always seemed to favor his two brothers over him. If he ever cried in front of his mother, he complained, she would simply order him to go to his room and stop crying. He said he found his neediness repugnant and disgusting. Whenever he thought about the relationship with the patient (which had ended by the time he was in analysis), he thought of how he had given to her. He did not like to think of himself as vulnerable and needing something from her. When the relationship was discovered, he became terrified of the consequences and confessed to his wife what had happened. He was amazed at how understanding she was, and he curled up in her arms like an infant suckling at the breast. He said he had never felt so needy in his life, and he was amazed and grateful that his wife could provide such succor. He said there was a palpable, almost tastable feeling of nurturance.

Like Ferenczi, Dr. I attempted to give to his patients what he did not receive from his own mother. Like Dr. H, even his sexual affair with his patient was couched in terms of what he was giving to her rather than what needs of his own were being met. A central conflict in Dr. I emerged when his regressive longing to be nurtured at the breast produced an overwhelming fear of passivity and vulnerability, leading him to defend against the wish with an attempt to be hypermasculine. He once commented that his wish to be held by his patient made him feel so vulnerable that he sexualized the relationship as a way of reasserting control.

It became apparent in the analysis that part of his fear of passivity was related to homosexual anxieties and insecurity about his maleness. He said that he had never gotten over the fact that he was supposed to be a girl. His mother had always conveyed to him that his maleness was unacceptable and had given him a first name that was gender-ambiguous. With each sexual liaison with his patient, Dr. I repeatedly reassured himself that he was not castrated, was not female, and was a desirable male.

In the initial phases of the analysis, Dr. I was completely unaware of any hostility in his relationship with the patient. As the treatment progressed, however, he began to recognize that a bitterness toward his mother for her childhood neglect of him had entered the equation. The experience of being shut out by his mother while she catered to his two brothers was reversed in his own situation, where he shut out his wife and directed all of his affection toward his patient, thus turning a childhood situation of humiliation and exclusion into one of adult triumph and revenge.

The reasons that Dr. I fell in love with a patient, rather than a woman who was not off-limits from an ethical standpoint, became clearer in the analysis when he examined his relationship with his father. He had little to say about his father, who had been emotionally unavailable to him throughout childhood. About 2 years into the analysis, Dr. I made a startling revelation almost in passing. He indicated that at one time his father had been a minister but had reportedly been ejected from his church after having an affair with one of his parishioners. The analytic work helped him to realize that he was unconsciously reenacting a pattern similar to his father's; Dr. I regarded that revelation with horror because he had always tried to make a point of being different from his father. He came to see the sexual relationship with the patient as a compromise formation involving the fulfillment of an oedipal wish to possess a forbidden incestuous object, coupled with an identification with his father that resulted in his disgracing himself, thus ensuring that he would not surpass his father.

Although Dr. I's situation focused largely on insecurities about his masculine identity, other cases involve conflicts about sexual orientation. In same-sex dyads, some analysts or therapists use a relationship with a patient as a way of exploring their own sexual orientation. In a study of 15 female therapist–female patient liaisons, 20 percent of the therapists identified themselves to patients as heterosexual, 20 percent as bisexual, and only 40 percent as clearly lesbian (Benowitz, 1995). Twenty percent said they had not been sexually involved with a woman before, and 33.3 percent demonstrated internal conflict concerning their sexual orientation or sexual behavior with women. John Gonsiorek (1989) noted a similar pattern in male therapist–male patient dyads.

Sexual transference and countertransference feelings are characterized by considerable fluidity in gender and sexual orientation (Gabbard, 1994f). A number of female therapists reported becoming sexually involved with female patients even though they did not find the patient sexually appealing or did not think of themselves as homosexual. They may have become so infatuated with the patient that they were willing to go along with a sexualization of the relationship just to stay in the company of the patient.

Although it is tempting to draw parallels between the forbidden aspects of the oedipal constellation in childhood and the boundary violations between therapist and patient as adults, the material reported in this chapter on the basis of clinical work with such therapists and analysts suggests that primitive preoedipal themes are often more prominent in cases of lovesickness (Gabbard, 1994d; Twemlow & Gabbard, 1989). One such theme is the wish to be transformed by the patient. Christopher Bollas (1987) noted that the mother is not initially experienced as a separate person but as a process of transformation: "In adult life, the quest is not to possess the object; rather the object is pursued in order to surrender to it as a medium that alters the self" (p. 14). Hence, at the most fundamental level, the therapist or analyst may harbor the fantasy that the patient will be a love object that serves as an agent of magical change. Indeed, the experience of Dr. I was that a loving and sexual relationship with his patient would bring him the happiness that he had never known and make him "a new man." He also used sexualization as a defense against more primitive wishes.

The sexual contact between analyst and patient is often rather dysfunctional. There may be impotence, inability to ejaculate, inability for the female partner to reach orgasm, or premature ejaculation. However, many of the therapists involved in such relationships stress repeatedly that sex was not really the point. Goldberg (1994), in writing about lovesickness, viewed sexualization as an effort to retain a linkage to a selfobject through a type of pseudosexuality. In his view, the sexual behavior defends against feelings of disintegration or an empty depression. Richard Chessick (1992) viewed the therapist in such situations as suffering from a severe narcissistic imbalance in which he attempts "a sadistically enforced control of an archaic self-object to restore that equilibrium" (p. 162). Many of the women who have been involved with male therapists or analysts sense that they were being used sexually to gratify the needs of their therapist. Some reported that they ultimately felt they were being used as a masturbatory aid. This perception of the patient, of course, fits with the formulation that the therapist has fallen in love with an idealized version of himself projected onto the patient.

MASOCHISTIC SURRENDER

Some analysts appear to be highly invested in their own suffering. Treating patients who are viewed as "difficult" or "impossible" by others may be the source of considerable masochistic gratification for the analyst who is able to "hang in there" when other colleagues have given up. These masochistic tendencies may be constructively channeled by some analysts in a manner that allows them to succeed ultimately with treatment of refractory patients. In others, however, the need to suffer leads inexorably down a self-destructive course to sexual boundary violations.

Some analysts repeatedly find themselves in a relationship with a difficult patient in which they feel tormented by the patient's demands. This pattern reflects a masochistic relational style that may have tragic consequences. These therapists appear to pursue humiliation and victimization in their work and often in their private lives as well. Probably the most common scenario involves the male analyst who allows himself to be intimidated and controlled by a demanding patient who badgers him into increasingly escalating boundary violations as a way to prevent suicide (Eyman & Gabbard, 1991). The patient is often an incest victim who suffers from dissociative disorder, posttraumatic stress disorder, or borderline personality disorder.

These clinicians characteristically have problems dealing with their own aggression. To assert their own rights or to set limits on the patient is viewed as cruel and sadistic, so all anger is turned inward in the form of self-defeating behaviors and attitudes. As the patient's demands escalate, the analyst uses reaction formation to defend against growing resentment and hatred toward the patient. Just at the point when the analyst's resentment is reaching monumental proportions, the patient may accuse the analyst of not caring. In such confrontations, analysts feel that their negative feelings have been exposed. The ensuing guilt feelings lead them to accede to the patient's demands so that aggression in either member of the dyad is kept at bay.

Psychoanalytic work with analysts in this category commonly reveals an overidentification of the therapist with the patient. Like lovesick therapists, those in this category may be reenacting their own childhood experiences of mistreatment at the hands of parents. They are well characterized by Arnold Cooper's (1993) description of narcissistic–masochistic personality disorders. Cooper noted that "these individuals assume that all objects close to them exist as a source of frustration and malice. In effect, they use the relationships in the external world to produce endless duplications of the refusing, cruel pre-oedipal mother that dominates their internal world" (p. 55).

Analysts who fit this profile are particularly susceptible to patients who present themselves as victims who are entitled to be compensated by the analyst for the suffering they experienced as children. On the surface, these analysts are drawn into gratifying the patient's demands to be compensated. Underneath the surface, they are distinguishing themselves through their suffering. They often harbor the conviction that their suffering is more severe and more prolonged than that of others and that therefore they deserve special recognition for it. As Cooper (1993) noted, such individuals may have a secret fantasy of themselves as innocent child victims of malicious parents who might yet love them if they are sufficiently submissive.

The analysts in this category often recognize the unethical nature of the sexual activity after it has occurred, and they attempt to stop the treatment and seek help for themselves. They may masochistically turn themselves in to licensing boards or ethics committees. When litigation enters the picture, they often fare far worse than colleagues who are psychopathic predators because they are much less manipulative and they deal with the proceedings in a straightforward and honest manner.

The Case of Dr. J

Dr. J was a 44-year-old male analyst who was treating a 28-year-old woman with long-standing posttraumatic stress disorder related to childhood experiences of physical and sexual abuse. Early in the treatment, the patient demanded to be held when she experienced flashbacks of abuse experiences. She said that only if she were held could she feel "grounded." Although reluctant at first, Dr. J put his arm around her shoulders and held her during the flashbacks; she said that this intervention helped her to get over the flashback and feel that she was in the present with him rather than in the past with her father.

Dr. J became concerned about this transgression of physical boundaries and tried to explain to the patient that they needed to use words in psychotherapy rather than touch. The patient became indignant at his suggestion and said, "Words don't help me! I need to be held and loved because I got no emotional support as a child!" Dr. J said that he understood what she was experiencing but that it would be important to talk about those wishes rather than to act on them repeatedly. The patient looked at him with a piercing glare and said, "You're not listening to me. You are treating me the way that *you* think I need to be treated rather than listening to what I need from you."

Dr. J felt the patient was extremely suicidal and needed his support to keep from killing herself. He acquiesced to her demands but soon learned that holding her around the shoulders was not sufficient. She began calling him late at night and demanding that he come to her house or she would kill herself. Dr. J reasoned with her that she needed to be in the hospital if she were that suicidal. She explained that she had no insurance for hospitalization and that the only thing that would keep her from killing herself was his presence. He reluctantly went over to her house, all the time feeling that he was crossing boundaries that should have remained intact. He justified what he did by telling himself that he was saving her life and that he was "unorthodox" and not bound by rigid rules of psychotherapy. He also would talk to her for as long as an hour in the middle of the night to the point that his wife became angry at him for keeping her up with his lengthy phone conversations in bed.

The patient also demanded that he treat her for free because she could no longer afford psychotherapy. He compromised and gave her a double session for the price of one, but she continued to intimidate him by telling him that he was like a prostitute who only cared about her because she paid him. Dr. J finally agreed not to charge a fee as he continued his descent down the slippery slope. Within the sessions, the embraces escalated to kisses and ultimately to genital fondling. At this point, the analyst said they would have to stop what they were doing because it was unethical. He attempted to transfer his patient to a colleague, and the patient promptly sued him for malpractice.

In treatment Dr. J recognized the extent to which he had been taken in by his patient, but he said that he felt there was something "noble" in his willingness to suffer to save her. He revealed a childhood identification with Christ, who had suffered for the sins of others. He reflected on how irresistibly he was drawn into the vortex with his patient, often fueled by the fantasy that his sacrifice of himself professionally by getting sexually involved with her would save her from suicide. He said, "It was almost as though I would die so she could live."

This kind of thinking is highly reminiscent of the relationship between Eros and Death spelled out by Sabina Spielrein 90 years earlier (see Chapter 5). This fantasy of altruistically "going out in a blaze of glory" had obvious oedipal underpinnings that became apparent as the treatment progressed. In other words, sex with this forbidden female would lead to his own death but by *his* hand rather than his father's.

Cooper (1993) observed that narcissistic and masochistic personality disorders typically have some version of superego pathology; the superego may be somewhat corrupt or excessively harsh. These individuals may flaunt rules of conduct but generally only in a way that results in their being caught and punished. Their superegos do not intervene to prevent self-destructive and damaging behavior but emerge after the fact to assist in the punishment.

The case of Dr. J also illustrates a specific projective–introjective pattern that frequently occurs in the masochistic surrender scenario. The sequence of events is best understood as the unfolding of a drama involving three principal characters: an abuser, a victim, and an omnipotent rescuer (Davies & Frawley, 1992; Gabbard, 1992). The analyst–patient relationship begins as a rescuer–victim paradigm until the analyst has "run the extra mile" by descending down the slippery slope to the point that he feels relentlessly tormented by the patient. At this point, the roles change and the patient becomes the abuser while the analyst becomes the victim. Finally, in an effort to rescue the patient, the analyst colludes with a reenactment of early abuse in which he becomes the abuser and the patient is once again the victim (Gabbard, 1994c; Gabbard & Wilkinson, 1994).

Another point demonstrated by the report of Dr. J's transgression is the terror of object loss underlying many instances of masochistic surrender. The concern that the patient will quit psychotherapy or commit suicide may resonate with earlier fantasied or real object losses that haunt the therapist. These clinicians may deny the loss by finding substitutes for the lost objects from the past in the form of patients. The therapist may cling to the patient, no matter how preposterous the circumstances, because the therapist's suffering is still preferable to loss of the object.

Analysts or therapists prone to masochistic surrender may be particularly vulnerable to unscrupulous patients with sadistic and psychopathic features. Occasional cases appear in which such patients (male or female) ask a therapist to come to their homes, where they then attempt to seduce the therapist while tape-recording the interaction. They subsequently contact an attorney and sue the therapist in hopes of winning a large financial settlement. We should point out, however, that regardless of the patient's pathology, the therapist or analyst is always responsible for maintaining appropriate boundaries.

THE COMMON GROUND OF NARCISSISM

In developing categories to understand analysts who engage in sexual boundary violations, we recognize that narcissistic problems of one kind or another are involved in almost all cases. Narcissistic issues occur on a continuum ranging from analysts with psychopathic structures to those who are vulnerable and needy for love. Herbert Strean (1993) discussed clinical work with four therapists who had had sex with their patients and reached the conclusion that all had serious problems with being able to love. They were all childishly narcissistic individuals who found it difficult to relate to others with sustained empathy. In each case, they had experienced ungratifying relationships with both of their parents and had considerable resentment that powerful wishes for physical and emotional contact had not been gratified.

A key manifestation of the analysts' struggles is the grandiosity inherent in virtually all these cases. A recurring theme is a conviction that "I alone can save (or heal) this patient." Altruistic wishes to rescue are transformed into omnipotent strivings to heal. Analysts who believe their love or their selfless sacrifices will cure the patient are essentially caught up in the fantasy that it is their *person* rather than their technique and knowledge that will help. Although the relationship is certainly part of the therapeutic action of psychoanalysis, the management of that relationship is a key aspect of analytic technique.

Another commonality striking to all observers of this phenomenon is the profoundly sadomasochistic core in these clinicians. In some cases the sadism toward the patient is more apparent, whereas in others, the self-destructive tendencies of the analyst are more prominent. In all cases, however, both are present in one form or another. Strean (1993) found that all four of the therapists he treated showed considerable self-hate, which often took the form of acting-out behavior that confirmed their self-contempt.

A third common denominator is some tendency toward action over reflection. Many of the analysts and therapists who get sexually involved with their patients have an ego impairment in the area of their capacity to engage in fantasy (Gabbard, 1994f). Dr. H personified this difficulty. In her own words, "There is a point in me where thought and fantasy disappear, and I just have to do something to resolve an internal conflict. This type of action is different from and often in opposition to the type of reasoned action needed to resolve a real external conflict." Helen Meyers (1991) made a similar observation about certain perverse patients, for whom action replaced fantasy. Other clinicians may be able to work through intense erotic countertransference through the productive use of fantasy. This impaired ability to fantasize is certainly not a universal feature of therapists or analysts who transgress sexual boundaries, but it is found often enough to warrant attention.

This proneness to action instead of fantasy in some cases overlaps with Hartmann's (1991) notion of "thick boundaries," discussed in Chapters 1 and 3. Therapists or analysts with thick inner boundaries find it difficult to enter an analytic space with the patient where fantasies and ideas can be played with or considered without the assumption of an action associated with them. These therapists may be inclined to respond to fantasies in their patients with concrete actions because of a failure to appreciate the difference between a transference wish and the gratification of that wish in reality. Both Dr. H and Dr. I had this difficulty. A particularly problematic situation in many cases of sex between therapist and patient is an incest-victim patient who has thin inner boundaries and an action-prone therapist or analyst who has thick inner boundaries. This situation may overlap with cases in which a narcissistic male therapist becomes sexually involved with a border-line female patient, reflecting the gender differences in boundaries that we described in Chapter 4.

Analysts or therapists with thick inner boundaries are paradoxically more prone to the perils of projective identification. Because they lack the capacity to play in a symbolic realm, they tend to perceive (or, more accurately, misperceive) an unbreakable tie between themselves and the object of the projections, the patient. When the patient has been damaged from a childhood of traumatic experiences, therapists with excessively thick inner boundaries may perceive that reparation must be made in a highly concrete form (Segal, 1994). The patient does not symbolically represent someone else, nor is the analyst represented as someone else in the patient's transference. There is an immediate sense of pressure to act because of the failure to symbolize. This dynamic explains why so many analysts and therapists who have had sex with their patients argue that they were simply being "the good father" in their efforts to love the patient back to health. They fail to recognize that the father is a symbolic representation rather than a literal figure.

Although certain clinicians can be characterized as having thick boundaries on an ongoing basis, it is also true that a paranoid–schizoid mode of mental functioning is present at some level in all of us (Ogden, 1986). Any therapist may regress to a more concrete mode of action in which projective identification predominates, particularly under the pressures of strong desires and yearnings in association with severe life stresses such as losses.

A fourth commonality is some form of superego disturbance. This impairment may be severe in the psychopathic predator but subtle in the lovesick analyst. Even the lovesick therapist, however, may not have fully internalized a set of values that prescribe ethical conduct and proscribe exploitation of others. Some of these clinicians feel the need for clear external guidelines and may work in institutional set-tings where employee policies and peer feedback help them maintain appropriate professional boundaries. Others have tyrannical, archaic superegos that lead them to act out as a veritable overthrow of the pro-hibiting parent. This understanding may help explain the common finding of histories of long-standing moral and ethical behavior to the point of asceticism in therapists who fall into the categories of lovesick-ness and masochistic surrender. When such a therapist transgresses sexual boundaries with patients, it creates tremendous cognitive disso-nance in colleagues, who may have experienced the clinician as a man or woman of great integrity. In more severe cases, some lovesick ana-lysts and some of those who fit the masochistic surrender category con-sciously experience the need to behave ethically as motivated by a fear of being punished or losing their license if they do not. Still others are able to compartmentalize moral or ethical proscriptions in the context of intense passion. Although part of them knows certain behaviors are potentially destructive to the patient, they keep that aspect of their awareness separate from the passionate aspect, which is compelled to action and sexual gratification.

A fifth common denominator is the analyst's perception of a deficit in the patient that requires some sort of enactment to be filled. This dimension is intimately linked to a confusion of role, in which the ana-lyst becomes a lover or parent instead of an analyst. Winer (1994) referred to this boundary line as the difference between being a con-sultant, which more accurately fits the role of the analyst, and a parent. Seeing the patient as having missed out on something in childhood may evoke powerful rescue fantasies in the analyst, who feels he or she must do more and more to fill the void left by the patient's parenting experience.

In identifying these common themes, we do not mean to imply that these factors definitively differentiate analysts who engage in sexual boundary violations from those who do not. The stress of divorce, death of a loved one, severe financial or professional blows, and other wounds to which all analytic flesh is heir can erode the smooth func-tioning of the ego, the superego, and the self, as well as the character-istic patterns of object relations. Although we would like to think that a thorough personal analysis is prophylactic for vulnerability to trans-gressions such as analyst–patient sex, experience suggests otherwise. Freud himself was pessimistic about the capacity for an analysis to pre-vent serious difficulties from arising in subsequent phases of the adult life cycle (Freud, 1937).

A recurrent theme found on examining analysts who have become sexually involved with their patients is an overvaluation of love and its power to heal both therapist and patient. Love may be as much a slayer as a healer. When we begin to feel that we can love our patients better than their parents did, we should acknowledge that we are at risk for succumbing to the siren song of the mythic power of love about which poets have cautioned us for centuries. As Leon Altman noted (1977),

> the need to disown hate might even be the root cause of our need to place so much emphasis on love, to ask so much of it. Demanding more from love than it can accomplish may bedevil our work as analysts. . . . Therapeutic zeal in this direction is as unwise and unanalytic as it is in any other. Love will not cure all. (p. 43)

CHAPTER 7

Nonsexual Boundary Violations

I N RECENT YEARS there has been a growing literature within psychiatry and psychology on nonsexual boundary violations (Borys & Pope, 1989; Epstein, 1994; Epstein, Simon, & Kay, 1992; Frick, 1994; Gutheil & Gabbard, 1993; Lamb, Strand, Woodburn, Buchko, Lewis, & Kang, 1994; Simon, 1992; Strasburger, Jorgenson, & Sutherland, 1992). Much of this literature evolved from a process of working backward from the study of sexual exploitation cases and observing that therapist–patient sex is the final outcome of a gradual erosion of nonsexual boundaries: the slippery slope phenomenon described in Chapter 6. It soon became apparent that considerable harm may be done to the patient and to the process even when the descent down the slope is aborted before sexual involvement takes place.

The psychoanalytic literature, on the other hand, has backed into this murky terrain from another direction, namely, the growing interest in transference–countertransference enactment. If one excludes the corrupt, psychopathic analysts from consideration, most nonsexual boundary violations can be understood as enactments. The recent emphasis on enactments grows out of a larger trend within psychoanalysis to view the process as a two-person endeavor in which the intrapsychic and interpersonal are inextricably linked. Passionate feelings, such as love and hate, arise in both persons as a result of mutual influence. There is also a recognition of the inevitability of the analyst's subjectivity as an influence on the analyst's behaviors and a concomitant acceptance that the positivist view of the "objective" blank screen analyst is increasingly untenable.

The awareness that greater human responsivity is an ingredient of good technique has resulted in the shunning of "by-the-numbers" approaches to analysis (Mayer, 1994a). Irwin Hoffman (1994) noted that many authors recently have reported some form of deviation from a traditional or more accepted way of working, what he has termed a feeling of "throwing away the book" (p. 188). He related this phenomenon to the spontaneous introduction of the analyst's subjectivity into the process. From a broader perspective, there is a widespread recognition in all quarters that the analyst is "sucked into" the patient's world through an ongoing series of enactments that dislodge the analyst from the traditional posture of quiet, reflective listening (Gabbard, 1995a).

With this acknowledgment of the ubiquitous nature of countertransference enactment, the definition of boundary violations becomes complex. A purist might argue that boundary violations are occurring all the time as the analyst is pulled first this way and then that in response to the evocative transference of the patient. However, such broadened use of the term erodes the narrower and preferred meaning of *violations*, which is egregious and potentially harmful transgressions. As we noted in Chapter 3, there is merit in distinguishing relatively harmless and perhaps even useful boundary *crossings* from serious and harmful boundary *violations* (Gutheil & Gabbard, 1993). Both may be understood as emerging from countertransference enactments, but the former is more attenuated than the latter and is subject to careful scrutiny by the analyst, the analytic dyad, or both. The determination of whether a particular boundary transgression is a crossing or a violation often must be postponed for a while as the analytic process unravels its meaning. As Robert Waldinger (1994) noted, "the intrapsychic meanings of a boundary crossing may be the only clues to understanding whether a violation has occurred" (p. 226). A useful starting point for our consideration of nonsexual boundary violations, therefore, is a detailed consideration of the concept of enactment.

COUNTERTRANSFERENCE ENACTMENT

Jacobs (1986) was instrumental in introducing the concept of *enactment* as a way of understanding subtle instances of interlocking transference–countertransference dimensions that operate outside of conscious awareness, often through nonverbal means, such as body postures. In an elegant review of the term, James McLaughlin (1991) noted the roots of the word in the notion of playing a part or simulating as well as persuading or influencing someone else in the interpersonal field. McLaughlin defined *enactment* broadly as "all behaviors of both parties in the analytic relationship, even verbal, in consequence of the intensification of the action intent of our words created by the constraints and regressive push induced by the analytic rules and frame" (p. 595). He also offered a more specific definition: "those regressive (defensive) interactions between the pair experienced by either as a consequence of the behavior of the other" (p. 595).

If we narrow our focus to *countertransference* enactments, because our concern in this discussion is the analyst's behavior, it becomes clear that the concept has much in common with the Kleinian notion of projective identification (Gabbard, 1995a; Gabbard & Wilkinson, 1994). Consider, for example, Judith Chused's (1991) definition: "Enactments occur when an attempt to actualize a transference fantasy elicits a countertransference reaction" (p. 629). Boesky (Panel, 1992) noted the similarities between enactment and projective identification, and he suggested that detailed study of enactments might allow for a better understanding of how projective identification works. Chused (Panel, 1992) stressed that implicit in the concept of projective identification is that any analyst would respond in approximately the same manner to specific behavior or material in the patient. Countertransference enactments, on the other hand, assume that the intrapsychic meaning of an interaction in the analysis could be entirely different for different analysts, who might then behave differently when presented with the same material by the same patient. McLaughlin (1991; Panel, 1992) suggested that in projective identification the analyst is viewed as virtually empty and is simply a receptacle or container for what the patient is projecting.

The distinctions made by Chused and McLaughlin may be more apparent than real (Gabbard, 1995a). Modern-day Kleinians, such as Elizabeth Bott Spillius (1992) and Betty Joseph (Joseph, Feldman, & Spillius, 1989), share the concern that it would be inappropriate to assume that all of the analyst's feelings derive from the patient. They would agree with Chused's perspective that individual analysts might have different countertransference enactments (or different variations of projective identification).

It is true that the more classical analysts, when writing about enactments, often focus to a greater extent on countertransference in the narrow sense, that is, experiences from their own past that are revived in the interaction with the patient (Jacobs, 1986). However, most would agree with the Kleinian notion that the analyst's countertransference may convey important information about the patient (Abend, 1989). As Jacobs (1993a) noted, "the inner experiences of the analyst often provide a valuable pathway to understanding the inner experiences of the patient." (p. 7). Similarly, Owen Renik (1993) described a countertransference enactment in which he felt immobilized and emphasized that the enactment was determined partly by his own childhood wish to save his mother and partly by his patient's need to elicit a rescue response in him.

Ralph Roughton (1993) also regarded countertransference enactments and projective identification as strikingly similar. He made a distinction, however, between an *enactment*, which simply involves putting an experience into behavior, and *actualization*, which he saw as

> subtle forms of manipulation on the part of the analysand that induce the analyst, often unknowingly, to act or to communicate in a slightly special way or to assume a particular role with the analysand that silently gratifies a transference wish or, conversely, defends against such a wish. This interactive aspect might also be called an enactment which has an actualizing effect. (p. 459)

Roughton acknowledged that this view of enactment as actualizing a countertransference response in the analyst is virtually the same as

Joseph Sandler's (1976) *role-responsiveness* and Ogden's (1979) under-standing of *projective identification.* He noted that the principal difference may be that the common use of the term *projective identification* is in the context of more primitive patients who are in somewhat regressed states during analytic treatment.

To summarize, the term *countertransference enactment* in the contem-porary psychoanalytic literature, like the term *projective identification,* implies that the analyst's countertransference is a *joint creation* by patient and analyst (Gabbard, 1995a; Gabbard & Wilkinson, 1994). The analysand evokes certain responses in the analyst, whereas the ana-lyst's own conflicts and internal self and object representations deter-mine the final shape of the countertransference response.

A consensus is emerging in the literature that such countertransfer-ence enactments are both inevitable and useful in the course of psy-choanalytic treatment. Morris Eagle (1993) presented a case vignette in which a transference–countertransference enactment in and of itself appeared to cure a symptom. He invoked the mastery–control theory of Joseph Weiss and Harold Sampson (1986) as an explanatory frame-work, assuming that the patient disconfirmed a core unconscious path-ogenic belief, which in turn led to symptom remission without insight.

Chused (1991) noted the value of enacting certain impulses within the analytic frame, only to catch oneself and retrospectively examine what happened. She stressed, however, that the value for the analysis is not in the enactment itself but in the observations and eventual understanding that derive from those enactments. As we noted previ-ously, this catching of oneself in the middle of the enactment and the retrospective examination of the behavior may also serve to differenti-ate a useful boundary crossing from a boundary violation. Jacobs (1993b) observed that both experience and insight operate together and cannot truly be separated from one another.

Renik (1993) argued that countertransference awareness always emerges *after* countertransference enactment. He shares Boesky's view that analysis may not proceed unless the analyst gets emotionally involved in ways that he or she had not intended. Renik has embraced a technique that allows for spontaneity of the analyst even though a certain degree of the analyst's subjectivity inevitably works its way into interventions. In this regard, he has aligned himself with constructivists such as Hoffman (1983, 1992, 1994), who recognize the inevitability of bringing subjectivity to bear in understanding the analytic interaction. The constructivist view also acknowledges that to some extent the analyst's behavior is shaped by influences from the patient. Both transference and countertransference would be regarded as joint creations within this view.

Central to the constructivist (or social-constructivist) perspective is the notion that enactments are going on continuously in the analytic setting and that analysts must continually monitor themselves for the possibility that they are unconsciously participating in an internal scenario scripted by the patient (Gill, 1991; Hoffman, 1992). Moreover, the process goes both ways in the sense that the analyst's actual behaviors influence the patient's transference to the analyst. Another implication of the constructivist understanding of transference–countertransference enactments is that the intrapsychic and interpersonal realms cannot be divorced from one another in the analytic dyad (Hoffman, 1991a, 1991b), a view also stressed by Coen (1992), who approached the issue from a more classical orientation.

The contemporary view of countertransference enactment as ubiquitous and useful presents a dilemma for the analyst. Where is the line between legitimate psychoanalytic work and exploitative boundary violations? The line cannot, of course, be definitively drawn. Nevertheless, a number of guidelines can assist the analyst in making the determination. As we noted previously, catching oneself as the enactment is *in statu nascendi* may serve to prevent a crossing from becoming a violation. Also, the capacity of both analyst and patient to discuss and analyze the incident may determine whether a behavior is productive or destructive. Conversely, if an enactment is not discussable for one reason or another, it may bode poorly for the process. A third principle concerns whether the enactment is repetitive and unresponsive to the analyst's own self-analytic efforts. Finally, a determination of harm to the patient or the process may assist the analyst in judging the enactment's exploitativeness.

As we noted in Chapter 3, the determination of whether an enactment is a boundary crossing or a boundary violation may be problematic, particularly when the enactment involves a relatively subtle, spontaneous reaction of the analyst. The following vignette illustrates such a case:

THE CASE OF MS. B

Ms. B, the patient described in Chapter 2, was a single, intelligent, and successful academic in her mid-30s who came to analysis because of difficulties maintaining relationships with men. She tended to choose sexually active but needy men who were somewhat socially and intellectually inferior to her. After an initial period of an intensely close, almost merging relationship, Ms. B would lose interest in her lover, and it became only a matter of time before she would throw him out. A good deal of analytic work addressed this repetitive pattern of using a sexual relationship primarily to satisfy fusional needs. The choice of needy men, who were also outsiders from her own social milieu, served both to ward off incestuous fears and to permit her to assert what she called her own "macho" toward her older brothers and her overpowering father.

In about the fourth year of her analysis, Ms. B went into a depressive state, lasting several months after breaking up with her last lover, a dreamy, ineffectual drifter. At the end of this period, a divorced male colleague asked her out for dinner. She became panicky in response to the invitation, a rather odd reaction given her active sexual history. She did accept the invitation but felt tense and anxious throughout the dinner. Old incestuous fears as well as the fear of submitting and becoming a "doormat" to husband and children, as her mother had been, began to surface during the dinner. To scare off her suitor, she acted "tough and macho" and openly discouraged further advances. On hearing this material, the analyst felt annoyed and disappointed with Ms. B; the analyst felt she was throwing away a positive opportunity to develop a more lasting relationship with a suitable male object. The analyst sensed irritation and some anxiety in herself, but she made no conscious attempt to understand the countertransference reaction.

By coincidence, the analyst was just about to embark on a few days of planned vacation. On her return to the analysis, Ms. B was apathetic and depressed. She reported a dream in which she was with her favorite sister. She was crying profusely, but the sister could not comfort her. In the ensuing few sessions, the patient and analyst discussed the patient's disappointment at the analyst's absence; however, the analyst made no effort to examine the possibility that the analyst's irritation might have contributed to the patient's depression.

A few days later, an opportunity presented itself for Ms. B to join a study group to which the male colleague also belonged. Ms. B was interested in joining, but to do so required changing the time of one of her analytic sessions. Although changing sessions had always been extremely complicated and difficult because both analyst and patient had relatively tight schedules, to the analyst's own surprise, she found herself agreeing immediately to Ms. B's request for another time, silently planning to herself a number of changes to accommodate Ms. B.

Ms. B accepted the analyst's suggestion but then called the same day to cancel the new schedule for 2 weeks. In the first appointment after the break, Ms. B came in with a new haircut, unusually short and even provocative. She talked of her stupidity to agree to such a haircut and questioned her motives. It became evident that cutting her hair so short was her way of postponing joining the study group. She now had to wait for at least 2 weeks before her hair would grow a bit longer. Cutting her hair short was also a way of asserting her "macho" (i.e., refusing to please men, who usually like long hair on women). The analyst suggested that her willingness to change the schedule so readily may have raised questions in the patient's mind about the analyst's motives.

The patient responded affirmatively and said that she had experienced the analyst's readiness as a way of urging her to enter into a relationship with the male colleague before trying to analyze her fears. The analyst had not only departed from neutrality, but also failed to consider the patient's anxiety and empathize with the patient's need to take some time to deal with her fears regarding a new relationship with a man who was different from most other men with whom she had had relationships in the past. The analyst gradually realized that her impatience and anxiety in the countertransference, expressed as therapeutic zeal, were experienced by the patient as a form of boundary crossing or boundary violation. Both Ms. B and her analyst were able to discuss and analyze the incident, which was not part of a repetitive pattern. Whether the patient was harmed as a result of the enactment was more difficult to determine. Ms. B did avoid the study group, where she might have continued to develop her relationship with the man who had taken her to dinner. Yet the patient appeared to experience no lasting or irreparable damage as a result of the interaction.

•   •   •

The analyst's spontaneous frame violation is an example of a common occurrence in the day-to-day ebb and flow of the analytic process. Interrupting a long silence with a question may be experienced by patients who are absorbed in reverie as a kind of trespassing by the analyst. On the other hand, failure to interrupt a silence may be experienced by certain patients as the analyst's way of taking distance from an uncooperative, irate, or stubborn patient. A spontaneous bit of self-disclosure by the analyst may be experienced as human and caring by one analysand and as a boundary violation by another. Even the analyst's insistence that the patient adhere to a somewhat rigid analytic frame can be experienced as a boundary violation by a sensitive patient with loose interpersonal boundaries. As we noted in Chapter 3, each analytic dyad establishes its own set of analytic boundaries.

This subtlety is completely missing in the more egregious cases of nonsexual boundary violations, in which a repetitive pattern continues without being subject to analytic scrutiny and clearly exploits the patient's vulnerability. The following case demonstrates how some patients respond in the face of these more severe violations.

THE CASE OF DR. K

When Dr. K started her analysis, she was a 29-year-old psychiatrist who had just finished her residency. Although she was analyzed by a highly respected analyst in the city where she practiced, her analysis soon became a nightmare of boundary violations. To convey her experience of the progressive transgressions she experienced, we will let her speak for herself in a first-person account of what happened (with her permission and endorsement, of course):

"When I began analysis, I was longing for someone who would 'understand' and 'know' me. To me, this meant someone who would not be put off by the intensity of my feelings and who could intellectually track the complexities of some of my thoughts. Although outgoing on the surface, I had been a private person inside and felt isolated emotionally.

"I was taken from the beginning with my analyst. He was emotionally warm, even in his neutrality. He was intellectually sharp. He seemed to grasp nuances of what I was trying to communicate. He offered associations of his own, rich in their imagery, in their compassion for patients he had treated, and in their acceptance of the offbeat or odd. He would weave in metaphors from his own avocation of painting and knowledge about artists he had met or read about. I felt I had, at long last, found a soul mate. He understood me. Years of internal loneliness welled up, and often I cried in sessions, grateful to feel understood and, by implication, accepted at last.

"The first year of the analysis was conducted in a relatively conventional manner; that is, there were no after-hours contacts either in person or by phone. Sessions ended on time. My analyst offered me no gifts or objects to take with me. Feelings about seeing my analyst in passing or from afar outside the session were analyzed in detail. I felt 'held' by the process and by him. I longed for more, and sometimes those longings were a bit like achings, but they were contained in the realm of fantasy. I knew the rules of treatment. I knew what the boundaries were. I talked about what I wished for from him. For his part, he allowed these wishes to blossom. In retrospect, it does seem he did little to interpret positive longings toward him, either as re-creations of past longings or as defenses against further growth. Maybe it was too early to do that. I don't know. But it did seem that he accepted as fact my experience that I had found in him something unique and special. He talked about this as something we did not need to interpret; something that was a rare 'gift' in life. He believed in unconscious communication, as did I, and we had the experience that sometimes my associations picked up on his unspoken associations (and vice versa).

"Thus we knew each other, sometimes without words. He affirmed that I had this ability with him. All of this felt supreme, magical, more than I ever imagined could be possible in real life. It was the most special relationship I had ever had, and, gradually, the relationship began to feel essential to my life. It was as if the emotional connection I felt with him in the sessions was life-giving water that I needed every day. He allowed me to feel and voice these things toward him. He allowed me to 'regress' in this way. All my life, I had conscientiously (albeit angrily at times) squelched such feelings within me in order to obey the expectation that I 'mature.' I entered school at a young age. I achieved superior grades. I moved relentlessly toward accomplishments, as if I were obeying a command to grow up and not make trouble by acting less than my age. I was praised for my maturity, and demands for emotional intimacy were reacted to as if they were threatening. Therefore, when he did not demand that I achieve, when he allowed me to need him, when he nurtured my longings for intimacy from him, I felt a thirst never quenched was now being slaked. And, perhaps most important, I felt it was being slaked by *him*. Not by the process. Not by something in me. I felt as if there must be something odd or unusual about me and about him that made this experience with him so rare in my life. He did not question this perception of mine.

"When he shared his personal thoughts and reflections with me, they felt like secret gifts. I had understood that an analyst was like a blank screen. He was somewhat neutral but was not blank. He sometimes told me vignettes from his life. I felt special, as if I knew things about him that others did not. I felt he was giving me presents. They felt a bit like contraband. I would jealously and a bit guiltily guard those presents of self-revelation. I would never talk about him to anyone outside analysis, never reveal the things he told me. That made them all the more precious; furthermore, it made me feel special and secretly loyal to him.

"He and I had a little secret life. None of this was voiced by me, nor raised by him for inspection. I did not consciously keep it hidden from analysis; it was more a part of the ego-syntonic fabric of our analytic work. It was the nature of our relationship, as it unfolded between us. I make these careful observations now only in retrospect. As I feel my way back into the past, I realize I was conscious then of feeling this way about what he told me, but I think I was afraid if I said anything about the effect it was having on me that he might stop it. And since it made me feel special, I did not want him to stop it. So I emphasized in my mind how special he was, as well as how special his technique was. Wasn't he a respected member of the analytic community? Weren't we analyzing things? This way he had with me, this warmth that felt seductive, his self-revelations and the internal impact they had on me, were simply part of his 'special style.' They were placed outside the realm of analysis.

"A line was crossed in the second year of analysis. The quality of the relationship, and the quality of the defenses against analyzing this relationship, did not change. Rather, the shift was one of moving from fantasy into action, for both of us. This crossing of the line, from fantasy into action, caused an unleashing of sorts. All sorts of actions tumbled into play, snowballing rapidly it seems (although in reality, this snow-balling took place over several years).

"I was the first to cross the line. Distraught over news that my father had passed away, I called him at home one night. The talk was brief. He was supportive but not overtly encouraging of my calling. How-ever, within the week, after I returned from the funeral, he sent flowers of condolence to my house, with a one-page handwritten note. I was stunned. Overwhelmed. My analyst had sent me flowers. With a note. In his handwriting. To me! He wrote of his thoughts about death and the preciousness of life. He shared his inner self. Stunned. That is how I felt. Like the time when I was 13, and a handsome boy, 2 years my senior, asked me to a special high school dance. How had he picked me? Was I indeed beautiful? I had done nothing, and suddenly a prince had appeared. What did this mean? Did it mean the way I felt it? Or was it commonplace and nothing extraordinary.

"There was a sort of split within me. A dream place in which my dreams were coming true and a prince was choosing me. And another level at which we acted as if nothing extraordinary had taken place. Why was I so stunned and excited? Whichever realm was the 'true' reality, I had to stay perfectly still for fear of upsetting the dream. If I showed what it meant to me, he might not come forward again. I had to hold myself quiet, perfectly still. I treasured that note. I read and reread it and allowed myself only the feeling of safety and harbor con-tained within it. I did not let myself fantasize or associate in romantic ways. Only now, as I write this, am I aware of the clearly romantic asso-ciations that go so readily with the feelings experienced back then. At the very moment the most important man in my life passed away, a prince appeared to replace him.

"I found myself calling my analyst again a week later. It was in the evening, and I had been weeping about my father, unable to sleep. He suggested that we meet at a restaurant equidistant from our houses. There we found a booth, away from the people and the noise, and I poured out my heart to him about my loneliness and the empty feeling my father's death had left. He reached over and touched me. A simple gesture. His hand over my hand. But again, in retrospect, I remember my heart standing still. I have clear images of that booth, the darkness of the low-lit restaurant, the touch of his hand. It was a turning point.

I had not forced myself on him. I had called, distraught and in tears. He had suggested we meet. Would any analyst have done that? Was it necessary at the time? I don't know. I also don't know if he could have conveyed acceptance and 'withness' over the phone in a way that could have sustained me, without my feeling rejected. It is easy to say, now, that he could have and should have. But to be honest, I don't know. What I do know is that he could have and should have analyzed my reactions to the event afterward, and I could have talked about it without feeling scared or rejected in any alliance-severing way.

"I would have felt safer, as if he were helping me contain my feelings instead of encouraging me to show him in action whatever I felt. He never asked me to analyze this event. He never asked me the internal impact it had on me. It was dealt with as if it had been a necessary intervention in the 'real relationship.' That was the name with which he then christened this new aspect of our work. Whatever was part of the real relationship was outside the realm of analysis. The real relationship did not need to be analyzed. It was a curative element in and of itself. It existed, and to subject it to analysis was to rigidly deny its validity. Instead, we were not to be threatened by the real feelings that existed between us. Greenson had pointed out that a real relationship always existed between analyst and analysand. Freud had fed the Rat Man. Within this rubric, now and for the rest of the treatment, came to be placed action after action, feeling and verbalization, safe from analysis, flouting the necessity for analysis.

"When my analyst did not ask me to analyze our restaurant meeting, I felt an increasing burden placed on me. I had to keep my reactions secret—the meaning the event had. And I had to be the one to regulate the impulses within me, alone. He was not going to provide a safe boundary between fantasy–impulse and action. He encouraged action. I had to be the one to say *stop*. I could not be myself. I could not push against the limits. I think I felt like an adolescent who was pushing against a limit and finding no safe wall against which to bounce. Instead, the burden for establishing limits was pushed back onto me. Whatever I asked for, from that point on, I got. At some level, I felt extremely angry with him that he was not helping me with my impulses, that he was not helping me learn mature ways of handling them. That all he was giving me were two options: Either don't voice the wish, or act the wish out. I was very angry about that. During the first phase of the acting out, I did not articulate this in words to myself, although the feeling was clearly there. During the second phase of the acting out, I was open and verbal about my anger with him and my irritation with what he was doing. But he kept doing it all the same.

"Each time he tried something new—finding the gourmet licorice I talked about often and sending a carefully selected tin of it to my office, laboring for days on a painting he had made of me from a photograph (and carrying it personally over to my house)—my reactions were a strange mix. Always the stunned feeling. To put that into words: He can't be doing this. This is not happening. What does this mean? Am I that incredibly special to him that he is breaking a boundary like this? The unadmitted romantic overtones of the older high school boy who had unexplainably singled me out seemed to be repeated.

"Then came a rapid, intellectualized rationalization: He is different. He is a good person. This is the way he does treatment. He is simply special. He knows what he is doing. He is a senior analyst. He is loved and respected by many. He does analysis better than others because he is not afraid of his own feelings and he is not afraid to show warmth. Above all: He is not acting nervous or dismayed by this; thus any anxiety must be my problem. And my anxiety was there. Mainly it showed itself in my fear that we/he would get caught. What if someone saw him coming over to my house? Other colleagues lived only blocks away in the same suburb: What if they saw his car parked in front of my house? What if we were seen together in a restaurant or a museum? Granted, we were moving through the environs of a major metropolitan area, but analysts and professionals-in-analysis tend to move in interconnecting circles and gravitate toward similar interests, so I was constantly on edge lest I/we be discovered.

"Then there was the feeling of being special. Glowing with a secret that had been told to no one. He loved me (even though I was averse to considering it a romantic love despite the fact that there was every indication that it was so). He loved me, and that armored me against the world. Whatever anyone said or did, I had an invisible shield of his love around me. No one but I knew it, but the knowledge of it made me sturdy in crowds of strange people. I was protective of my secret. I wanted to hear nothing about him from others and directly asked people who might be gossiping about him in front of me to stop. I said nothing of my analysis to anyone. This isolation of the relationship, this act of keeping it to myself, added somehow to its sense of purity and specialness for me. Not unlike an adolescent's first love.

"Was I ever scared of the implications of his behavior? Scared of what it said about his mental stability and the viability of the analysis? Rarely could I face directly my fears about his mental stability. However, after the acting out had occurred over a few years, I was able to allow some anxiety about the effect all this was having on the treatment to come into awareness. I would raise my anxieties about the appropriateness of the treatment with him. He felt my concerns were unjustified and that I exaggerated the import of his actions. He assured me that he regularly discussed his cases in confidence with a trusted colleague and that he was always told that everything he was doing was fine. I can remember my mixture of relief and uneasiness when he told me this. I was relieved because one part of me had felt sure that were anyone to be told of what he was doing and the nature of our work, he would be asked to take leave of my case and I would have to find a new analyst. However, simultaneously I was uneasy about what it meant that we were doing what we were doing and what it meant that no one seemed uneasy about it. If my reactions had been explored in depth at the time, many splits within me would have been revealed. I felt all this was wrong.

"The constant secrets were not elements of sexual excitement for me, although he frequently reported that such was the case for him. Instead, they were alarms to the 'nice Jewish girl' within me that something was not right. However, when I would raise my discomfort with him, he would gently tease me and indirectly belittle me for my prudishness. In analytic sessions, these responses took the form of interpretations about how harsh my superego was. Outside the sessions, he began writing me fond letters in which he would describe in terms of belittlement masked by affection that he 'found my modesty touching and sweet.' What he did was relentlessly thrust himself on me through his gifts, his personal thoughts, and his insistence that I needed him, even when I said no or when I said I wasn't enjoying it.

"Sadly, this hit a point of weakness within me: As a child, I had not had a clear sense of my right to tell someone not to do something, nor of my accuracy of judgment in not wanting them to do it. Instead, I was made to feel foolish for being a 'prude' or 'prissy' or a 'party pooper.' Now, in my adult life, my analyst was, in so many words, saying the same things to me. And once again, I doubted. I doubted my perceptions (was I, because of a rigid superego or repressed sexual impulses, indeed reading sexual meaning or illicit overtones into behavior that was merely kindness and supportive warmth?), and I doubted my judgment (was I nothing after all but that unwanted prude of my childhood who did not fit in?). I split awarenesses within me.

"When my analyst once gave me a red, short-cut silk kimono, delicately wrapped in perfumed paper, I saw what I was looking at. I knew it was a revealing, silk kimono. But my analyst was giving it to me. If the kimono were sexual, then our relationship was truly illicit, and something might be mentally unbalanced about him. I hadn't asked for it. Or had I? My mind played tricks on me: Was my seeing it as sexual merely an exposure of some kind of perversity within me? Therefore, it could not be sexual. He was not acting as if it were sexual. He was saying he was giving it to me as a father to a daughter—trying to affirm my femininity in a somewhat avuncular fashion. Telling me it was okay to be a woman. He always told me the truth. He never lied to me. He was so well analyzed—surely he knew his own motivation. To point the finger at him as being 'seductive' and taking advantage of me would hurt him. He would withdraw. He always did when I rejected his many other gifts. He acted hurt and made me feel guilty. Then, relentlessly, he would offer them again a few days later, as if all I had said had blown over. I learned to try to titrate the gift-giving. I'd accept a few here and there, hoping that if I did, then perhaps he would ease up on his relentlessness.

"A few times during the analysis, I would wonder about something that I would doggedly try to push away: What if he were sick? Then I was laying my psyche bare to an ill man. I was entrusting my soul to an ill person. It would be like suddenly realizing in the middle of undergoing brain surgery that the person operating was a charlatan who had falsely represented himself as a qualified surgeon. Seeing him as ill brought fear. It also brought a sudden moment of stunned hopelessness: a momentary feeling of being stopped in one's tracks. The person you thought was a hero is actually unstable. The stuff that simultaneously frightens and dulls all senses in a psychological horror movie. I pushed aside any thoughts of 'he is acting ill.' I was unable to handle that perception. The burden of his weight on me, like a drunk father one is helping up the stairs at night, was too much to bear for more than a moment. To expose him to others and see the image of this man I idealized fragment into pieces before me was too much to consider.

"Why didn't the so-called trusted colleague see what was going on? Why didn't he (interesting that I always assumed it was a *he*) see anything wrong with an analyst meeting his patient in the evenings? Holding her hand? Kissing her forehead? How did that trusted colleague rationalize this away? Self-doubt again fought with paranoia. Is it me? Are my perceptions off? Or is there a sinister brotherhood of men out there who refuse to see the implications of what they are doing and instead insist on the 'illness' of their female patients who aren't appreciating what they are doing for them? Again, this paranoia was too frightening for me to entertain. And my sense of self and my right to personal boundaries as a woman had not been forged well enough for me in childhood for me to feel clear about my perceptions and unswerving in my right to speak out as an adult.

"Where were *my* wishes in all this? Was I asking for all this? My internal conviction is that I was not. I wanted an analyst, not a lover or a father. He had been a superb analyst when he stayed in that role. I was rageful at him that he was taking that away from me. But self-doubt still lingered. I thought to myself that others would blame me for all this or wonder what part I played in this. When I finally risked filing a complaint with the ethics chair of the district branch psychiatric society, she repeatedly asked me why I had not gone to someone sooner. How difficult it was to explain to her, much less to myself, the confusing mix of perceptions, compartmentalized splits, and mixed feelings that together made possible my living in the analysis yet being afraid of what was happening.

"Even my analyst asked, after I had confronted him, 'Was everything you said to me and gave to me fake then?' How can I explain to him that I was trying to end with him? That I was trying to preserve his self-esteem? That I was trying to preserve my own belief that the analysis was okay, and that 5 years were not warped, and that tens and tens of thousands of dollars had not been thrown down a sinkhole. How could I explain to myself my smiling face and my statements of adulation? How could those exist in the same world as my fear, my guilt, my worry, and (now realized) my rage. One thing is clear: I said all this to him while I was in analysis with him. I presented all the contradictions within me to him; however, he did not help me sort them out. It was as if they were never dealt with. Did I repress his attention to them? Or did he, as I believe he did, simply not deal with whatever threatened his continued acting out of his internal scenario.

"The most chilling perception of all is the realization that he was on a course driven by his own needs. That despite his endless avowal of love for me and his frequently proclaimed willingness to die for me, it was being said out of some peremptory urges within himself. He was not seeing me. He was forcing me to exist for him. It feels now as if he used me to masturbate himself with and had himself convinced not only that I wanted it and that it made me feel better but that I needed it.

"There was a phase, toward the end of the analysis, when I grew consciously irritated with his insistence on being real within my life. In retrospect, I realize this irritation, this annoyance and anger, coincided with my announcement that I would finally get married. I had avoided marriage throughout my adult life. My ability to make a commitment had been long in coming. I felt a sense of pride in my accomplishment. My analyst felt differently. It was as if he had been a loving, if not overly expressive father and I his darling daughter. But now I wanted to be free of him, yet he was hanging on, metaphorically peering in my windows and following my moves. I felt like I was Lolita in the novel. I had been oddly naive as to the sexualized nature of our relationship and, instead, nestled within what felt to be attentive, doting, caretaking arms. Then, as Lolita did, I reached puberty. Developmentally speaking, I wanted to move on. The arms that had felt enfolding, now felt restraining. The doting smile that had warmed me, now imprisoned me. I wanted out.

"When I brought up sexual fantasies, he used them as springboards for editorializing about how a man *should* treat me, how *he* would treat me if he could. He jumped at every opportunity to make sadistic barbs about the man I had chosen to marry. My anger grew, and soon I hated him. But I never let myself fully realize that. I just wanted him off my back. I felt that he, like Humbert in *Lolita*, was exposing himself as a doddering old fool as he pursued me further. Full of ambivalence, I did not know how to leave him. He was not helping me terminate. The analysis was dragging on.

"The rage emerged fiercely at this point, when I realized that a necessary piece of this drama for him was to see me as ill, to convince me of my illness, and to keep that perception alive between us in order to justify his actions toward me. He rationalized his behaviors as necessary because of how deficit-ridden I was. He seized on an isolated comment in the write-up of a preanalysis consultation I had undergone with one of his colleagues as proof that I needed extraordinary means to get through analysis. He liked to think of himself as saving me from suicide. He viewed his treatment of me as changing someone who was ridden with deficits to someone who was now strong. What broke into my awareness for the first time, when hearing myself speak aloud as I filed the formal complaint, was the startling realization that I had been presenting myself as emotionally labile and unstable to protect myself and him from the alternative: the exposure of him as the unstable one. When I finally could acknowledge how sick he truly was, the revelation was frightening and tragic, as if I were saying the emperor truly had no clothes. I wrestled with the rage within me that wanted to shame him. Why had he done this to me? Why was he ill? When Abraham lay naked on his bed, one son wanted to cover him up in sad embarrassment. The other laughed and scoffed at him, perhaps out of his anxious rage that the man had such feet of clay. I felt like both brothers at once. I wanted to shield my analyst from the eyes of the world, but at the same time I ragefully wanted to expose him to all who would look.

"I hate him, but he is now within me, and I have to resolve what I am going to do about the *him* within me. Who was he for me? Where was the good? Was my love for him real? Does my gratitude have any basis? These are questions I have yet to answer. I am trying to sort them out. One thing I know he gave me was the chance to be heard and, through being heard, the chance to know myself. I am rarely afraid to speak what is inside me now. But I am also cynical now, easily demeaning, with an undercurrent of crust. I am angry. I am plagued by transferences that were never analyzed and some that were iatrogenic to the analysis. I still shake inside when I begin to talk about what happened, and after I talk, I am filled with shame and guilt. I want to hide these things from others and erase them, as if they expose me as 'damaged goods.'

"After 5 years of analysis, I am left with having to sort it all out again.

I gave my life to him, and he cheated me. He used me. He wasn't what he seemed and I didn't know it, and when a part of me knew it, I didn't have the strength to say it out loud to someone else. I want to forget all this. But I know I shouldn't try to. Because it stays. It festers. I wish he would know what he did to me. But it is clear to me that he does not, because what I had thought was my long-sought-for, 'magical'-seeming empathy was nothing more in the end but his admiring his own reflection in me, projecting his own needs into me and seeking to meet them. If he had truly 'loved' me, he would have helped me to be free of crippling infantile longings, not try to use them to tie me to him.

"I need to do what is best for me now. And realize that life is not fair. That I'm going to make mistakes. That this was a big one. But that I am determined to grow and get better and be better because of it. This is the only way I have at present to handle it."

DISCUSSION

Although this poignant and revealing account provides only one side of the story, the events described were largely corroborated by the analyst. Dr. K's ordeal also offers a number of penetrating insights into an analysis characterized by ongoing pervasive boundary violations. The enactments occurring were clearly in the realm of violations rather than crossings for several reasons: (1) they were not attenuated, that is, the analyst did not catch himself as they emerged and attempt to understand them; (2) despite the patient's efforts to make him analyze what was going on, the analyst steadfastly refused to subject the enactments to analytic scrutiny; (3) the enactments were certainly not isolated, but rather were pervasive and repetitive; and (4) the analyst's behaviors certainly caused harm to the patient and destroyed any pretense of a viable analysis. One of the striking aspects of the account, however, is Dr. K's desperate efforts to deny the harm in what was happening to her. She evidently engaged in a form of defensive splitting or disavowal in which she simultaneously knew and did not know that she was being harmed by a seriously misguided analyst. Much like the child who is subjected to incest, she needed to believe in the transgressor's benevolence, so she engaged in a dissociative maneuver to keep the malignant nature of the boundary violation out of her awareness.

The analogy to incest brings us to another observation about the analysis. Despite the fact that no actual sexual contact took place between Dr. K and her analyst, the similarity to the dynamics of sexual boundary violations is striking. The incestuous meaning of the enactments is apparent in Dr. K's analogy to Lolita and in the sexualization of the gifts and self-disclosures of her analyst. Also, like an incest victim, Dr. K struggled with blaming herself for somehow seducing her analyst because of her ambivalently held wishes to be special to him. From Dr. K's account, her analyst appears to have been a classical case of the lovesick analyst. The boundary violations began with self-disclosures that made the patient feel special. The fantasy of being soul mates who could know each other's thoughts without having to voice them followed. The analyst clearly confused his own needs with the patient's needs, as Dr. K ultimately realized. His rescue of her was actually an attempt to rescue himself. She experienced this as though she were being used as part of his masturbatory fantasy.

Another similarity between this case and those of sexual boundary violations is the loss of the "as if" in the transference–countertransference dimensions of the analysis. Dr. K's analyst steadfastly assured his patient that the idealizing transference did not need to be analyzed: *He* was what she needed, *he* was what slaked her thirst, not analysis. To treat her special feelings as transference would be to acknowledge that he was not unique, not special, but merely a stand-in for someone else (Gabbard, 1994f). The exclusivity of the relationship would be shattered. After her father's death, he *became* the lost father. It was not *as if* he were her father in the transference. On the contrary, he told her that he was being a loving father who was trying to help his daughter. Within this paradigm, he attempted to heal her with love, although she clearly experienced the underlying contempt in his "love" as well as the real agenda, which was to gratify his own narcissistic needs. Dr. K's analyst, like most analysts who engage in egregious boundary violations, apparently lost track of the distinction between an analyst and a parent.

A related feature of this case is the analyst's apparent misuse of the concept of the real relationship. This notion was repeatedly invoked by him whenever Dr. K raised concerns about what was going on, always with the emphasis that the real relationship was something outside the transference and therefore did not need to be analyzed. In fact, there is considerable interpenetration between reality-based perceptions and transference (Greenberg, 1991; Hoffman, 1983), and teasing out the real relationship from the transference is a formidable challenge. Dr. K's analyst used the distinction in the service of denying and minimizing his patient's need to analyze the bizarre enactments she was witnessing. In addition, the "real relationship" concept was employed as a way for the analyst to avoid looking at his own countertransference issues. Indeed, in an empirical study of analytic discourse, Victoria Hamilton (1993) found that analysts' use of the "real relationship" construct negatively correlated with a perspective that countertransference examination was useful in the analytic process.

The observation that the dynamics of nonsexual boundary violations resemble those of sexual boundary transgressions applies in the majority of cases, confirming the soundness of the slippery slope concept. Indeed, this case appears to be one in which the patient herself needed to maintain limits to prevent a descent into a more overtly sexual relationship. Clearly, both sexual and nonsexual boundary violations represent a form of corruption of the analytic process. Arnold Rothstein (1994) drew a comparison between the seductiveness of sex and of money in the transference. He stressed that the patient who wishes to make a donation of money to the analyst or to the institution with which the analyst is affiliated presents the same fundamental problem as the patient who offers sex. In fact, wealthy patients may evoke countertransference wishes to be taken care of in the same way that seductive patients do. Both hold out the promise of gratifying frustrated pleasure strivings. The analyst who accepts offers of sex or money from the patient has acted on a countertransference wish to exploit the patient.

Much of the psychoanalytic literature on gifts has focused on the problems with accepting presents from patients. In the case of Dr. K's analysis, however, the *analyst* was the one offering gifts. Analysts are advised to be wary of accepting gifts because they may be efforts to bribe the analyst to avoid certain unpleasant issues in the analysis or to buy the analyst's gratitude for a variety of quid pro quos (Calef & Weinshel, 1983). Much of the same pressure was experienced by Dr. K, who felt she must collude with the gift-giving or hurt her analyst's feelings. The gifts also seemed to keep her from acknowledging the analyst's contempt for her and the process more directly, at least until the end of the analysis.

As noted in Chapter 6, the perception of deficit-based pathology often appears to be involved in sexual boundary violations. The same is true in nonsexual boundary violations. In Dr. K's analysis, it even became the subject of explicit discussions between analyst and patient. The analyst apparently justified his departure from standard analytic technique by rationalizing that the patient was deficit-ridden and suicidal. His love was supposed to fill the void left by the insufficient nurturance of her childhood environment.

We are clearly not in a position to know to what extent Dr. K's pathology was deficit-based. However little or much it was in actuality, the point we wish to stress is that the descent down the slippery slope often begins with the analyst's conviction that the patient has deficits and that those deficits need to be filled by the analyst's heroic efforts. The well-publicized case of Dr. Margaret Bean-Bayog's failed attempt to treat Paul Lozano created a sensation in the media because of her unorthodox methods of trying to save him from suicide. In his Presidential Address to the American Association of Suicidology, Terry Maltsberger (1993) defended her efforts and rightfully accused the press of plundering her career without a fair hearing of her side of the case. He spoke of the need for extraordinary involvement to prevent suicide in severely regressed patients. Even he, however, raised questions about her portraying herself to her patient as though she were his mother.

Although Maltsberger persuasively makes the case that there were no sexual relations between Bean-Bayog and her patient, he describes an alarming series of nonsexual boundary violations and an inability on Bean-Bayog's part to set limits.

Although Dr. K's analysis and the Bean-Bayog/Lozano case are quite different in many respects, there is a similar lesson to be learned from both. This lesson involves the confusion between a shift from expressive to supportive technique, on the one hand, and complete erosion of professional boundaries, on the other. There are certainly patients who appear to require support at times during their analyses. There are also those who begin analysis with an analyst who has overestimated the extent of their ego resources and their capacity to make good use of an analytic process. Indeed, Robert Wallerstein's (1986) investigation of outcomes in the Menninger Psychotherapy Research Project found that some patients who did well in treatment had benefited from supportive interventions and that these measures resulted in structural changes that were as durable as those produced by expressive methods. Many of the analyses had begun with excessively high expectations of the patient's ability to use an analytic approach and were characterized by a progressive shift to more supportive techniques.

Supportive strategies, however, involve a shift away from interventions like transference and extratransference interpretations toward clarifications, confrontations, empathic validation, advice and praise, and limit setting (Gabbard, 1994c). They also call for the analyst to bolster adaptive defenses and serve as an auxiliary ego when specific ego functions are not operating smoothly. Supportive strategies do not involve countertransference-ridden enactments of gross boundary violations. Although flexibility is needed with patients who are suicidal or deficit-based, throwing limits out the window and gratifying the wish to be rescued may actually make the patient worse (Eyman & Gabbard, 1991; Gabbard & Wilkinson, 1994; Gutheil & Gabbard, 1993). Countertransference enactments and boundaries must be monitored even more closely in supportive treatments because they are more complex and ambiguous in view of the fact that a modicum of transference gratification is part of the technique (Rockland, 1992).

In the case of Dr. K's analysis, the patient first experienced her analyst's rescue operation as gratifying, but she soon felt imprisoned and robbed of her own autonomy and freedom. With a good deal of insight, she eventually reached the highly disconcerting conclusion that she had been conforming to a role in which her analyst had cast her to protect him. As long as she presented herself as labile and unstable, he could justify his actions as providing her the necessary support to keep her functioning. If she stopped participating in this folie à deux, they would both have to face the fact that he was out of control and acting out of his own needs. Who was treating whom? As in most cases of lovesick analysts, a role reversal had occurred. This case represents an illustration of the interlocking enactments of rescue fantasies that Roberta Apfel and Bennet Simon (1985) noted.

The issue of deficit-based pathology and the analyst's response to it raises fundamental questions about the analyst's role and the therapeutic action of psychoanalysis. As we emphasized in Chapter 3, although Loewald (1960) and others have invoked the concept of reparenting as a component of the analytic process, the notion is often misconstrued to mean becoming an idealized parent to make up for the deficiencies of the actual parents of childhood. This countertransference response is particularly likely in patients who experienced severe neglect and abuse in childhood.

Yet if the analyst does not allow himself to be experienced as the old object from the past, the patient's efforts to work through experiences from childhood will be compromised. Casement (1985) described a female patient who expressed a wish to hold his hand. As a child she had undergone surgery after being scalded. During an operation, her mother, who had been holding her hand, fainted and thus let go of her hand. He initially consented to holding her hand, but he later retracted his promise after subjecting his countertransference to self-analysis. He recognized that his holding her hand would be colluding with her in an attempt to become a better parent who would make up for the failures of the actual mother. He also emphasized that it was important for his patient to experience him *as she did her mother* in addition to experiencing him as a new and different object to work through the trauma.

It would, of course, be reductionistic to conclude from this vignette that any form of touch or hand-holding is always technically incorrect in analytic work. The variability of the analytic situation is too great to make inductive leaps from one situation to all situations. McLaughlin (1995) described a situation in which an impulsive patient grabbed onto his hand for several minutes as she sobbed. He reported that the enactment was a crucial breakthrough for the patient. She experienced it as a sign that the analyst was there for her and did not view her as untouchable. She felt enhanced trust and could then tell him some reservations she felt about his technique. In the same paper, McLaughlin reported that he has accepted occasional hugs initiated by the patient without damage to the process.

This discussion shades into that dark nether region known as the art of psychoanalysis, where rigid rules are not particularly useful. Many professional boundaries can be crossed for good reason on occasion. Most analysts would not meet patients outside the office, but Elizabeth Lloyd Mayer (1994b) reported a moving case of treating a dying patient during which the last few sessions took place in the patient's home because she was too weak to come to the analyst's office. This boundary crossing seemed entirely appropriate in the context of the treatment.

By contrast, the repeated hand-holding in Dr. K's analysis and the frequent extraanalytic meetings were confusing, traumatic, and ultimately devastating to the analytic process and to Dr. K herself.

Although it might be tempting to dismiss Dr. K's analyst as simply an impaired clinician who should have been prevented from practicing, the situation is more complex. He was a highly respected analyst in the professional community where he practiced, and his poor judgment, like that of many lovesick analysts, seemed to be confined to the treatment of Dr. K. As part of the ethics committee investigation of the district branch psychiatric society, his other patients were systematically interviewed. All gave accounts of perfectly acceptable analytic work. They were flabbergasted to hear of the ethics charges against him.

Although Dr. K was not in a training analysis, the violations she encountered in her treatment are an extreme form of problems known to occur in training analyses. Phyllis Greenacre (1966) wrote of the frequency with which exceptions and indulgences occur in training analyses and how difficult it is for the student analysand in those situations to bring up the special favor as something to be analyzed. She also observed that these acts of benevolence are most commonly performed by older analysts of considerable repute. She attributed the phenomena to narcissistic blind spots protected by the defense mechanism of isolation. These analysts may be similar to the analysts described in Chapter 6 who feel that they have achieved such stature in the field that the usual rules do not apply to them. In any case, the effect of such indulgences is often to bind the patient to the analyst indefinitely, as is discussed in Chapter 8.

In some quarters, there has been skepticism expressed about the harmfulness of nonsexual boundary violations. Dr. K's frank discussion about the impact of her analyst's behavior is an elegant description of the harm done by the analyst who loses track of the analytic task and the analytic role. Although there is little doubt that part of the healing process in analysis involves the analyst–patient relationship itself, the analyst who steps outside the analytic role raises false hope in the patient that will inevitably be shattered as time goes on. The analyst cannot be a parent or a lover without destroying the essence of the analytic process. The analyst who tries to love his patient to health and thus offers hugs, round-the-clock availability, and professions of affection has confused the concrete with the symbolic. Analysis is about the *wish* to be loved and hugged and the feelings stirred up by the impossibility of the analyst's gratifying those wishes. The most effective and powerful gift we have to offer the patient is the analytic setting itself.

CHAPTER 8

The Fate of the Transference: Posttermination Boundaries

THE APPROPRIATE BOUNDARIES of the posttermination relationship between analyst and patient have never been consensually defined by psychoanalysts. Different analysts view the posttermination period from significantly different perspectives. Indeed, few aspects of professional boundaries are more controversial than posttermination restrictions.

Much of the disagreement stems from disparate views regarding the analysis itself and what can reasonably be accomplished. If the analysis is seen as completely resolving and eradicating the transference neurosis, postanalytic relationships might be perceived as uncontaminated by residual transference and therefore much the same as other relationships.

If some version of the transference neurosis is regarded as persisting beyond the termination of the analysis, however, similar prohibitions to those that apply *during* analysis should apply *after* analysis. A more current view is that the concept of transference neurosis has outlived its usefulness and should be discarded (Brenner, 1982; Cooper, 1987). In this regard, one might speak of transferences that may or may not be resolved rather than the interpretive resolution of the transference neurosis.

Another issue relevant to the controversy is that some boundaries may make more sense than others in the posttermination period, especially as time passes. Even sexual relationships, some would argue, might be acceptable if a suitable interval had passed. Indeed, a lead article in the *American Journal of Psychiatry* suggested a 1-year posttermination ban on sexual relationships between therapists and their patients, arguing that any extension of that time frame could be seen as an infringement on one's constitutional right to associate with whomever one wishes (Appelbaum & Jorgenson, 1991). Similarly, in 1992 the American Psychological Association, although prohibiting sexual intimacy between therapist and patient for at least 2 years after termination, declined to impose a complete ban on posttermination sexual relationships (American Psychological Association, 1992). This decision allows for the possibility that no exploitation occurred because of unusual circumstances.

In analytic work, a strong argument can be made that posttermination sexual relationships should be regarded as unethical and clinically ill-advised in virtually every situation. This point of view is most persuasively supported by the research on the fate of the transference after termination of analysis. However, there are other considerations that also argue against the sexualization of a relationship between a former patient and his or her analyst. We consider these issues after our examination of the literature on the vicissitudes of transference following termination.

THE PERSISTENCE OF TRANSFERENCE

Although psychoanalytic writing has traditionally placed great emphasis on the interpretive resolution of the transference neurosis as the cornerstone of the analytic process, research in the last 3 decades has consistently demonstrated that transference persists beyond termination. Arnold Pfeffer (1963), in the course of follow-up research on previously analyzed subjects, encountered two unexpected but striking phenomena in his interviews. First, patients dealt with the analyst conducting the follow-up interview as though he or she were their own analyst. In other words, transference was instantly reestablished. Second, the symptoms for which analysis was originally sought appeared to recur during the follow-up interviews. The patients appeared to return to the last point of their analyses and to continue analyzing the loss of the analyst and the analysis, a process that was not fully accomplished at the time of termination.

In contemporary psychoanalytic thinking, we would conceptualize Pfeffer's (1963) observations somewhat differently. In an era in which the analyst's participation in the patient's transference is widely acknowledged, we suggest that the same transference that existed in analysis is not what is established with the interviewer. Because the two participants are not exactly the same, the nature of the transference cannot be identical. Rather, a basic *transference disposition* is reestablished. In other words, there is a *readiness* to reexperience the transference with other clinicians and certainly with one's former analyst.

Pfeffer also concluded that even in a successful analysis, the patient retains a complex mental representation of the analyst. This representation appeared to be related to *resolved* aspects of the transference neurosis as well as transference residues that were not as thoroughly addressed in the analysis. Because this observation applied to all the patients studied, it was not considered idiosyncratic or reflective of special circumstances in the analysis.

In a subsequent paper, published 30 years after the original contribution, Pfeffer (1993) noted that the phenomenon he observed (which, incidentally, has come to be known as the "Pfeffer phenomenon") can be understood as a capsule recapitulation of the patient's analysis, with both the recurrence and the recovery from the transference neurosis represented. In this regard, the analyst is represented as both an old object (a residual displacement from past figures) and a new object (on the basis of new integration of conflicts integral to the transference neurosis). He also stressed that both mental representations remain indefinitely. Nathan Schlessinger and Fred Robbins (1974) also observed that many former patients make consistent use in fantasy of the "benign presence" of the analyst to facilitate the solution of conflicts after analysis.

Although one might think this internal process would wane in the years following completion of analysis, a study of 97 psychotherapists who had been in either analysis or therapy suggested that it does not (Buckley, Karasu, & Charles, 1981). The authors found that thoughts about the therapist or analyst reached a peak during the 5- to 10-year period after termination and that these thoughts were related to a gradual working through of unresolved transference issues. These subjects all considered returning to treatment at some point during this period.

One must even allow for the possibility that the transference actually *intensifies* after termination. Rita Novey (1991) described a male patient who returned to see his female analyst following termination and experienced intense erotic feelings toward her. The author, commenting on the case, noted that the transference did not peak until a full 2 years after termination.

In a study of five former analysands, Haskell Norman, Kay Blacker, Jerome Oremland, and William Barrett (1976) interviewed each of the subjects four or five times at weekly intervals, much as Pfeffer had done. Also like Pfeffer, they observed that every former patient readily reestablished the transferences that had occurred in their analyses and related to the interviewers as though they were their analysts. These authors shared the view that analysis does not obliterate the transference neurosis. They also noted that each patient experienced varying degrees of control over the transference neurosis, so that it could be viewed as a new psychic structure under the purview of the unconscious ego. They concluded that "the transference neurosis remains as a latent structure which may, under certain conditions, be revived, repeated, and rapidly mastered" (p. 496).

A recent investigation using a more rigorous methodological approach offered further support for the notion that the central transference paradigms emerging in the analytic process do not disappear as a result of analytic work (Luborsky, Diguer, & Barber, 1994).

Luborsky and his colleagues compared the core conflictual relationship theme in the first quarter of analysis with that of the last quarter of the treatment. In the 13 analytic patients studied, there was remarkable consistency between the transference themes at the early and late periods. The authors concluded that basic transference dispositions remain despite increased understanding, expansion of the ego, and greater mastery of conflict. They suggested that Freud was correct when he noted in his 1912 paper, "The Dynamics of Transference," that the transference is a lifelong template.

We should clarify in this context that the studies we have reviewed *do not* suggest that nothing changes as a result of analysis. Although the transference dispositions persist, they are much more thoroughly understood and mastered. As Joseph Schachter (1992) noted, follow-up studies of analyzed patients indicate that whereas transferences are not necessarily resolved, they are modulated to the point that patients can deal with them more effectively. Transference wishes remain, but the expectations of how others will react to those wishes are significantly altered.

This review of the literature is not a selective one. Studies demonstrating the obliteration of the transference following termination of analysis do not exist. If transference makes analyst–patient sexual relations symbolically incestuous, potentially harmful, and clearly unethical *during* analysis, the same considerations should apply to posttermination sex. An analogy vividly makes the point: Father–daughter incest is abhorrent no matter how much time has passed since the daughter lived in the same household as the father and regardless of their status as "mutually consenting" adults (Gabbard, 1993; Gabbard & Pope, 1989).

POSTTERMINATION RELATIONSHIP AS RESISTANCE

The persistence of transference is only one of several arguments for a "once a patient, always a patient" attitude regarding posttermination sexual relationships. The mere possibility of such a relationship can serve as the nidus of a formidable resistance. For example, if a patient were aware that a future relationship with the analyst was an outcome that was not subject to ethical censure, he or she might knowingly or unknowingly approach the analysis as though the primary goal of the treatment were to win over the analyst's affection. Aggressive transference themes might be avoided. Sexual conflicts might be minimized. Shameful or embarrassing life events might be swept under the rug because of the patient's concern that revealing them would jeopardize a future relationship with the analyst.

Similar issues might arise in the analyst's countertransference if a future sexual relationship were regarded as acceptable by the profession. Analysts experiencing intense loving feelings for a patient might foster idealization in hopes of persuading the patient that they were a match made in heaven.

Confrontation of painful or unpleasant material might be eschewed in the service of preserving the "real relationship" without contamination from the patient's anger or resentment. Most important of all, a necessary mourning process might be entirely avoided by presenting oneself as the magically healing future partner who will transform the patient's suffering into unending bliss.

An essential element in a successful psychoanalytic experience is the renunciation of long-held yearnings for incestuous objects. There is no viable shortcut that bypasses the painful mourning and working through that must accompany this giving up process. Analysis can be effective largely because it involves a relationship confined to a circumscribed time each day in which understanding is the goal. As Freud (1915a) emphasized, it is a relationship for which there is no model in real life. The more the analytic relationship is allowed to blur into other forms of relationship outside the analytic context, even potential relationships in the future, the more the analysis will be undermined.

The analyst must never forget that it is precisely because the relationship with the patient will never be anything other than what it is that patients can feel free to say whatever comes to mind. As we stressed in Chapter 3, the analytic role, along with its concomitant analytic boundaries, creates an atmosphere of safety and holding in which the patient can feel free to play with ideas and feelings without fear of adverse consequences. The knowledge that the analyst will never use the information gleaned from the patient in any other context is a crucial component of the analytic setting that frees up the patient.

Many patients, particularly those in the mental health professions, approach analysis with a secret agenda of paving the way for a post-analytic relationship—sometimes sexual, sometimes not—that will allow the analyst to be a "real person." Interpretation of this fantasy paves the way for the necessary grief process. Any hint of collusion with it, either through avoidance or subtle encouragement of it, may leave a crucial sector of the personality unanalyzed. One female analysand in her 20s was consumed with erotic feelings for her male analyst and asked him if he would sleep with her. His response was that he did find her sexually attractive and that perhaps sometime in the future there might be a possibility of that kind of relationship but that it was absolutely off-limits for now because it would be unethical. The patient held onto his words—that it might be possible in the future—and could think of nothing else. All the other issues in the analysis paled by comparison, and she viewed the analysis as something that had to be endured until they could finally get to a romantic, nonanalytic relationship. The analyst's response not only was unethical, it also was poor analytic technique.

Termination is a particularly high-risk time for the enactment of sexual longings between analyst and analysand. It is the bane of the analytic profession that practitioners must become extraordinarily close to their patients, only to lose them. Termination is a real loss for both participants. It represents the finiteness of the relationship and even the unbearable impermanence of life itself. Associations that link termination to death are a regular occurrence during the termination phase of analysis. Both analyst and analysand may wish to short-circuit the grief associated with loss and death and share in a manic defense designed to deny the definitive nature of the ending.

The analyst may self-disclose more, offer more advice, become more informal, and even invite the patient to enter into a social relationship as a way of communicating something like the following: "We don't really have to dwell on the mourning inherent in the loss of this relationship because we are embarking on a new relationship that will be better. This is not an ending; it is a beginning."

Just as Freud (1915a) pointed out that the analytic relationship is one for which there is no model in real life, Martin Bergmann (1988) stressed that the experience of termination in analysis is highly unique in the sense that it is without parallel in any other realm of human relationships. Where else does one end an extraordinarily intense, lengthy, and intimate human relationship without an understanding that there will be ongoing contact of some kind? Jack Novick (in press) argued that termination was essentially inconceivable by the early analysts, and modern analysts have inherited a legacy that involves ignoring and denying the feelings surrounding termination. A number of authors

(Dewald, 1966; Limentani, 1982; Novick, 1982; Viorst, 1982) have noted the fact that termination is a loss for the analyst as well as for the patient. Just as the patient may use the defensive fantasy of postanalytic contact as a way of fending off mourning, the analyst may similarly avoid dealing with the loss and therefore reinforce the patient's denial (Novick, in press).

Victor Calef and Edward Weinshel (1983) observed that many analytic patients terminate with a feeling of "unfinished business." When such patients are analyzed in second analyses, it becomes apparent that the feeling often relates to a wish for sexual consummation with the analyst as oedipal parent. If the analyst is vague or provocative with the terminating patient, the analyst's behavior may unwittingly encourage the patient to focus on future consummation rather than the impossibility of ever having the desired relationship.

THE RETURN OF THE PATIENT

In a study of 71 successfully analyzed patients reported by George Hartlaub, Gary Martin, and Mark Rhine (1986), two-thirds had contacted their analysts within 3 years of termination. Hence there is a practical, common-sense reason for abstaining from sexual involvement with former patients: Most of them are likely to require the analyst's services again. In the sample studied by Hartlaub and his colleagues, the patients clearly did not return because their analyses were incomplete or ineffective. They were generally doing well in their personal and professional lives but needed a consultation or two to solidify gains from the analysis. Some needed to work on continued de-idealization of the analyst, whereas others required assistance in reactivating their self–analytic function. Still others felt a need to report developmentally important accomplishments and thereby continue the process of restructuring internal self and object representations, a procedure that one might term "getting new paint on old introjects."

When one has the opportunity to analyze these returns in some detail, a common theme is the analysand's guilt about the possibility of harming the analyst through termination. Ending the analysis and renouncing the infantile object in the transference relationship with the analyst may be experienced unconsciously as a form of parricide (Loewald, 1980; Winer, 1994). Leading a successful life after the analysis may also have that meaning, and the return of the patient to the analyst may in part be designed to appease the analyst, who has been surpassed, abandoned, or left behind (Schafer, 1992). These returns may be preceded by flare-ups of old symptoms, but fears regarding greed, competitiveness, and grandiosity may be at the heart of the flare-up. Schafer viewed these symptomatic returns as a variant of survivor guilt in relation to the analyst. Fearing that the analyst may retaliate against them in envy, they return for more treatment as a way of placating the enraged analyst of their fantasy.

ARGUMENTS AGAINST AN ABSOLUTE PROHIBITION

Whereas analysts agree that engaging in sexual relations with a current patient is unequivocally unethical, there is some disagreement about the need for an absolute ethical prohibition against sexual relationships with former patients. In many institutes, leading figures have married former patients, and there is often a concern that a condemnation of such relationships would have a devastating effect on these esteemed teachers, supervisors, and training analysts. As noted in Chapter 6, these marriages are often pointed to in an effort to argue that every case is not uniformly harmful.

Even if these unions were thoroughly evaluated and some were found to be of questionable harmfulness, the need for an ethical standard would not be eliminated: Ethical standards do not require a demonstration that a particular behavior always results in harm (Gabbard, 1994e). Most analysts can conceive of cases in which confidentiality might be broken, for example, but because the instance was circumscribed and did not get back to the patient, no apparent harm occurred. Nevertheless, all would agree that breaking confidentiality is unethical. Ethics codes are generally based on the *potential* for harm. Moreover, such standards are created to apply to the vast majority of instances, not to take into account every possible exception. By analogy, most individuals cannot drive safely while intoxicated, so we have laws prohibiting such behavior. Some heavy drinkers might argue that they regularly drive home from a bar after consuming a fifth of hard liquor and have never had an accident. The law remains a sound one because most people cannot drive safely after imbibing that much alcohol.

Another argument for a more lenient view of posttermination sexual relationships is that prohibition of such unions is inherently unconstitutional (Appelbaum & Jorgenson, 1991). In other words, just as individuals have a right to assemble and a right to pursue happiness, they also have the right to romance whomever they wish without infringement from professional organizations. This argument confuses the definition of a professional's acceptable behavior according to ethical guidelines with the citizen's more general constitutional rights. Professionals automatically submit to additional responsibilities and legal mandates when they enter a profession (Gabbard, 1994e). For example, an analyst does not exercise the right to free speech regarding privileged communication from a patient because there are legally mandated prohibitions against violating confidentiality as well as ethical codes proscribing such behavior. Moreover, if law alone were the basis on which professionals determined their conduct, there would be no need for ethics codes in the professions. Finally, if the constitutional argument were taken seriously, one could extend it by saying that a professional organization has no constitutional right to prevent sex with a *current* patient.

Finally, one other argument occasionally brought to bear is that the flesh is weak, drive pressures are powerful, and, as Woody Allen would say, "You can't help whom you fall in love with." In other words, if analyst–patient sex can never be completely eliminated because of human nature, why should we have the expectation that analysts refrain from posttermination sexual relationships? The answer is twofold. First, no ethics codes are established with the assumption that they will deter all unethical behavior. Second, analysts may not be able to control whom they fall in love with, but they can certainly control whom they fall in bed with. If they cannot keep themselves from sleeping with a former patient, something is awry. When one considers the fact that numerous other partners are available, an all-consuming infatuation with a former patient—someone who unconsciously represents a forbidden, incestuous object—should prompt concern in the profession, if not in the analyst.

Despite the persuasive arguments against sex with former patients presented here, organized psychoanalysis has been reluctant to adopt ethics codes that stipulate that former patients are off-limits. There are other reasons for this reluctance, in addition to the resistance to renouncing incestuous objects inherent in all people. Financial considerations

tend to loom large in such decisions (Gabbard, 1994e). Ethics committees are already unable to investigate many cases thoroughly because
of the costs incurred in such investigations, particularly when attor-
neys become involved. Expanding the purview of ethics committees to
include posttermination relationships would be even more costly.

Finally, most of us see ourselves in those who have transgressed sexual boundaries. We all struggle with intense feelings toward our
patients, and we are inclined to view colleagues charged with sexual
misconduct, at least at some level, by thinking, "There but for the grace
of God go I." Hence a reluctance to adopt an ethics code that would
proscribe posttermination involvement may reflect a wish to be easy on
ourselves in matters of the heart.

OTHER POSTTERMINATION RELATIONSHIPS

In Chapter 7, the potential harm of nonsexual boundary violations to
the analytic process and to the patient was discussed in detail. However,
much less has been written about the nonsexual boundaries of *postanalytic* relationships. In principle, the arguments marshaled to support an
absolute prohibition of posttermination sexual relationships might be
applicable to other kinds of dual relationships. In practice, however, the
nonsexual areas are murky, and certainly no consensus exists.

All analysts must deal with postanalytic relationships in one way or
another. In the absence of clear guidelines, they develop their own,
often based on the way that their own training analyst managed the
posttermination period with them.

Some analysts assume that the transference persists and that the
patient may return for further treatment, so that they maintain the analytic boundaries in much the same form as during treatment. Others feel
that there is no longer a professional relationship, so that they feel free
to develop closer ties and even move in the direction of a friendship.
Still others take a middle ground, in which they maintain sufficient professional distance to avoid difficulty if the patient should return for further treatment; however, they are less formal and more self-disclosing
(in a limited way) when they run into their former patients on social or
professional occasions.

The problem in all these posttermination relationships is knowing
where to draw the line. Should analysts engage in business relation-

ships with former patients? Should they eat lunch together periodically? Should they entertain each other in their homes or play golf or tennis together? In some areas the persistence of transference appears to be of greater concern than in others. For example, should analysts accept large contributions for their own projects or those of their institute or society from a former patient who wishes to express gratitude? One could argue that the ongoing transference compromises the patient's ability to make a rational judgment or an informed decision about the choice of the recipient.

Rothstein (1994) is unequivocal in his view of this situation. Espousing a perspective that transference and countertransference are both interminable, he argues that there are no "former analysands." The mind is forever in conflict, in Rothstein's view, so that offers by patients of contributions to the analyst after termination should be regarded as a seduction in the postanalytic phase of an ongoing analysis rather than a simple expression of gratitude. Similarly, an analyst's acceptance of such gifts is regarded as a countertransference enactment in which the behavior is rationalized, usually involving the thought that the money is for a higher cause.

Many other forms of postanalytic boundary violations may also present themselves. For example, should one accept a referral from a former patient who is also a professional? Should one refer a patient to a former analysand? Should an analyst accept an invitation to a social occasion from a former patient?

Schachter (1990, 1992) systematically studied posttermination patient–analyst contact. He conceptualized analysis as part of an ongoing developmental process with the goal of facilitating the analysand's capacity for psychological growth. His primary emphasis was on the value of a planned posttermination consultation in the analyst's office, not a social relationship. However, he also suggested that there are situations in which an analyst and a former patient may develop a genuine friendship as an outgrowth of a good therapeutic alliance during the analytic process. He suggested that these relationships in some cases may be psychologically healthy and do not necessarily have strong neurotic underpinnings.

All of these issues are greatly clouded by the unique dimensions of the training analysis. As we noted in Chapter 7, there is a dual relationship inherent in the training analysis that must be taken into account when considering the posttermination period. The former analysand becomes a colleague of the training analyst and will be involved in many activities, such as committee membership, scientific meetings, and teaching, alongside the former analyst. As Ricardo Bernardi and Marta Nieto (1992) observed, "the paradox is that while no one would take a patient with whom such an enterprise was shared, in this case, this is precisely what is necessary" (p. 142).

Recognizing the potential for boundary problems, many institutes arrange it so that the candidate is neither supervised nor didactically taught by his or her training analyst. However, a number of analysts who were supervised by their training analyst after termination speak of the experience in positive terms. They particularly emphasize the value of the experience in promoting a de-idealization of the analyst. The encounter with the analyst in the supervisory setting, they argue, assists them in the ongoing work of consolidating the analytic experience and mourning its loss. In short, it facilitates the posttermination work.

Skeptics of this view argue that persisting transference makes post-termination supervision highly problematic. The candidate's capacity to evaluate critically the supervisor's observations about the case or the candidate's technique may be significantly impaired. Disagreements about the patient or the optimal approach may be suppressed by the candidate, or alternatively, negative transference residues may be reactivated, so that there is a subtle or not-so-subtle power struggle in the supervisory process.

The problems arising from using one analysis for both training and analyzing have been discussed exhaustively. As long ago as 1964, David Kairys concluded that some analysts "have come to believe that the problems of analyzing within a training program are intrinsically insoluble and no longer worth discussing" (p. 485). Nevertheless, we must consider the complexities of the training analysis, and particularly the posttermination period, or we can easily fall into the trap of a double standard, in which we are advocating one set of posttermination boundaries for nontraining analyses and another for candidates. At the very least, a training analysis should provide a good analytic experience. If the posttermination phase, and therefore the termination phase itself, is handled differently by the training analyst, the training analysis may color the candidate's management of termination issues with other patients.

Yet a great many analysts have argued that the termination process is irrevocably different in a training analysis than in other analyses. Edith Weigert (1955) suggested that in training analyses there is not a definite separation as in other analyses because of the candidate's need to live and work in the same professional environment as the training analyst.

Joan Fleming (1969) was explicit in her view that an advantage of a training analysis over a personal analysis is the opportunity for a continuing relationship between candidate and training analyst on a basis that is different from that of the analytic situation: "Having worked so hard at being a patient, the student–analyst must now work equally hard at shifting to another level, that of colleague and friend" (p. 79). She argued that those who oppose this view are selling analysis short. She accused them of negating the reality principle and invoked the parent–child metaphor to make her point. She suggested that they are viewing the former analysand as "once a child, always a child" and refusing to accept that their analytic "child" has grown up, thus perpetuating a patriarchal culture in the profession.

Fleming, in our view, oversimplified the issues of the termination of a training analysis. The assumption of a parent–child paradigm as a guiding metaphor feeds right into the patient's transference wishes. After analysis, one can finally grasp the elusive, longed-for relationship that was out of reach during the analysis. This view of termination as a relatively smooth transition from an analyst–analysand paradigm to a friendship or mentoring paradigm encourages a postponement and ultimately avoidance of the grief work that is necessary to complete the analytic experience. A period of internalization and mourning is necessary for the candidate to work through the termination, and analysts who establish immediate friendships with their terminated analysands do not provide that necessary time and space (Torras de Beà, 1992; Treurniet, 1988).

A fundamental problem in the training analysis is that patient and analyst will *in reality* have an ongoing relationship of some nature after termination. To be sure, the character of this relationship will differ from one dyad to the next. Nevertheless, the fact that they will become colleagues makes the training analysis different from other analyses. Novick (in press) emphasized that an inherent risk in the way analysts are trained is that the analytic candidate's own termination in the setting of a training analysis may be taken as a model for conceptualizing *all* terminations. This potentiality is particularly problematic if both training analyst and candidate have colluded in denying the extent of the loss with the knowledge that they will continue to have a collegial relationship. All candidates must recognize that there is a fundamental difference between their own experience and that of their patients around termination.

Oremland, Blacker, and Norman (1975) studied "incompleteness" in analyses that were apparently successful by arranging a series of follow-up interviews with several patients in the posttermination period. In one case, there was a discrepancy between the analyst's and the patient's view of the termination. The training analyst viewed the ending as orderly and without incident. The patient, on the other hand, felt that his training analyst was attempting to prolong the analysis. He also felt that the analyst was behaving more like a mother than an analyst. He did not mention this reaction to the analyst, and the investigators observed that he then carried an unanalyzed idea of the analyst with him beyond termination.

The abstinence required of the analyst takes its toll, and some analysts long to be known as a "real person" as termination approaches. However, becoming more "real" or more like a parent has a host of risks associated with it, as Oremland et al. (1975) noted. Such a message from the analyst to the analysand can be heard as an injunction to remain loyal to the analyst as a child would to a parent. What about the patient's autonomy? What about the analysand's freedom to choose *not* to be a friend of the analyst because of the wish to preserve him or her as a potential analyst for the future should problems arise?

Evidence of the loyalty pressures produced by this view of the analysand as a kind of grown-up child of the analyst is ubiquitous. In one of the worst scenarios, one sees former analysands literally taking care of their former training analyst. This caretaking may take the form of sending referrals to the training analyst, who may actually be too feeble or too demented to practice, or it may manifest itself in looking in on him at his home, taking care of his physical needs, and driving him to medical appointments. In a more typical scenario, the candidate feels obligated to become something of a disciple of the training analyst and may forcefully endorse the analyst's theoretical or technical precepts while vehemently denouncing those of rivals. This "convoying" of former patients has been a widespread problem throughout the history of psychoanalysis. Accounts of the Controversial Discussions of the 1940s in the British Society provide ample evidence of this demand for loyalty from former analysands.

Greenacre (1966) cited the training analyst's wish to maintain the candidate's allegiance after termination as one of the three main areas of countertransference in training analyses (the other two were overzealousness regarding the analysand's academic performance and active participation in training matters pertaining to one's analysand). She noted that rationalizations involving "saving" a promising younger colleague for the future of psychoanalysis may be conjured up to justify the training analyst's narcissistic need to control the candidate.

Ramon Ganzarain (1991) noted that a common difficulty encountered between candidate and former training analyst is the continued attempt to establish analytic activity in a nonanalytic setting. Candidates may "free associate" with their former training analyst in a social situation. Similarly, analysts may foster such behavior by continuing to interpret unconscious meanings to their former patients. Ganzarain pointed out that this approach may reflect the analyst's wish to have continued influence and authority over the patient.

Increased freedom of thought should be one goal of analysis, whether a personal treatment or a training analysis. Analysts who insist that their analysands must think about analysis or other matters as the analyst does rob patients of the opportunity to enhance their own autonomy and the freedom to think their own thoughts. The identification process intrinsic to every training analysis can be seriously misguided by the training analyst who places his or her own narcissistic needs above the needs of the patient. Greenacre (1966) observed that this dynamic may take the form of subtle indulgences by the training analyst that gratify instead of frustrate the patient's transference wishes. When the analyst happens to be prominent, the analysand often assumes that such indulgences must be appropriate, however unorthodox they are, as described by Dr. K in her account in Chapter 7. Greenacre noted: "The force of this undesirable authority is apt to be greatest where the analyst is well known for his ability, and yet provides these indulgences. The influence of these combined factors is almost unshakable" (1966, p. 562).

The loyalty bind deriving from the training analyst's indulgences not only breeds discipleship in the posttermination period; it also estab-lishes an intergenerational cycle that is difficult to break. Young ana-lysts repeat the behavior of their training analysts, even when they do not fully understand it or approve of it. Greenacre (1966) argued that there is inadequate attention devoted to the subtle narcissistic pres-sures in the analysis of candidates as well as to the reciprocal self-analysis of the training analyst. Sadly, nearly 30 years later, the same problems persist and suffer from the same lack of attention.

Postanalytic contact between analysand and training analyst is, of course, inevitable. Some of those contacts may facilitate the candidate's continued psychological growth. Others may be more problematic and compromise the candidate's autonomy. Clearly, both the candidate and the training analyst may play a role in determining the frequency and the nature of those posttermination contacts. How they are handled is not entirely out of control. The optimal boundaries in the posttermina-tion period are controversial and cannot be established by fiat. Only systematic discussions within the profession based on the collection of data from various sources will help to achieve some form of consensus.

In the meantime, the crucial importance of the analyst's role in ana-lyzing the patient's fantasies about the postanalytic relationship cannot be overstated. Many patients actively resist looking at such fantasies because they fear that analysis of them will make their fulfillment an impossibility. To facilitate this optimal disillusionment, analysts must first come to terms with their own wish to hold onto their patients and to fend off the loss inherent in the psychoanalytic enterprise.

CHAPTER 9

Boundaries in Psychoanalytic Supervision

PSYCHOANALYTIC SUPERVISION has become the focus of consider-able theoretical inquiry in recent years. The Sixth International Psychoanalytic Association Conference of Training Analysts in Amsterdam, held July 1993, was devoted to this subject. Because the complexity of the issues is such that one conference was insufficient to deal with the subject, the Organizing Committee of the Seventh IPA Conference of Training Analysts in San Francisco, held July 1995, again adopted the theme of psychoanalytic supervision.

It has long been recognized that the personal analysis of the candidate and the supervised analyses during training constitute the two "enabling" processes of training. These two aspects of training are in contrast to the didactic, theoretical seminars, which, valuable as they are, belong to a different type of learning, one that is less dependent on interpersonal transactions. In recent decades, the majority of psychoanalytic institutes have gradually abandoned the practice of monitoring the personal analysis of the candidates. Earlier practices requiring that the evolution of the candidate's analysis be "reported" to the training committees have gradually been abandoned by most institutes. The burden of the evaluation of the candidate's clinical ability, therefore, has now been placed almost entirely on the supervision of control cases.

Supervision is the process par excellence for the articulation of theory and practice during the training. The functions of supervisors demand that they question and validate not only the dynamics of the patient–analysand and the process and procedure of the analysis as it is being taught, but also the theoretical basis of such dynamics and technical procedures.

At the 1993 training analyst conference on supervision, the participation of the candidates was solicited. A group of candidates prepared a position paper (Casullo & Resnizky, 1993), the final version of which was circulated among the participants. This beautifully written communication by the two candidates superbly portrays the complexities and the potentials of supervision as it is viewed from the candidates' vantage point. The candidates wrote:

> The proposition is to let things emerge instead of making an imprint upon them, to let the encounter take place. It is expected of supervisor and supervised to cover together the same road towards transformation. Their aim is the encounter, defined as the moment in which the supervising analyst is able to find the adequate answer to the needs of the candidate, helping him to emerge, creating a propitious situation for the development of a new psychological structure in both of them, since no one remains unmodified after being creative in some way. (p. 3)

Later in their document, they made the following observation:

> If we think a session is unrepeatable, what is re-created with the supervisor is a new emotional experience with the material. A new drama emerges. Under the supervisor's eye the candidate will begin to find it possible to contain his uncertainty, and if the supervisor is able to put up with his own misgivings in so far as the scope of his theories and his capacity to transmit them, he will then be in a position to guarantee the

supervision space and [to accompany] the candidate down the road to doubting one's beliefs and the collapse of one's certainties. (p. 6)

Freud, the first psychoanalytic educator, supervised his "candidates" concurrent with analyzing them, often during evening walks through the streets of Vienna. Siegfried Bernfeld (1962), as quoted by Rudolph Ekstein (1960), recalled that Freud dismissed Bernfeld's reservations about starting his first analysis of a patient without benefit of supervision and said, "Nonsense, you go right ahead. You will get into trouble, and then we will figure out what to do about it" (p. 501). At this stage of the development of psychoanalytic theory and method, Freud saw no boundaries between analysis and supervision.

Ekstein (1960) used the term *ahistorical* to describe this early period of psychoanalytic education, during which the roles of analyst and supervisor were often combined in the same person, that of a "senior" analyst. Michael Balint (1954) described the same period as *prehistori cal*. No written records of the training procedures of this period exist.

As training centers developed, and with the founding of the Berlin Institute in the early 1920s, a number of teachers became available. Gradually it became feasible and desirable to separate the role of training (personal) analyst from that of the candidate's supervisor. For a number of years, the Hungarian group argued against this separation of roles as initiated by the Berlin Institute. Vilma Kovács (1936) argued that the analysis of the candidate's countertransference would best be accomplished by the training (personal) analyst, at least for the first control case.

Publication of this position by the Hungarian analysts led to a sharp controversy that continued for several years. Opposing this view was the Viennese position, represented primarily by Edward Bibring (1937). Bibring and his colleagues in Vienna stressed that the primary function of the supervisor was to teach and that the focus of supervision should be the candidate's grasping of the dynamics of the patient and learning of correct technical approaches to such dynamics. Eventually, the Viennese position prevailed in most analytic centers, and the two functions, that of the training analyst and that of the supervisor, have remained separate ever since.

In North America, Fleming (1969), who wrote extensively on psychoanalytic supervision, came close to advocating an updated version of the Hungarian position by suggesting that training analysts should take an active part in the evaluation of their analysands and that supervisors should also feel free to interpret the candidate's countertransference, at least in cases in which such intervention was deemed necessary.

INTERACTIVE PROCESSES IN SUPERVISION

Although we still lack a common language when discussing the multiple issues involved in interaction and interactive processes in analysis (Richards, 1991), no one presently disputes the fact that the interactive and intersubjective points of view have been gaining prevalence in psychoanalytic theory over the past few decades. Interactive processes, which Helen Gediman and Fred Wolkenfeld (1980) called the multidirectional reverberations, are constantly in evidence during supervision. Supervisor and supervisee are continuously switching from the intrapsychic perspective of the patient on the couch to a variety of interactions that develop during supervision, including those between candidates and their supervisor; those among candidates, their analyst, and their supervisor; and those among candidates, their supervisor, and other supervisors. At any one time during supervision, a number of triads are in motion, guaranteeing complexity, confusion, and boundary crossings among the various individuals and institutional groupings that make up the system.

Because analysis is an interactive process, boundaries in supervision are seen predominantly as interpersonal, external boundaries. By the very nature of the supervisory process, specific types of interpersonal boundaries are at play: educational boundaries (i.e., those developing and upholding professional standards), boundaries based on a fiduciary relationship, and finally, the various types of interpersonal boundaries described in Chapters 1 and 3, representing only one dimension of boundaries encountered in supervision. In what follows, we do not deal specifically with extreme boundary violations, such as supervisor–supervisee sexual relations, that are unethical because of the asymmetry of power in a trusting relationship. Such violations, as have been described in the literature (Gabbard, 1989), have much in common with boundary transgressions in other fiduciary relationships. Instead, we deal with boundaries specific to psychoanalytic supervision.

BOUNDARY ISSUES

TREAT OR TEACH

The main issue in this controversy is the distinction between upholding the educational goals of the supervision and the occasional need to
inquire into the supervisee's psychic reality to be able to understand
better and convey to the candidate the dynamics of particular
exchanges in the patient's analysis. The controversy between only
teaching versus treating and teaching in supervision has been extensively discussed in the literature and usually has been presented as a
dichotomy: treat *or* teach. Stated briefly, this position maintains that the
two functions should not overlap. The function of the supervisor
should be only to teach. When candidates show signs of a countertransference reaction, their supervisor should refer the candidates to
their analyst. Otherwise, the handling of the candidate's countertransference would constitute a crossing of the supervisory boundaries,
which are seen exclusively as educational (i.e., as those between a
teacher and a pupil). Violation of educational boundaries, it is maintained, inevitably leads to a "wild" analysis; the supervisor cannot and
should not try to enter into the candidate's conflicts or unconscious
fantasy.

Leon Grinberg (1970), in an effort to avoid the dichotomous thinking,
distinguished between two types of issues in relation to the candidate's
countertransference: (1) cases in which obvious countertransference is
at play and in which the supervisor refers candidates to their analyst
and (2) cases in which projective counteridentification is taking place.
In the latter, Grinberg stated, the supervisor should step in and deal
directly with the candidate's difficulties. Grinberg drew a clear distinction between countertransference proper, always the responsibility of
the candidate's analyst, and projective counteridentification, which
remains the responsibility of the supervisor.

Countertransference proper, Grinberg (1970) argued, develops when
the material the patient brings to the sessions stirs up the candidate's
own conflicts. When the "affective response [of the candidate] can be the
result of what the patient has projected into him" (p. 379), however, one
is dealing with projective counteridentification. The candidate unconsciously identifies with a "given aspect of an internal object or with certain parts of the patient's self" (p. 379), which has been projected into

him. This identification accounts for the fact that the candidate experiences emotions belonging to the patient or enters into enactments suggestive of the patient's internal self and object representations.

What Grinberg (1970) implied in this communication is that countertransference reactions are of a "deeper" origin, requiring analytic scrutiny on the couch, whereas the presence of projective counteridentification is easy to detect in supervision because it is right there. Furthermore, Grinberg believed that these processes of projections and identifications may take place between candidate and supervisor as well. Not only do candidates in supervision reenact their unconscious interactions with the patient, but owing to the particular nature of the supervisory situation, they also evoke similar experiences in the supervisor. Grinberg was referring, of course, to the phenomenon of parallelism between the analysis and the supervision, a phenomenon broadly discussed in the literature in recent years (Arlow, 1963; Doehrman, 1976; Gediman & Wolkenfeld, 1980; Sachs & Shapiro, 1976).

We maintain that the mechanism of parallel process is not substantially different from that of enactment, whether in the session or on the outside. In all these cases, patients, candidates, or supervisors enact (or "experience") what they resist remembering. We believe that whether it is called projective counteridentification or a parallel reenactment in supervision, the unconscious identification of the candidate with the patient represents an aspect of the countertransference to the patient that is then reenacted in the supervision.

Projections are not a one-way phenomenon. Just as the patient projects into the analyst, so does the analyst project into the patient. Similarly, in analytic supervision the supervisor may at times project self and object representations, as well as the affects connected with them, onto both the supervisee and the patient. Another dimension of parallel process, therefore, is that the supervisor may project onto the supervisee in a way that parallels the analyst's projections onto the patient. For example, supervisors who find themselves "taking over" and telling the supervisee what to do and how to do it may be viewing the supervisee as passive, helpless, and dependent, in the same way that the supervisee views the patient as incapable of self-initiative and as requiring outside help from the analyst to become more effective and competent.

Yet another parallelism in supervision and analysis is the containing function. The analyst must contain and "detoxify" painful affects projected by the patient. Through a process of tolerating those affects, articulating their meaning, and linking them with various self and object representations, the analyst facilitates the patient's re-introjection of the projective contents in modified form (Carpy, 1989; Gabbard, 1991b; Ogden, 1982). Something analogous happens when the analytic candidate is having a good deal of difficulty with the patient's projections. Certain affects may then be evoked in the supervisor that resemble those with which the supervisee is struggling. The supervisor contains those affects and tries to find ways to help the supervisee use them productively in the process (Gabbard & Wilkinson, 1994). Above all, the supervisor seeks to translate the affects into words that are useful to the supervisee in understanding the process. In this regard, it may be helpful in some instances for the supervisor to self-disclose fantasies and affects that are evoked by the supervisee's account of the analysis.

Parallel processes represent two complex boundary crossings: (1) analytic boundary crossings between the candidate and the patient and (2) educational boundary crossings between the candidate and the supervisor. As stated in recent communications (Gabbard & Wilkinson, 1994; Lester & Robertson, 1995), we maintain that a restricted approach to the candidate's countertransference in the supervision (i.e., dealing only with instances in which countertransference is reenacted in the supervision as a parallel phenomenon) is not justified. In the great majority of cases, the supervisor becomes aware of the candidate's countertransference *without the evidence of a parallel process.* In other words, we maintain that the educational boundaries of the supervisory process are not clearly and firmly delineated from analytic or interpersonal boundaries, as the "treat or teach" dichotomy would imply.

Francis Baudry (1993) maintained that the supervisor does not address the specific problems the student is having with the patient. We find this statement too general to be of value to the supervisor. We believe the supervisor does indeed approach such problems by inviting the candidate to explore them. Supervisors use their own reactions to the material *and* the candidate's reactions to it to point out the candidate's blind spots, overreactions, and countertransference enactments. What supervisors do not do, in our opinion, is give *genetic interpretations to the candidate.*

This model of supervision depends, of course, on the existence of a sufficient level of trust and acceptance such that the supervisee feels comfortable with a good deal of self-disclosure. This trust may be interrupted because of the evaluative nature of the supervisory relationship. The progress made in the institute will be greatly influenced by the impressions of the analytic candidate's supervisor. Hence the supervision is always vulnerable to contamination by the supervisee's superego projections onto the supervisor (Doehrman, 1976). Psychoanalytic candidates have been known to omit important material and even alter the events of the analysis because of their fear that their supervisors may in some way retaliate or punish them with a negative evaluation or verbal censure (Chrzanowski, 1984). Shame, in particular, is a powerful affect relevant to the supervisory situation that may inhibit supervisees from fully disclosing their interventions with their patients as well as their feelings about the process (Wallace & Alonso, 1994).

THE PHENOMENON OF MULTIPLE TRIADS

As previously mentioned, a number of triads are in motion during psychoanalytic supervision. Professional, educational, interpersonal, and analytic boundaries are involved in the process, and boundary leakage is often the result. The triad of candidate, training analyst, and supervisor is the most familiar ground of subtle and not-so-subtle acting out. The most frequently observed acting out of candidates in this context is the splitting of their transference between their analyst and their supervisor. Oedipal antagonisms, preoedipal conflicts, and other types of pathology may be enacted within this triad. Analytic boundaries between candidates and their analyst, as well as educational–professional and interpersonal boundaries between candidates and supervisors, are confused and crossed in several directions, and this often results in serious consequences for the training of candidates.

One of the commonly described boundary crossings in this triadic system may take place when the training analyst and the supervisor belong to competing theoretical groups. Both the supervisor and the training analyst may, with varying degrees of intensity, transgress analytic, educational, and interpersonal boundaries in an effort to win the loyalty of the candidate. Such transgressions inevitably interfere with both the personal analysis and the supervision of the candidate.

Educational and interpersonal boundaries also are transgressed quite readily in the triads involving the candidate and two or more supervisors competing with each other for the loyalty and the mind of the candidate. Finally, the interactional plane may include the candidate, the supervisor, and the institute, especially in cases in which competing ideologies and theoretical positions create uncertainty and anxiety in the candidate.

As we noted earlier in the chapter, we have chosen to focus our discussion here on boundaries specific to psychoanalytic supervision rather than to deal with the more general issues of sexual exploitation in fiduciary relationships. Nonetheless, the conditions of the supervisory setting have much in common with those in psychoanalysis itself. Both involve private relationships in which a good deal of intense emotion is shared in intimate detail. Transferences and countertransferences are operating, and a clear power differential is in evidence. In recent years, complaints of sexual boundary violations by supervisors have begun to surface in psychoanalytic institutes. In private, other candidates have acknowledged that supervisors have made inappropriate sexual comments to them or have even made physical advances, but these incidents have gone unreported because the candidates fear that their advancement in training might be jeopardized by reporting such behavior to the education committee of the institute.

The manner in which professional boundaries are respected (or disrespected) by supervisors has far-ranging significance for the candidate's development. An internalization process occurs in supervision that begins with a superficial imitation, or "playing supervisor" with one's patient (Doehrman, 1976), and eventually becomes consolidated as part of one's analytic identity. If the analytic supervisor models a seductive or provocative interpersonal style in the supervision, this quality may be subtly assimilated and eventually enacted with patients in the analytic process. In one study of graduate students in psychology, Kenneth Pope, Hanna Levenson, and Leslie Schover (1979) noted that those who had had sexual relationships with supervisors or teachers had a higher subsequent incidence of sexual boundary violations with their patients.

Jacob Arlow (1963), quoting the 1955 Rainbow Report of the American Psychoanalytic Association's Committee of the Board on Professional Standards, described supervision as the "psychoanalysis of a psychoanalysis" (p. 583), thus capturing in a few words the vast complexities of the process. Despite these complexities, however, supervision is not taught in the institutes or anywhere else, and every training analyst is expected on election to the institute to function as a supervisor. A similar situation exists in the educational bodies of departments of psychiatry, where training in various forms of dynamic psychotherapy is given. It is often the case that the assignment of supervision is made to professionals who are less aware of the complexities involved than those within the psychoanalytic institutes. With the accelerating decrease in the numbers of analytically trained teachers in departments of psychiatry or psychology, the training and supervision of dynamic psychotherapy may become more problematic.

We believe that a theoretical grasp of the psychoanalytic process and procedure is not sufficient for the optimal functioning of supervisors. We maintain that an understanding of the interactive processes taking place during supervision, their reverberation, and the potential for boundary leakage are fundamental to the functioning of the competent supervisor.

CHAPTER 10

Institutional Responses

THE RESPONSE OF PSYCHOANALYTIC institutes and societies within the United States and Canada to boundary violations by their members has been slow in coming. There is an irony in the fact that psychoanalytic organizations and training facilities have done so little about an aspect of the field that has caused devastating damage to the public's opinion of psychoanalysis, to the patients who undertake the treatment, and to the trainees and young practitioners who are disillusioned by the "clay feet" of their teachers and supervisors.

This denial and avoidance may reflect a deep-seated conviction that psychoanalysts are not supposed to have these kinds of problems. Is it not a goal of the training analysis to assist young clinicians in the task of mastering and understanding their own needs and wishes so that they do not profoundly interfere with those of their patients? A boundary transgression by a colleague raises doubts within all of us about the effectiveness of our analytic work. Freud himself was rather modest about the therapeutic outcome of analysis. Specifically, he doubted that an analysis in one's young adulthood would be likely to prevent problems in future adult developmental phases (Freud, 1937).

For many years, when transgressions occurred, the accused analyst would be pulled aside and quietly told that he or she should return for more analysis. The needs of patients were often ignored, and every effort was made to avoid publicity and not to air dirty laundry in public. The analyst who was referred back to the couch was generally not reevaluated and often not even supervised in his ongoing work. Analysts have long had difficulty saying a behavior is "wrong" or "bad." Instead, they often try to understand and excuse; hence a return to analysis is the solution.

Colleagues have been reluctant to confront one of their own for a multitude of reasons. Long-standing friendships may be destroyed. The analyst who blows the whistle may fear a lawsuit for defamation of character. In addition, many analysts who have raised concern about a colleague have had their own motives called into question and have been told, in essence, to mind their own business.

Psychoanalytic institutes have been dragged kicking and screaming into confronting the issue of boundary violations in recent years, largely because the other mental health professions (psychiatry, psychology, and social work) have been involved in major efforts to understand and prevent them and to discipline practitioners who have crossed professional boundaries with their patients. Also, just as the women's movement was influential in bringing the devastating effects of incest to the public's attention, the larger numbers of women trainees in psychoanalytic institutes have contributed greatly to the increased awareness of sexual exploitation of patients.

Both the Canadian and American psychoanalytic organizations have ethics policies that allow for ethics committees at the level of local institutes or societies. Nevertheless, many institutes and societies still do not have standing ethics committees and prefer to pass on the responsibility of dealing with boundary violations to state and provincial licensing boards and ethics committees of other professional organizations. Although concerns about the cost of litigation are certainly justified, Marvin Margolis (in press) noted that this abrogation of responsibility in some ways is a repetition of the secrecy and denial regarding experiences of incest that typify the families of many of the patients who experience sexual involvement with their analyst.

Despite the reluctance of many institutes to become involved in the quagmire of boundary violations, a number of institutes have been actively engaged in developing guidelines to deal with such problems and accumulating hard-earned experience on strategies of approaching both the analyst and the patient. In this chapter, we break down the institutional response into four principal areas: management of complaints, response to the victim, assessment and rehabilitation, and prevention. We present a model that we believe is optimal and therefore represents an ideal rather than the standard procedures implemented by institutes and societies throughout North America.

MANAGEMENT OF COMPLAINTS

In many cases of sexual misconduct, a formal complaint is filed only after years of rumors and innuendos about an analyst. Incriminating information about the analyst may have come to colleagues through confidential sources. The colleague who hears about a transgression from a patient on the couch is faced with an ethical dilemma. Is the analyst–patient confidentiality of such crucial importance to the psychoanalytic enterprise that it must be preserved even at the cost of knowing that the patient or patients of a colleague are being seriously harmed?

Many states have already passed legislation that provides specific guidelines on this ethical dilemma. For example, some states have mandatory reporting laws that require the clinician to report any instance of sexual exploitation of patients even when the source is a confidential one. Other states have more narrowly defined reporting laws, in which doctor–patient confidentiality overrides the requirement to report.

Analysts should certainly be familiar with the reporting laws in their state, but ethical concerns often require the analyst to make difficult decisions that are not necessarily governed by state laws. For example, what about instances of nonsexual boundary violations that are in a gray area, which may or may not be harmful? What about allegations of sexual misconduct that stem from the distant past? Also, what about the conflict between professional ethics and state law? There are several instances of analysts who have chosen to go to jail rather than breach patient confidentiality.

Often the most useful recourse is to consult with a knowledgeable colleague about one's options. An attorney may also be useful if legal issues are worrisome. In some cases involving egregious behavior, one may break confidentiality to report a colleague to the licensing board or an ethics committee even though one risks being sued for violating confidentiality by one's patient or for defamation of character by the accused colleague.

Although some would argue that it is always preferable for the patient to file a formal complaint to relieve the analyst of that responsibility, patients who have taken that course of action have often found it highly unpleasant. Some have compared the hearing before an ethics committee to a rape trial in which they feel that their entire sex life is on trial. Others have found that the publicity stemming from such hearings has ruined their marriage or personal life. In addition, many patients who have been sexually involved with their analyst are still deeply in love or at least intensely ambivalent, and they do not want to act in any way that might be harmful to their analyst.

Faced with a patient who is not willing to bring forth a complaint, an analyst who hears of a boundary violation should at least have a designated person in the institute or society to whom he or she can turn. In the ideal situation, institutes or societies should have ombudspersons who are knowledgeable and can deal confidentially with rumors, innuendos, concerns, questions, and complaints from both patients and analytic colleagues. In some cases, this person may be the chair of the local ethics committee. Alternatively, two or three individuals forming the nucleus of that committee may meet with patients or professionals who have concerns. Then, a group of colleagues can come to a consensus about the best course of action in a particular case. The advantage of having an ethics committee member serve as the ombudsperson is that these individuals are likely to have the most knowledge of and experience in the subject. The disadvantage is that members who have heard confidential information in their role as ombudsperson may have to recuse themselves if the complaint goes on to reach the ethics committee.

Many institutes or societies do not have standing ethics committees and prefer to deal with complaints either through ad hoc committees or through the education committee as a whole. Although this approach has the advantage of involving a larger group of colleagues with a broader based knowledge of the analyst in question, the disadvantages tend to outweigh the advantages. First, there is generally a lack of expertise on ethics issues if there has been no specific individual, small group of faculty, or members designated to develop an ethics committee as well as procedures. Each time a complaint is filed, there may be a feeling of reinventing the wheel. There may also be a greater tendency to develop splits and factions in the education committee on the basis of whether the analyst in question is viewed as reprehensible or as depressed and in need of help. Often these factions have been preexisting, and the allegation of misconduct serves as a lightning rod to widen the splits.

Also, if there is no ethics committee with a set of standard procedures, there is a greater risk of accusations regarding failure of due process. The appearance (or reality) of harsh treatment may exist for an unpopular analyst and a lenient approach to a popular colleague. Having a standing committee with a clear set of procedures goes a long way toward establishing fair and consistent dealings with all complaints.

Regardless of whether a standing ethics committee or an alternative group handles the complaint, outside consultation should be sought. Often such committees are paralyzed because of various transferences to the accused analyst. He or she may be a leader in the analytic community who analyzed or supervised members of the ethics committee. Committee members may be largely incapable of viewing the situation with any kind of dispassionate objectivity. Similarly, smoldering resentments and enmities between members of the institute or society may get in the way of a fair and impartial hearing of the complaint. The members of the local society may be reticent to take necessary action because of these preexisting feelings toward the accused analyst, and a fresh, outside consultant may empower them to do what needs to be done. Ethics experts in different institutes or societies may be ideal consultants, particularly when they do not have any significant relationship with the analyst against whom the complaint is brought. Also, national ethics committees of the American or Canadian parent organizations may be valuable resources for local groups.

After a complaint has been filed or a rumor has been aired, the ethics committee needs to discuss the optimal manner in which to inform the accused colleague. Some committees prefer to send a letter with a copy of the complaint and a request for a written response. If a decision is made to inform the analyst in person, more than one member of the ethics committee should visit the analyst personally and let him or her know of the concerns. This responsibility should not fall to a single member of the committee because the exchange in any one-to-one meeting between the committee member and the accused colleague may boil down to a contested conversation to which there are no witnesses. Most ethics committee members find it highly supportive to have a colleague to share such a stressful task.

Whether or not the colleague who has been charged acknowledges the boundary violation, some form of ethics hearing usually needs to follow for the purpose of gathering information. Both the patient and the analyst are allowed to present their side of the story (usually separately) to the same small group of society or institute members. In such cases there is often intense pressure from candidates, faculty, and other colleagues to reveal what is going on, but the patient's and the analyst's right to confidentiality and privacy must, of course, take precedence.

To complicate matters further, there may be parallel investigations or actions going on at the same time. In 14 states therapist–patient sex has been criminalized, and the accused analyst may be facing criminal charges. A lawsuit may be filed against the analyst as well. Although most malpractice insurance companies do not cover sexual misconduct, suits may be filed for mismanagement of the transference. Ethics committees of the psychiatric or psychological associations may also be investigating. Finally, the state or provincial licensing board may be doing its own review as well. The interface between these various agencies has not been well delineated, and ethics committees can find it difficult to figure out who is responsible for what. Impaired-practitioner committees of local medical societies and the like may have had the analyst referred to them for treatment in a confidential setting removed from any disciplinary considerations; the committee needs to be aware of this resource as well.

Because of all these parallel investigations, ethics committees of psychoanalytic organizations may prefer to postpone their own process until after other bodies have collected the evidence and reached a conclusion. In Canada, the provincial college of physicians and surgeons has considerable experience in dealing with such matters, so that the ethics committees are often guided by the rulings of the college. In the United States, the investigations of state licensing boards may be helpful to ethics committees. A practical consideration is the enormous expense that ethics committees may incur in a full investigation because of the need for legal assistance. In the United States, serious boundary violations resulting in censure by an ethics committee must now be reported to the National Practitioner Data Bank. Analysts are aware of this requirement and often choose to fight the complaint with all legal means available.

RESPONSE TO VICTIMS

As we noted in Chapter 5, patients were often blamed historically for the sexual indiscretions of the analyst. Even today, patients who report violations are often regarded as "defective" or "manipulative" and viewed as troublemakers. Hence if they have the courage to step forward and report details of their analyst's boundary violations, they are often treated with reactions ranging from contempt to minimization to defensive aloofness by the analyst to whom they report. The ethics committees are obligated to create an environment in which a patient with a complaint can be given a fair hearing. Because the majority of the victims are female, the institute or society would do well to have female members represented on ethics committees or in the role of ombudsperson. It is helpful and supportive to express gratitude and admiration to patients who have the courage to speak up (Margolis, in press).

In the past, the major concern of institutes and societies was for the analyst. It is essential in the current climate that we address the patient's needs as comprehensively as we address those of the analyst. For example, referral to another clinician, either for analysis or for psychotherapy, can be offered by the society or institute to facilitate a low-fee treatment because resources have been exhausted in a treatment that was essentially unethical. This referral process may be complicated by difficulty finding a therapist or analyst willing to accept the patient. Well-publicized cases of accusations by the accused therapist against the subsequent therapist for fomenting the patient have made some clinicians reluctant to get involved.

Another form of intervention is a mediation process (Gabbard, 1994g; Margolis, in press; Schoener et al., 1989). In this approach, an analyst (often from another institute) with expertise and knowledge regarding the sequelae of sexual boundary violations agrees to meet with the accused analyst and the accusing patient. Mediation provides an opportunity for the patient to explain how he or she felt exploited and betrayed by the analyst. The analyst must sit still long enough to hear the patient out. In a great many cases, the analyst has rationalized the boundary violations in such a way that he or she is convinced that the patient was helped by the deviations from standard practice. Mediation creates a situation in which the analyst's denial comes face to face with the patient's insistence that harm was done.

The mediation process also provides an opportunity for the analyst to offer an apology to the patient. Victims of sexual transgressions by analysts often have never experienced any acknowledgment from the analyst, the institute, or the society that something terribly wrong has happened. Legal advice to institutes often takes the form of suggesting that no one acknowledge any wrongdoing lest there be an increased risk of liability. Victims generally find it exceedingly important to receive an apology both from the institution and from the analyst (Wohlberg, in press).

In many cases a good deal of healing takes place during a mediation process. Pent-up feelings are finally expressed. The analyst may have the opportunity to express regret and remorse. Margolis (in press) stressed that a genuine apology also implies a willingness to offer restitution, not just to acknowledge guilt. Reimbursing the patient for the analytic fees spent on a process that ended up being harmful and traumatizing may promote healing as well.

ASSESSMENT AND REHABILITATION

As the ethics committee (or other body) conducts its investigation of the complaint, the issue of whether the accused analyst should continue in practice is of paramount concern in the minds of everyone involved. The determination of the analyst's suitability for a rehabilitation effort is greatly assisted by an independent, outside assessment (Gabbard, 1994g; Schoener et al., 1989). If such an evaluation is performed by an outside clinician, it is important to make it clear to everyone that the evaluation for amenability to rehabilitation must be clearly separated from any disciplinary measures. Punishment or discipline is the purview of the ethics committee or possibly the licensing board, if that state agency has become involved. The assessment for rehabilitation is done in a clinical setting by clinicians who are knowledgeable about boundary violations and who are trained to reach reasonable conclusions about suitability. If the allegations have been substantiated but the analyst emphatically denies any boundary violations, the rehabilitation assessment can be a charade as well as a waste of time, energy, and money. There is a sense of absurdity in trying to evaluate someone for a rehabilitation plan when the individual insists that there is nothing for which to be rehabilitated.

The ideal assessment is a thorough psychiatric evaluation that may or may not include psychological testing. The end result of such an evaluation is a determination of the viability of a rehabilitation plan, as well as the formulation of an individualized plan most useful for the particular analyst (Gabbard, 1994g; Schoener et al., 1989). The psychodynamic classification outlined in Chapter 6 can be useful in making this determination. The vast majority of analysts who fall into the category of predatory psychopathy and paraphilias are not amenable to any rehabilitation effort. The severe compromises of the superego, lack of remorse, lack of motivation, and sadistic orientation to the treatment situation make the analyst unsuitable for a clinical career. These individuals should be advised to consider a career change.

Many analysts who fall into the categories of lovesickness and masochistic surrender are highly suitable for a rehabilitation effort. Those in the latter category are frequently filled with remorse and realize that they have acted in a highly self-destructive way. They are therefore motivated to prevent transgressions from occurring again (Gabbard, 1994d). Some lovesick analysts may initially be rather refractory to considerations of rehabilitation because they are still madly infatuated with their patient. They may be puzzled that anyone would suggest that they need treatment, because they have rationalized that the sexual relationship with the patient had nothing to do with transference or countertransference. Rather, they view the episode as "true love" and cannot understand why such a time-honored state of ecstasy should require treatment. After the "dew is off the rose," and the analyst regains his or her judgment, the rehabilitation effort may have more meaning, and the analyst may then be highly motivated to collaborate in such an effort.

Psychotic disorders are rarely involved in cases of boundary violations.

If a bipolar illness is clearly treatable with medication and psychotherapy, the analyst may be able to return to work, but individuals with more refractory psychoses require redirection toward another career.

A basic rule of thumb in assessing analysts who have been charged with sexual misconduct is that the information about the boundary violation must come from more than one source. If the evaluating clinician relies only on the self-reporting of the analyst, a skewed version of the events may influence the evaluator's opinion in such a way that an erroneous conclusion is reached. Transcripts of any ethics hearings or licensing board investigations should be made available to the evaluating clinician. Also, any written complaint by the patient should be included as relevant information to assist in the evaluation.

The analyst (or other mental health professional) performing the assessment must attempt to identify the stressors that may have been at work in contributing to the boundary violations. He or she must also identify the key psychodynamic themes involved in the transgression and determine to what extent they are situational versus long-standing. Sexual history is also highly relevant to the situation. Analysts who have a history of several boundary violations as well as predatory sexual activities outside the analytic setting generally represent a considerable risk for future practice. On the other hand, analysts who have suffered a severe loss before the boundary violation and have no record of other transgressions may represent minimal risk to future patients. Long-standing patterns of object relatedness may offer significant clues to what happened in the analytic setting in terms of a repetition of an externalization of internal object relations patterns. The intactness of the analyst's marriage or other key personal relationships must also be taken into consideration as part of the assessment. In some cases, strengthening that support system may be a critical ingredient in a successful rehabilitation plan.

After completion of the assessment, the findings should be presented to the analyst who has been evaluated as well as to the ethics committee or other agency that has requested the evaluation (Gabbard, 1994g; Schoener et al., 1989). The ethics committee of the institute may proceed with the rehabilitation plan if all participants have accepted it and, of course, if it is not at odds with any other stipulations by licensing boards or other bodies. Each rehabilitation plan is individually tailored to the needs of the analyst, but several key components are usually present in one form or another, and these are discussed in the following sections in varying degrees of detail.

It should be clear at this point that this model of assessment and rehabilitation assumes a cooperative and motivated analyst as its subject. In the American Psychoanalytic Association, the ethics committees have limited sanctions, including censure, suspension from membership in the Association for up to 3 years, separation from the rolls with the potential for new application at a later date, and permanent expulsion from membership. They cannot mandate practice limitations, supervision, treatment, or the like. Only licensing boards have that kind of justification. Ethics committees can merely recommend such a program to an analyst who wishes to be rehabilitated (and who wishes to continue as a member of the society or institute).

In the Canadian Psychoanalytic Society, the hearing panel of the ethics committee has somewhat greater authority. Any sanction considered reasonable may be imposed. These may include reprimand, recommendation for supervision or other sanctions, and the reporting of those sanctions. Also, if the member attempts to resign after a complaint has been filed against him or her, the resignation will not be accepted. Even with this broadened authority, however, little recourse other than expulsion is available concerning the analyst who refuses to cooperate with a rehabilitation plan. Appeal processes *are* available in both the Canadian and the American systems.

PRACTICE LIMITATIONS

A central question in any rehabilitation plan is "rehabilitation for what?" The fact that the analysts under consideration have devoted their professional career to the practice of psychoanalysis does not automatically mean that they should be returned to that practice. A determination may be made that because of chronic narcissistic vulnerability, superego pathology, ego weaknesses, or entrenched patterns of internal object relations, the analyst might do better pursuing other aspects of professional work. For example, brief structured psychotherapies may be regarded as posing less of a risk. If the analyst is a psychiatrist, a general psychiatry practice could be considered. Administrative jobs within the mental health professions may be deemed more suitable as well. Often the nature of the patient population is stipulated. Some analysts may be viewed as doing competent work as long as they confine themselves to patients of one gender. Others may do well with a geriatric population.

The rehabilitation plan must walk a fine line between meeting the needs of the analyst who is being rehabilitated and protecting the public from potential exploitation. The analyst may make powerful pleas to be allowed to return to a more or less full-time analytic practice, and local colleagues may wish to give in to the analyst's wish because of their long-standing affection for him or her. The value of an outside consultant is that the analyst's vulnerabilities may be more apparent, and the safety of the public may be given greater importance because the evaluator has no history of a close relationship with the analyst that might blind him or her to the limitations of the analyst. At the same time, local colleagues may have valuable information about the analyst's long-standing patterns of behavior and character that could assist the consultant in the evaluation. The ideal situation involves a close collaborative relationship between the ethics committee and the outside evaluator. If the decision is made that a practitioner should avoid analytic work and pursue an alternative form of practice or administration, the rehabilitation plan should probably be monitored by the licensing board or ethics committee of the psychiatric or psychological society.

SUPERVISION

Supervision is a component of almost every viable rehabilitation plan. The analyst who returns to the practice of analysis or intensive psychotherapy often wishes to choose his or her supervisors. In general, the ethics committee would be well advised to maintain control of that decision. Analysts who are allowed to choose for themselves may select long-time friends or mentors who are particularly sympathetic and who may minimize the extent of the analyst's problems with boundary violations. Indeed, a supervisor may be selected for exactly those reasons. The supervisor or supervisors chosen by the ethics committee must make a point of focusing on countertransference in general and boundary issues in particular in the course of the supervision. Although the rehabilitation plan is based on the principle that the analyst will collaborate in reporting such difficulties, supervisors must be alert to omissions from the supervisory process that may be highly significant.

ASSIGNMENT OF A REHABILITATION COORDINATOR

The rehabilitation coordinator is a key figure in the overall plan. This individual is often a member of the ethics committee. He or she may also be someone outside the local institute or society. In any case, the rehabilitation coordinator should, at the very least, be someone who is highly knowledgeable about issues of boundary violations and ethics procedures. This individual must be fully informed of the analyst's professional activities and should receive regular reports from the clinical supervisors and any administrative supervisors (if the analyst is affiliated with an institution). The rehabilitation coordinator is the official liaison to the ethics committee and makes periodic reports (every 6 months or so) to the committee regarding the progress of the rehabilitation effort. The coordinator may also perform various other functions, such as prescribing psychotropic medication for the analyst if necessary. Many analysts who are accused of sexual misconduct become seriously depressed and even suicidal as the disparity between ideals and reality becomes apparent to them. As Edward Bibring (1953) pointed out, depression may result from the recognition that the aspirations one has long held will not be fulfilled and the recognition of the reality of one's limitations. Some rehabilitation coordinators may wish to assign the role of pharmacotherapist to someone else.

One role that explicitly is not under the purview of the rehabilitation coordinator is that of psychotherapist or psychoanalyst. This deliberate separation of the coordinator role from the psychotherapist role allows the treating clinician, whether psychoanalyst or psychotherapist, to preserve confidentiality.

PERSONAL THERAPY OR ANALYSIS

Part of the rehabilitation assessment is a careful evaluation of the optimal psychotherapeutic approach to the analyst. More analysis may be indicated in many cases. Sometimes a more structured intensive psychotherapy process appears to be the preferred modality. If serious difficulties in the analyst's marriage or support system need to be addressed, a combination of individual and marital therapy may be recommended. As noted previously in the discussion of supervision, analysts undergoing rehabilitation should not be in a position of choosing the therapist or therapists completely on their own. In some cases, the ethics committee may view it as optimal for the analyst to return for more analysis with his or her previous training analyst. In other cases, a new analyst may be a better option. To provide the analyst with some say in the matter, ethics committees may wish to provide several choices and allow the analyst to make the final decision.

In any case, the psychotherapist* must see his or her primary task as providing understanding for the patient (Gabbard, 1994a, 1994b; Strean, 1993). By delegating the reporting function to the rehabilitation coordinator, the psychotherapist can maintain a confidential relationship and the analyst–patient can be assured that any sexual fantasies or feelings voiced in the treatment will remain in the treatment. If the psychotherapist has any reporting obligation to the ethics committee or licensing board, the treatment is compromised, because the analyst undergoing treatment feels that the therapist is a double agent of the ethics committee rather than an individual devoted to insight and understanding. Sometimes psychotherapists have limited communication with the rehabilitation coordinator, but such an arrangement must be carefully discussed with all persons involved to be certain that the treatment is not seriously compromised.

Even when confidentiality is preserved and no reporting is required of the psychotherapist, the transference–countertransference dimensions of the treatment setting provide a host of formidable challenges. Psychotherapists in such settings may feel they must police the profession in addition to helping their patients understand themselves. This countertransference posture may be exacerbated by the transference of the analyst–patient, who may be suspicious of the therapist's intentions despite reassurances of complete confidentiality. The suspiciousness may make it difficult for the patient to open up completely to the therapist, who then may become increasingly hypervigilant about what the patient is concealing. This posture may manifest itself in sub-

*We are using the term *psychotherapist* here to avoid confusion with the term *analyst*, which is applied to the person who is being rehabilitated.

tle forms of contempt toward the patient and a feeling that one must "catch" the patient before another boundary violation occurs (Gabbard, 1995c). It may also take the form of lecturing the patient on the unethical nature of his or her behavior.

Part of this countertransference paradigm is a conscious or unconscious feeling of moral superiority that places greater distance between the psychotherapist and the analyst–patient. The psychotherapist may be attempting to control his or her own impulses by taking a punitive position vis-à-vis the patient. The therapist can disavow sexual temptations by seeing them only in the patient and then playing the role of cop or jailer to stop the patient from acting on such impulses ever again.

Another countertransference tendency is for psychotherapists to collude with various subtle forms of corruption initiated by the analyst–patient. The analyst may wish to become more informal and casual and to treat the psychotherapist as a colleague rather than a therapist. The therapist may collude with the patient's transference wish to become an equal with the therapist and with the denial of the obvious aggression in these efforts to bring the therapist down to the level of a friend or colleague. In response to these efforts to compromise professional boundaries, the therapist may react by becoming excessively rigid. Therapists may find themselves behaving in a more remote and less empathic manner compared to their usual posture with patients. In many cases this corruption of boundaries takes the specific form of erotization in both the transference and countertransference. There appears to be something particularly tempting in treating an analyst who has done the unthinkable.

Part of the allure in these situations is the unconscious fascination with and envy of a colleague who has entered forbidden territory that is symbolically equated with the incest taboo. Strean (1993) noted that in one case he had to face his envy of his patient, who had the "freedom to give immediate expression to his id impulses without examining them" (p. 57). One response to this envy may be moral indignation, which, as the saying goes, is jealousy with a halo.

Some analysts who have been charged with sexual misconduct have been deeply traumatized by the process of being brought up before an ethics committee. By the time they come to psychotherapy or analysis, they are suffused with a profound sense of shame and may approach treatment as a confessional where absolution for one's sins is granted. In addition to their shame at having engaged in highly self-destructive and unethical behavior, they may also feel mistreated, betrayed, and unfairly judged by their peers on ethics committees. They may appear to be pleading their case with their psychotherapist, whom they hope will take up their cause and rescue their good name by speaking to judgmental peers about "the other side of things."

A common development, especially with male analysts who have had sexual relations with female patients, is that the analyst feels no one has appreciated his positive motives for crossing boundaries with the patient. He may have felt that he was saving the patient's life and that his peers have focused only on how he harmed the patient. In the evolving transference, he may desperately seek for the psychotherapist to become a figure who will validate and affirm his essential goodness as well as absolve him of his transgressions.

Another frequent dimension of the accused analyst's feelings is the sense that he has been exploited by the patient. From an ethical standpoint, of course, one can never blame the patient for the analyst's violation of sexual boundaries. The analyst may nonetheless feel that he has been manipulated by a patient who made demands on him and then turned around and reported him after he gave in to her demands. In pleading his case with his psychotherapist, the male analyst may also want validation of his role as victim, for the exploitation he felt by the patient and for the mishandling of the case he experienced by the ethics committee.

Strong countertransference pulls may arise as a result of these pleas. When the analyst is a female and the patient was a male with antisocial tendencies, there is an even stronger tendency to see the female analyst as a victim of a smooth con artist rather than as a professional acting out of her own sense of agency and violating ethics codes (Averill et al., 1989; Gabbard, 1994d; Gutheil & Gabbard, 1992). Therapists may empathize with the analyst they are treating and begin to see the disciplinary system as a collection of insensitive ogres. This countertransference wish to rescue the patient often grows out of an unconscious collusion with the patient in denying the role of his or her aggression and sadism in the ethics violation (Gabbard, 1995c). Many lovesick analysts are blinded to the harm they do to patients when they become sexually involved with them. In treating such analysts, one must make

an effort to help them reintegrate that aggression rather than external-
ize it onto the disciplinary bodies that are dealing with them. One can
err in being overly empathic as well as overly punitive.

An ongoing struggle for psychotherapists treating analysts who
have been charged with sexual misconduct is in dealing with the wish
to reassure the patient. Therapists may have powerful urges to tell the
patient that he or she is essentially honest and well intentioned. They
may even find themselves struggling with powerful urges to reach out
and touch the analyst as a way of overtly demonstrating acceptance of
the patient.

Another countertransference issue that is related to the therapist's
feelings of moral superiority and the sense of policing the profession is
an intrusive voyeuristic tendency. There is something morbidly fasci-
nating about colleagues who have acted on fantasies that we all harbor.
This struggle may manifest itself as excessive curiosity about the
details of the sexual relationship, even when the analyst–patient is
working on other issues. The therapist's wish to find out more about
why the analyst transgressed boundaries may interfere with the establishment of a solid therapeutic alliance and the optimal exploration of
the patient's psychological concerns.

RETURN TO UNSUPERVISED PRACTICE

The duration of the rehabilitation program cannot be arbitrarily set.
Reports of the rehabilitation coordinator to the ethics committee provide the opportunity for periodic (every 6 months or so) assessment of
how the program is working out. Supervisors may be asked to attend
such meetings if their written reports raise some questions. It is often
useful to taper the number of meetings between the analyst and the
rehabilitation coordinator as the program continues. Similarly, supervision can be tapered rather than stopped abruptly. Many highly motivated analysts wish to continue supervision after the rehabilitation
program is officially ended. The personal psychotherapy must be negotiated between the analyst and the psychotherapist. The duration of a
typical rehabilitation plan ranges from 3 to 6 years. Before a complete
return to unsupervised practice is sanctioned, the analyst must have a
careful reassessment. Occasionally, the outside evaluator who made
the original assessment may be used.

PREVENTION

Although prevention of all sexual and nonsexual boundary violations is a goal that institutes and societies undoubtedly aspire to, we acknowledge that such a goal is unrealistic. As Apfel and Simon (1985) suggested, because of the very nature of privacy and intimacy in the analytic relationship, complete prevention of sexual boundary violations is probably impossible. Education is clearly a cornerstone of preventive efforts, but analytic candidates with severe narcissistic or antisocial character pathology will be relatively impervious to educational interventions and will probably exploit the analytic situation to gratify various sadistic wishes. More careful screening of applicants to analytic institutes is needed to keep such individuals out of the analytic profession, but history has taught us that no form of assessing applicants is foolproof.

Education begins in the classroom, and there is some indication that few institutes offer courses in ethics. In a survey of the 28 institutes and 40 societies in the American Psychoanalytic Association, just over half had ethics committees, and only 6 had regular courses in ethics in their curricula (Engle, 1995). The members of some institutes felt strongly that teaching about such matters as erotic transference and countertransference, boundaries, and boundary violations should be incorporated into courses on technique rather than consigned to courses specifically focused on ethics. The advantage of teaching such issues in an ethics course is that various boundary problems might be discussed more explicitly. This setting also provides an opportunity to present model cases and promote open discussion about them.

Regardless of whether the issues are taught in ethics courses or technique courses, psychoanalytic strategies of dealing with erotic and erotized transference must be stressed in the context of the vulnerability we all have to violating boundaries. Similarly, countertransference, especially of an erotic nature, should be taught as an expected part of the analytic process that grows out of various enactments that inevitably occur in the analytic process. In other words, permission must be provided to discuss such countertransference issues without fear of censure.

With the current interest in intersubjectivity, constructivism, and the redefining of terms like *abstinence* and *neutrality*, institute faculty should be wary of unwittingly fostering an "anything goes" attitude in candidates. Although lack of spontaneity is a frequent problem in beginning analysts, a jazz musician must learn the scales before improvising. Senior faculty who espouse radical departures from orthodoxy may be misunderstood by their students.

Supervisors must similarly be open to exploration of countertransference, at least in terms of the here and now as we described in Chapter 9. If erotic or rescue fantasies are omitted from the supervisory process, supervisors should feel free to raise questions proactively about the absence of such material from the analysis. Also, as we noted in Chapter 9, supervisors must model a sense of professional boundaries so that the supervisee internalizes a feeling of clarity and safety in the supervisory relationship.

Theodore Jacobs (1994a) suggested that a thoroughgoing attempt to prevent boundary violations requires a hard look at the way that training analyses are conducted. He speculated that we may be all too ready to explore psychodynamic themes and underlying causes for antisocial behavior or unethical tendencies instead of confronting candidates with the consequences of their behavior and the impact it has on others. He noted that we can err on the side of being too empathic and too nonjudgmental and thus unconsciously collude with a candidate's deception. Jacobs also noted that training analysts need to be particularly alert for any problems that candidates encounter in using self-scrutiny and self-reflection in their work. These difficulties act as "red flags" for a tendency to act rather than analyze and reflect on what is happening intrapsychically.

Psychoanalysis takes place in isolation. Unfortunately, the very isolation that makes the process viable also severely limits the analyst's opportunities for feedback from colleagues. Hence the privacy of the setting contributes to the perils of being drawn into a folie à deux in which rescuing the patient seems like the only viable option open to the analyst. The need for regular consultation cannot be stressed strongly enough. Analysts must be wary of the feeling that they are all alone in the consulting room and must figure out all situations for themselves. By monitoring early signs of nonsexual boundary violations that suggest countertransference enactments that deviate from their usual practice, analysts can recognize the need for consultation with a colleague. This can be done in a one-to-one setting or in an ongoing peer supervision group. One advantage of the latter is that the colleagues get to know one another so well that they can immediately spot typical countertransference problems as they develop.

Waldinger (1994) noted that whereas seeking a consultation may be highly useful, there are no guidelines for such consultations. Although his own suggestions are designed for psychotherapists, they have considerable applicability to psychoanalysts. He advised those who seek consultation to present the frame of treatment as part of the discussion without assuming that the consultant knows the exact architecture of the frame that applies to a specific treatment. The analyst could help the consultant to understand the situation better by describing in detail the deviations from usual technique or boundaries as well as the rationale for doing so. Waldinger also recommended that a consultant with expertise in boundary issues be sought out. Finally, if there is concern in the process about the possibility of boundary violations, the consultant could see the patient separately. When sexual misconduct has actually occurred, consultants need to be aware that they may share in any liability that results if they do not take action to stop it or report.

Another form of isolation has occurred in various parts of the country where analysts become estranged or alienated from their institutes, societies, and even the profession itself (Jacobs, 1994a). Many analysts who have graduated from training but have small or part-time analytic practices may have little contact with analytic colleagues and may as a result develop an idiosyncratic style of treatment that develops without benefit of feedback or critiques from colleagues. The same group of analysts may become increasingly disappointed and resentful that they have not advanced to training analyst as part of their career progression. The combination of bitterness toward the institute, disillusionment with psychoanalysis, and a sense of personal failure and despair may be a fertile field for the development of boundary violations.

Prevention can also involve the public. Analysis has developed in a highly insular way, and providing more public information about the nature of analytic boundaries and the analytic frame could be a useful preventive measure. Committees or ombudspersons could also be available for any patient who might have questions or concerns about an analyst. Telephone numbers of these committees and individuals could be made widely available by placement in waiting rooms or in other ways, such as through the news media. These measures might provide an early warning system through which preliminary signs of boundary crossings or violations could be addressed by designated analysts in each community. This active intervention could also alert analysts to a particular colleague who may need to be supervised regularly. Similarly, analytic institutes and societies need to have an open-door policy regarding the airing of complaints or the expression of concern about gossip. A small group of analysts on the designated committee could keep the information from spreading widely by immediately talking to the colleague in question and keeping that dialogue confidential, while proceeding with an investigation of the rumor.

The final preventive measure is one that cannot be legislated quite so easily as some of the others. It has to do with the way analysts choose to construct their lives. From early in their training, they become geared to a procedure in which they carefully put their own needs aside in the service of trying to tune into the needs of their patients. A certain cost is incurred in this demanding and arduous procedure. The practice of analysis can subtly become a masochistic exercise in self-neglect and self-sacrifice.

Many analysts see their first patient at 6:00 or 7:00 a.m. and do not finish their office hours until well into the evening. They may then have little time for family interaction or fulfillment of their own needs for love and succor. Their primary contact with others involves seeing patients in the privacy of the consulting room. Their needs for human contact gradually may become directed toward their patients as they grow increasingly distant from the loved ones that ought to constitute their support system. Many analysts spend more time thinking about their patients than about their marriages. Although it should be obvious, most analysts neglect to see the connection between having an emotionally gratifying personal life and their effectiveness as analysts.

A supportive spouse or partner does not merely provide the analyst with the love (and sexual gratification) needed to face another day of grueling analytic work. He or she also helps the analyst to develop the necessary humility to deal with the intense transference–countertransference passions stirred up in the analytic crucible. When analysts feel they are indispensable and irresistible to the patient who desperately needs them, a loving spouse may remind them that they are not really so exceptional as they think. In fact, they are more human than otherwise.

References

Abend, S. M. (1989). Countertransference and technique. *Psychoanalytic Quarterly, 48,* 374–395.

Abend, S. M. (1990). The psychoanalytic process: Motives and obstacles in the search for clarification. *Psychoanalytic Quarterly, 59,* 532–549.

Akhtar, S., & Thompson, Jr., J. A. (1982). Overview: Narcissistic personality disorder. *American Journal of Psychiatry, 139,* 12–20.

Alexander, F. (1950). Analysis of the therapeutic factors in psychoanalytic treatment. *Psychoanalytic Quarterly, 19,* 482–500.

Almond, R. (1995). The analytic role. *Journal of the American Psychoanalytic Association, 43,* 469–494.

Altman, L. L. (1977). Some vicissitudes of love. *Journal of the American Psychoanalytic Association, 25,* 35–52.

American Psychological Association (1992). Ethical principles of psychologists and code of conduct. *American Psychologist, 47,* 1597–1611.

Anzieu, D. (1989). *The skin ego* (C. Turner, Trans.). New Haven and London: Yale University Press.

Apfel, R. J., & Simon, B. (1985). Patient–therapist sexual contact: I. Psycho-dynamic perspectives on the causes and results. *Psychotherapy and Psychosomatics, 43,* 57–62.

Appelbaum, P. S., & Jorgenson, L. (1991). Psychotherapist–patient sexual contact after termination of treatment: An analysis and a proposal. *American Journal of Psychiatry, 148,* 1466–1473.

Appignanesi, L., & Forrester, J. (1992). *Freud's women.* New York: Basic Books.

Arlow, J. A. (1963). The supervisory situation. *Journal of the American Psychoanalytic Association, 11,* 576–594.

Arvanitakis, K., Jodoin, R. M., Lester, E. P., Lussier, A., & Robertson, B. M. (1993). Early sexual abuse and nightmares in the analysis of adults. *Psychoanalytic Quarterly, 62,* 572–587.

Averill, S. C., Beale, D., Benfer, B., Collins, D. T., Kennedy, L., Myers, J., Pope, D., Rosen, I., & Zoble, E. (1989). Preventing staff–patient sexual relationships. *Bulletin of the Menninger Clinic, 53,* 384–393.

Bacal, H. A., & Newman, K. M. (1990). *Theories of object relations: Bridges to self psychology.* New York: Columbia University Press.

Baker, R. (1993). The patient's discovery of the psychoanalyst as a new object. *International Journal of Psycho-Analysis, 74,* 1223–1233.

Balint, M. (1954). Analytic training and training analysis. *International Journal of Psycho-Analysis, 35,* 157–162.

Barron, J. W., & Hoffer, A. (1994). Historical events reinforcing Freud's emphasis on "holding down the transference." *Psychoanalytic Quarterly, 63,* 536–540.

Baudry, F. D. (1993). The personal dimension and management of the supervisory situation with a special note on the parallel process. *Psychoanalytic Quarterly, 62,* 588–614.

Beebe, B., Lachman, F., & Jaffe, J. (1991, April). *Mother–infant interaction structures and presymbolic self- and object-representations.* Paper presented at the meeting of the Ontario Psychoanalytic Society, Toronto.

Belicki, K. (1986). Recalling dreams: An examination of daily variations and individual differences. In J. Gackenbach (Ed.), *Sleep and dreams: A source book* (Vol. 296, pp. 187–206). New York: Garland.

Benowitz, M. S. (1995). Comparing the experiences of women clients sexually exploited by female versus male psychotherapists. In J. Gonsiorek (Ed.), *Breach of trust* (pp. 213–224). Thousand Oaks: Sage.

Bergmann, M. S. (1988). On the fate of the intrapsychic image of the psycho-analyst after termination of the analysis. *Psychoanalytic Study of the Child, 43,* 137–153.

Bernardi, R., & Nieto, M. (1992). What makes the training analysis "good enough"? *International Review of Psycho-Analysis, 19,* 137–146.

Bernfeld, S. (1962). On psychoanalytic training. *Psychoanalytic Quarterly, 31,* 453–482.

Bibring, E. (1937). Symposium on the theory of the therapeutic results of psycho-analysis. *International Journal of Psycho-Analysis, 18,* 170–189.

Bibring, E. (1953). The mechanism of depression. In P. Greenacre (Ed.), *Affective disorders: Psychoanalytic contributions to their study* (pp. 13–48). New York: International Universities Press.

Bick, E. (1968). The experience of the skin in early object–relations. *International Journal of Psycho-Analysis, 49,* 484–486.

Black, D. M. (1993). What sort of a thing is a religion? A view from object-relations theory. *International Journal of Psycho-Analysis, 74,* 613–625.

Blatt, S. J., & Ritzler, B. A. (1974). Thought disorder and boundary disturbances in psychosis. *Journal of Consulting and Clinical Psychology, 42,* 370–381.

Bleier, R. (1991). Gender ideology and the brain: Sex difference research. In M. T. Notman & C. C. Nadelson (Eds.), *Women and men: New perspectives on gender differences* (pp. 63–73). Washington, DC: American Psychiatric Press.

Blos, P. (1980). The life cycle as indicated by the nature of the transference in the psychoanalysis of adolescents. *International Journal of Psycho-Analysis, 61,* 145–151.

Blum, H. P. (1973). The concept of erotized transference. *Journal of the American Psychoanalytic Association, 21,* 61–76.

Blum, H. P. (1994). The confusion of tongues and psychic trauma. *International Journal of Psycho-Analysis, 74,* 871–882.

Boesky, D. (1990). The psychoanalytic process and its components. *Psychoanalytic* Quarterly, 59, 550–584.

Bollas, C. (1987). *The shadow of the object: Psychoanalysis of the unthought known.* New York: Columbia University Press.

Borys, D. S., & Pope, K. S. (1989). Dual relationships between therapist and client: A national study of psychologists, psychiatrists, and social workers. *Professional Psychology: Research and Practice, 20,* 283–293.

Bouvet, M. (1958). Technical variation and the concept of distance. *International Journal of Psycho-Analysis, 39,* 211–221.

Brabant, E., & Falzeder, E. (Eds.). (in press). *The correspondence of Sigmund Freud and Sándor Ferenczi* (Vol. 2, 1914–1919; P. T. Hoffer, Trans.). Cambridge, MA: Harvard University Press.

Brabant, E., Falzeder, E., & Giampieri-Deutsch, P. (Eds.). (1994). *The corre-*

spondence of Sigmund Freud and Sándor Ferenczi (Vol. 1, 1908–1914; P. T. Hoffer, Trans.). Cambridge, MA: Harvard University Press.

Brenner, C. (1982). *The mind in conflict*. New York: International Universities Press.

Brenner, C. (1994). Personal communication.

Breuer, J., & Freud, S. (1893–1895/1955). Studies on hysteria. In J. Strachey (Ed. and Trans.), *The standard edition of the complete psychological works of Sigmund Freud* (Vol. 2, pp. vii–xxxi, 1–311). London: Hogarth Press.

Browne, A., & Finkelhor, D. (1986). Impact of child sexual abuse: A review of the research. *Psychological Bulletin, 99,* 66–77.

Buckley, P., Karasu, T. B., & Charles, E. (1981). Psychotherapists view their personal therapy. *Psychotherapy: Theory, Research and Practice, 18,* 299–305.

Burbiel, I., Finke, G., & Sanderman, G. (1994). Measuring narcissism and boundaries of borderline patients. *Dynamic Psychiatry, 144/145,* 8–23.

Calef, V., & Weinshel, E. M. (1983). A note on consummation and termination. *Journal of the American Psychoanalytic Association, 31,* 643–650.

Carotenuto, A. (1982). *A secret symmetry: Sabina Spielrein between Jung and Freud* (A. Pomerans, J. Shepley, & K. Winston, Trans.). New York: Pantheon Books.

Carpy, D. V. (1989). Tolerating the countertransference: A mutative process. *International Journal of Psycho-Analysis, 70,* 287–294.

Casement, P. J. (1985). *On learning from the patient*. London: Tavistock.

Casement, P. J. (1990). The meeting of needs in psychoanalysis. *Psychoanalytic Inquiry, 10,* 325–346.

Casement, P. J. (1994). *Psychoanalysis as process*. Paper presented at the meeting of the Quebec English Psychoanalytic Society, Montreal.

Casullo, A. B., & Resnizky, S. (1993, July). *Psychoanalytic supervision: A clinical approach or shared clinical reflections*. Paper presented at the Sixth IPA Conference of Training Analysts, Amsterdam, Holland.

Celenza, A. (1991). The misuse of countertransference love in sexual intimacies between therapists and patients. *Psychoanalytic Psychology, 8,* 501–509.

Chasseguet-Smirgel, J. (1973). Essai sur l'Idéal du Moi: Contribution à l'étude de la "maladie d'idéalité." *Revue Francaise de Psychanalyse, 37,* 709–927.

Chessick, R. D. (1992). Review of the book *Sexual exploitation in professional relationships* by G. O. Gabbard. *Journal of the American Academy of Psychoanalysis, 20,* 161–163.

Chrzanowski, G. (1984). Can psychoanalysis be taught? In L. Caligor, P. M. Bromberg, & J. D. Meltzer (Eds.), *Clinical perspectives of the supervision of psychoanalysis and psychotherapy* (pp. 45–58). New York: Plenum Press.

Chused, J. F. (1991). The evocative power of enactments. *Journal of the American Psychoanalytic Association, 39,* 615–639.

Coen, S. (1992). *The misuse of persons: Analyzing pathological dependency.* Hillsdale, NJ: Analytic Press.

Cohen, D. B. (1974). Toward a theory of dream recall. *Psychological Bulletin, 81*, 138–154.

Cohn, J. F., Campbell, S. B., & Ross, S. (1992). Infant response in the still-face paradigm at 6 months predicts avoidant and secure attachment at 12 months. *Development and Pathology, 3*, 367–376.

Compton, A. (1990). Psychoanalytic process. *Psychoanalytic Quarterly, 59*, 585–598.

Cooper, A. M. (1987). Changes in psychoanalytic ideas: Transference interpretation. *Journal of the American Psychoanalytic Association, 35*, 77–98.

Cooper, A. M. (1992). Psychic change: Development of the theory of psychoanalytic techniques. *International Journal of Psycho-Analysis, 73*, 245–250.

Cooper, A. M. (1993). Psychotherapeutic approaches to masochism. *Journal of Psychotherapy Practice and Research, 2*, 51–63.

Cooper, J. (1993). *Speak of me as I am: The life and work of Masud Kahn.* London: Karnac Books.

Craik, D. M. A. (1859). *Life for a life.* New York: Harper.

Davies, J. M., & Frawley, M. G. (1992). Dissociative processes and transference–countertransference paradigms in the psychoanalytically oriented treatment of adult survivors of childhood sexual abuse. *Psychoanalytic Dialogues, 2*, 5–36.

Dewald, P. A. (1966). Forced termination of psychoanalysis: Transference, countertransference, and reality responses in five patients. *Bulletin of the Menninger Clinic, 30*, 98–110.

Doehrman, M. J. G. (1976). Parallel processes in supervision and psychotherapy. *Bulletin of the Menninger Clinic, 40*, 3–104.

Dupont, J. (Ed.). (1988). *The clinical diary of Sándor Ferenczi.* (M. Balint & N. Z. Jackson, Trans.). Cambridge, MA: Harvard University Press.

Dupont, J. (1994). Freud's analysis of Ferenczi as revealed by their correspondence. *International Journal of Psycho-Analysis, 75*, 301–320.

Eagle, M. N. (1987). *Recent developments in psychoanalysis: A critical evaluation.* Cambridge, MA: Harvard University Press.

Eagle, M. N. (1993). Enactments, transference, and symptomatic cure: A case history. *Psychoanalytic Dialogues, 3*, 93–110.

Edmunds, L. (1988, April). His master's choice. *Johns Hopkins Magazine*, 40–49.

Eissler, K. R. (1983). *Victor Tausk's suicide.* New York: International Universities Press.

Ekstein, R. (1960). A historical survey on the teaching of psychoanalytic technique. *Journal of the American Psychoanalytic Association, 8*, 500–516.

Emde, R. N. (1988). Development terminable and interminable: I. Innate and motivational factors from infancy. *International Journal of Psycho-Analysis, 69*, 23–42.

Engle, R. (1995). Personal communication.

Epstein, R. S. (1994). *Keeping boundaries: Maintaining safety and integrity in the psychotherapeutic process.* Washington, DC: American Psychiatric Press.

Epstein, R. S., Simon, R. I., & Kay, G. G. (1992). Assessing boundary violations in psychotherapy: Survey results with the Exploitation Index. *Bulletin of the Menninger Clinic, 56*, 150–166.

Eyman, J. R., & Gabbard, G. O. (1991). Will therapist–patient sex prevent suicide? *Psychiatric Annals, 21*, 669–674.

Fairbairn, W. R. D. (1963). Synopsis of an object-relations theory of the personality. *International Journal of Psycho-Analysis, 44*, 224–225.

Farber, S., & Green, M. (1993). *Hollywood on the couch: A candid look at the overheated love affair between psychiatrists and moviemakers.* New York: William Morrow.

Faulkner, H. J., & Pruitt, V. D. (Eds.). (1988). *The selected correspondence of Karl A. Menninger, 1919–1945.* New Haven: Yale University Press.

Federn, P. (1952). The ego as a subject and object in narcissism. In E. Weiss (Ed.), *Ego psychology and the psychoses* (pp. 283–322). New York: Basic Books.

Feldman-Summers, S., & Jones, G. (1984). Psychological impacts of sexual contact between therapists and other health care professionals and their clients. *Journal of Consulting and Clinical Psychology, 52*, 1054–1061.

Finell, J. S. (1985). Narcissistic problems in analysts. *International Journal of Psycho-Analysis, 66*, 433–445.

Fleming, J. (1969/1987). The training analyst as an educator. In S. S. Weiss (Ed.), *The teaching and learning of psychoanalysis: Selected papers of Joan Fleming* (pp. 62–80). New York: Guilford Press.

Freinhar, J. P. (1986). Oedipus or Odysseus: Developmental lines of narcissism. *Psychiatric Annals, 16*, 477–485.

Freud, S. (1896/1984). Letter of December 12, 1896. In J. M. Masson (Ed.), *The complete letters of Sigmund Freud to Wilhelm Fliess 1887–1904* (pp. 207–215). Cambridge, MA: Belknap Press.

Freud, S. (1905/1953). Fragment of an analysis of a case of hysteria. In J. Strachey (Ed. and Trans.), *The standard edition of the complete psychological works of Sigmund Freud* (Vol. 7, pp. 1–122). London: Hogarth Press.

Freud, S. (1905/1953). Three essays on the theory of sexuality. In J. Strachey (Ed. and Trans.), *The standard edition of the complete psychological works of Sigmund Freud* (Vol. 7, pp. 123–245). London: Hogarth Press.

Freud, S. (1912/1958). The dynamics of transference. In J. Strachey (Ed. and Trans.), *The standard edition of the complete psychological works of Sigmund Freud* (Vol. 12, pp. 97–108). London: Hogarth Press.

Freud, S. (1913a/1953). The claims of psycho-analysis to scientific interest. In J. Strachey (Ed. and Trans.), *The standard edition of the complete psychological works of Sigmund Freud* (Vol. 13, pp. 163–190). London: Hogarth Press.

Freud, S. (1913b/1958). On beginning the treatment (further recommendations on the technique of psycho-analysis I). In J. Strachey (Ed. and Trans.), *The standard edition of the complete psychological works of Sigmund Freud* (Vol. 12, pp. 121–144). London: Hogarth Press.

Freud, S. (1914a/1963). On narcissism: An introduction. In J. Strachey (Ed. and Trans.), *The standard edition of the complete psychological works of Sigmund Freud* (Vol. 14, pp. 67–102). London: Hogarth Press.

Freud, S. (1914b/1963). On the history of the psycho-analytic movement. In J. Strachey (Ed. and Trans.), *The standard edition of the complete psychological works of Sigmund Freud* (Vol. 14, pp. 1–66). London: Hogarth Press.

Freud, S. (1915a/1963). Instincts and their vicissitudes. In J. Strachey (Ed. and Trans.), *The standard edition of the complete psychological works of Sigmund Freud* (Vol. 14, pp. 109–140). London: Hogarth Press.

Freud, S. (1915b/1958). Observations on transference-love (further recommendations on the technique of psycho-analysis III). In J. Strachey (Ed. and Trans.), *The standard edition of the complete psychological works of Sigmund Freud* (Vol. 12, pp. 157–173). London: Hogarth Press.

Freud, S. (1925/1959). An autobiographical study. In J. Strachey (Ed. and Trans.), *The standard edition of the complete psychological works of Sigmund Freud* (Vol. 20, pp. 1–74). London: Hogarth Press.

Freud, S. (1930/1960). Civilization and its discontents. In J. Strachey (Ed. and Trans.), *The standard edition of the complete psychological works of Sigmund Freud* (Vol. 21, pp. 57–145). London: Hogarth Press.

Freud, S. (1931/1960). Letter 258 to Stefan Zweig. In E. Freud (Ed.), *Letters to Sigmund Freud* (pp. 402–403; T. Stern & J. Stern, Trans.). New York: Basic Books.

Freud, S. (1937/1964). Analysis terminable and interminable. In J. Strachey (Ed. and Trans.), *The standard edition of the complete psychological works of Sigmund Freud* (Vol. 23, pp. 209–253). London: Hogarth Press.

Frick, D. E. (1994). Nonsexual boundary violations in psychiatric treatment. In J. M. Oldham & M. B. Riba (Eds.), *Review of Psychiatry: Vol. 13* (pp. 415–432). Washington, DC: American Psychiatric Press.

Friedman, L. (1991). A reading of Freud's papers on technique. *Psychoanalytic Quarterly, 60,* 564–595.

Friedman, L. (1994). *Ferrum, Ignis and Medicina: Return to the crucible.* Plenary Address, Annual meeting of the American Psychoanalytic Association, Philadelphia, PA.

Fromm-Reichmann, F. (1989). Reminiscences of Europe. In A. Silver (Ed.), *Psychoanalysis and psychosis* (pp. 409–418). Madison, CT: International Universities Press.

Gabbard, G. O. (1989). *Sexual exploitation in professional relationships.* Washington, DC: American Psychiatric Press.

Gabbard, G. O. (1991a). Psychodynamics of sexual boundary violations. *Psychiatric Annals, 21,* 651–655.

Gabbard, G. O. (1991b). Technical approaches to transference hate in the analysis of borderline patients. *International Journal of Psycho-Analysis, 72,* 625–637.

Gabbard, G. O. (1992). Commentary on "Dissociative processes and transference–countertransference paradigms" by Jody Messler Davies & Mary Gail Frawley. *Psychoanalytic Dialogues, 2,* 37–47.

Gabbard, G. O. (1993). Once a patient, always a patient: Therapist–patient sex after termination. *The American Psychoanalyst, 26,* 6–7.

Gabbard, G. O. (1994a). Commentary on papers by Tansey, Hirsch, and Davies. *Psychoanalytic Dialogues, 4,* 203–213.

Gabbard, G. O. (1994b). On love and lust in erotic transference. *Journal of the American Psychoanalytic Association, 42,* 385–403.

Gabbard, G. O. (1994c). *Psychodynamic psychiatry in clinical practice: The DSM-IV edition.* Washington, DC: American Psychiatric Press.

Gabbard, G. O. (1994d). Psychotherapists who transgress sexual boundaries with patients. *Bulletin of the Menninger Clinic, 58,* 124–135.

Gabbard, G. O. (1994e). Reconsidering the American Psychological Association's policy on sex with former patients: Is it justifiable? *Professional Psychology: Research and Practice, 25,* 329–355.

Gabbard, G. O. (1994f). Sexual excitement and countertransference love in the analyst. *Journal of the American Psychoanalytic Association, 42,* 1083–1106.

Gabbard, G. O. (1994g) Sexual misconduct. In J. M. Oldham & M. Riba (Eds.), *Annual review of psychiatry* (pp. 433–456). Washington, DC: American Psychiatric Press.

Gabbard, G. O. (1995a). Countertransference: The emerging common ground. *International Journal of Psycho-Analysis, 76,* 475–485.

Gabbard, G. O. (1995b). The early history of boundary violations in psychoanalysis. *Journal of the American Psychoanalytic Association, 43.*

Gabbard, G. O. (1995c). Transference and countertransference in the psychotherapy of therapists charged with sexual misconduct. *Journal of Psychotherapy Practice and Research 4*, 10–17.

Gabbard, G. O. (1995d). When the patient is a therapist: Special challenges in the psychoanalytic treatment of mental health professionals. *Psychoanalytic Review, 82*, 709–725.

Gabbard, G. O., & Pope, K. S. (1989). Individual psychotherapy for victims of therapist–patient sexual intimacy. In G. O. Gabbard (Ed.), *Sexual exploitation in professional relationships* (pp. 89–100). Washington, DC: American Psychiatric Press.

Gabbard, G. O., & Wilkinson, S. M. (1994). *Management of countertransference with borderline patients*. Washington, DC: American Psychiatric Press, 1994.

Ganzarain, R. (1991). Extra-analytic contacts: Fantasy and reality. *International Journal of Psycho-Analysis, 72*, 131–140.

Gediman, H. K., & Wolkenfeld, F. (1980). The parallelism in psychoanalysis and supervision: Reconsideration of triadic systems. *Psychoanalytic Quarterly, 49*, 234–255.

Gedo, J. E. (1993). *Beyond interpretation: Toward a revised theory for psychoanalysis* (Rev. ed.). Hillsdale, NJ: Analytic Press.

Gill, M. M. (1991). Indirect suggestion: A response to Oremland's *Interpretation and interaction*. In J. D. Oremland (Ed.), *Interpretation and interaction: Psychoanalysis or psychotherapy?* (pp. 137–163). Hillsdale, NJ: Analytic Press.

Gilligan, C. (1982). *In a different voice: Psychological theory and women's development*. Cambridge, MA: Harvard University Press.

Goldberg, A. (1994). Lovesickness. In J. M. Oldham & S. Bone (Eds.), *Paranoia: New psychoanalytic perspectives* (pp. 115–132). Madison, CT: International Universities Press.

Gonsiorek, J. C. (1989). Sexual exploitation by psychotherapists: Some observations on male victims and sexual orientation issues. In G. R. Schoener, J. H. Milgrom, J. C. Gonsiorek, E. T. Luepker, & R. M. Conroe (Eds.), *Psychotherapists' sexual involvement with clients: Intervention and prevention* (pp. 113–119). Minneapolis, MN: Walk-In Counseling Center.

Green, A. (1986). *On private madness*. Madison, CT: International Universities Press.

Greenacre, P. (1966). Problems of training analysis. *Psychoanalytic Quarterly, 35*, 540–567.

Greenberg, J. R. (1986a). The problem of analytic neutrality. *Contemporary Psychoanalysis, 22*, 76–86.

Greenberg, J. R. (1986b). Theoretical models and the analyst's neutrality. *Contemporary Psychoanalysis, 22*, 87–106.

Greenberg, J. R. (1991). Countertransference and reality. *Psychoanalytic Dialogues, 1*, 52–73.

Greenberg, J. R. (1995). Psychoanalytic technique and the interactive matrix. *Psychoanalytic Quarterly, 64*, 1–22.

Greenberg, J. R., & Mitchell, S. A. (1983). *Object relations in psychoanalytic theory.* Cambridge, MA: Harvard University Press.

Grinberg, L. (1970). The problems of supervision in psychoanalytic education. *International Journal of Psychoanalysis, 51*, 371–383.

Grosskurth, P. (1986). *Melanie Klein: Her world and her work.* New York: Knopf.

Grossman, W. I. (1992). Hierarchies, boundaries, and representation in the Freudian model of mental organization. *Journal of the American Psychoanalytic Association, 40*, 27–62.

Grotstein, J. S. (1994). "The old order changeth"—A reassessment of the basic rule of psychoanalytic technique: Commentary on John Linden's "Gratification and provision in psychoanalysis." *Psychoanalytic Dialogues, 4*, 595–607.

Grubrich-Simitis, I. (1986). Six letters of Sigmund Freud and Sándor Ferenczi on the interrelationship of psychoanalytic theory and technique. *International Review of Psycho-Analysis, 12*, 259–277.

Gunderson, J., & Ronningstam, E. (1991). Is narcissistic personality disorder a valid diagnosis? In J. Oldham (Ed.), *Personality disorders: New perspectives on diagnosis* (pp. 107–119). Washington, DC: American Psychiatric Press.

Gutheil, T. G., & Gabbard, G. O. (1992). Obstacles to the dynamic understanding of therapist–patient sexual relations. *American Journal of Psychotherapy, 46*, 515–525.

Gutheil, T. G., & Gabbard, G. O. (1993). The concept of boundaries in clinical practice: Theoretical and risk-management dimensions. *American Journal of Psychiatry, 150*, 188–196.

Hale, N. G. (Ed.). (1971). *James Jackson Putnam and psychoanalysis: Letters between Putnam and Sigmund Freud, Ernest Jones, William James, Sándor Ferenczi, and Morton Prince, 1877–1917.* Cambridge, MA: Harvard University Press.

Hamilton, V. (1993). Truth and reality in psychoanalytic discourse. *International Journal of Psychoanalysis, 74*, 63–79.

Hartlaub, G. H., Martin, G. C., & Rhine, M. W. (1986). Recontact with the analyst following termination: A survey of seventy-one cases. *Journal of the American Psychoanalytic Association, 34*, 885–910.

Hartmann, E. (1991). *Boundaries in the mind: A new psychology of personality.* New York: Basic Books.

Haynal, A. (1994). Introduction to *The correspondence of Sigmund Freud and Sándor Ferenczi* (Vol. 1, 1908–1914; P. T. Hoffer, Trans.). In E. Brabant, E. Falzeder, & P. Giampieri-Deutsch (Eds.). Cambridge, MA: Harvard University Press.

Hoffer, A. (in press). Introduction to *The correspondence of Sigmund Freud and Sándor Ferenczi* (Vol. 2, 1914–1919; P. T. Hoffer, Trans.). Cambridge, MA: Harvard University Press.

Hoffman, I. Z. (1983). The patient as interpreter of the analyst's experience. *Contemporary Psychoanalysis, 19,* 389–422.

Hoffman, I. Z. (1991a). Discussion: Toward a social-constructivist view of the psychoanalytic situation. *Psychoanalytic Dialogues, 1,* 74–105.

Hoffman, I. Z. (1991b). Reply to Benjamin. *Psychoanalytic Dialogues, 1,* 535–544.

Hoffman, I. Z. (1992). Some practical implications of a social-constructivist view of the psychoanalytic situation. *Psychoanalytic Dialogues, 2,* 287–304.

Hoffman, I. Z. (1994). Dialectical thinking and therapeutic action in the psychoanalytic process. *Psychoanalytic Quarterly, 63,* 187–218.

Horowitz, M. J., Duff, D. F., & Stratton, L. O. (1964). Body buffer zone. *Archives of General Psychiatry, 11,* 651–656.

Jacobs, T. J. (1986). On countertransference enactments. *Journal of the American Psycho-analytic Association, 34,* 289–307.

Jacobs, T. J. (1990). The corrective emotional experience: Its place in current technique. *Psychoanalytic Inquiry, 10,* 433–454.

Jacobs, T. J. (1993a). The inner experiences of the analyst: Their contribution to the analytic process. *International Journal of Psycho-Analysis, 74,* 7–14.

Jacobs, T. J. (1993b). Insight and experience: Commentary on Morris Eagle's "Enactments, transference, and symptomatic curing." *Psychoanalytic Dialogues, 3,* 123–127.

Jacobs, T. J. (1994a, December). Discussion of boundary violations. Presented to the Panel on Enactments of Boundary Violations at the meeting of the American Psychoanalytic Association, New York, NY.

Jacobs, T. J. (1994b, April). *Impasse and progress in analysis: On working through and its vicissitudes in patient and analyst.* Paper presented to the Quebec English Psychoanalytic Society, Montreal.

Jacobson, E. (1964). *The self and the object world.* New York: International Universities Press.

Jaggar, A. M. (1983). *Feminist politics and human nature.* Lanham, MD: Rowman & Allanheld.

Jones, E. (1955). *The life and work of Sigmund Freud: Vol. 2. The years of maturity, 1901–1919.* New York: Basic Books.

Jones, E. (1957). *The life and work of Sigmund Freud: Vol. 3. The last phase, 1919–1939.* New York: Basic Books.

Joseph, B., Feldman, J., & Spillius, E. B. (Eds.). (1989). *Psychic equilibrium and psychic change: Selected papers of Betty Joseph.* London: Tavistock/Routledge.

Kairys, D. (1964). The training analysis: A critical review of the literature and a controversial proposal. *Psychoanalytic Quarterly, 33,* 485–512.

Keller, E. F. (1985). *Reflections on gender and science.* New Haven, CT: Yale University Press.

Keller, E. F. (1986). Making gender visible in the pursuit of nature's secrets. In I. de Lauretis (Ed.), *Feminist studies/critical studies* (pp. 67–77). Bloomington: Indiana University Press.

Kernberg, O. F. (1977). Boundaries and structure in love relations. *Journal of the American Psychoanalytic Association, 25,* 81–114.

Kernberg, O. F. (1984). *Severe personality disorders: Psychotherapeutic strategies.* New Haven: Yale University Press.

Kernberg, O. F. (1993). The psychotherapeutic treatment of borderline patients. In J. Paris (Ed.), *Borderline personality disorder* (pp. 261–284). Washington, DC: American Psychiatric Press.

Kerr, J. (1993). *A most dangerous method: The story of Jung, Freud, and Sabina Spielrein.* New York: Knopf.

Kerr, J. (1994). Personal communication.

Kluft, R. P. (1989). Treating the patient who has been sexually exploited by a previous therapist. *Psychiatric Clinics of North America, 12,* 483–500.

Kohlberg, L. (1981). *The philosophy of moral development: Essays in moral development.* San Francisco: Harper & Row.

Kohut, H. (1984). *How does analysis cure?* A. Goldberg (Ed.). Chicago: University of Chicago Press.

Kovács, V. (1936). Training- and control-analysis. *International Journal of Psycho-Analysis, 17,* 346–354.

Kris, A. O. (1982). *Free association: Method and process.* New Haven: Yale University Press.

Kubie, L. S. (1950). *Practical and theoretical aspects of psychoanalysis.* New York: International Universities Press.

Lamb, D. H., Strand, K. K., Woodburn, J. R., Buchko, K. J., Lewis, J. T., & Kang J. R. (1994). Sexual and business relationships between therapists and former clients. *Psychotherapy, 31,* 270–278.

Landis, B. (1970). Ego boundaries. *Psychological Issues Monograph, 6(4),* 1–177.

Langs, R. (1977). *The therapeutic interaction: A synthesis.* New York: Jason Aronson.

Lester, E. P. (1985). The female analyst and the erotized transference. *International Journal of Psycho-Analysis, 66,* 283–293.

Lester, E. P. (1990). Gender and identity issues in the analytic process. *International Journal of Psycho-Analysis, 71,* 435–444.

Lester, E. P. (1993). Boundaries and gender: Their interplay in the analytic situation. *Psychoanalytic Inquiry, 13,* 153–172.

Lester, E. P., Jodoin, R.-M., & Robertson, B. M. (1989). Countertransference dreams reconsidered: A survey. *International Review of Psycho-Analysis, 16,* 305–314.

Lester, E. P., & Robertson, B. M. (1995). Multiple interactive processes in psychoanalytic supervision. *Psychoanalytic Inquiry, 15,* 211–225.

Levin, R., Galin, J., & Zywiak, B. (1991). Nightmares, boundaries, and creativity. *Dreaming, 1,* 63–74.

LeVine, R. A. (1991). Gender differences: Interpreting anthropological data. In M. T. Notman & C. C. Notman (Eds.), *Women and men: New perspectives on gender differences* (pp. 1–8). Washington, DC: American Psychiatric Press.

Lewin, K. (1936). *Principles of topological psychology.* New York: McGraw-Hill.

Limentani, A. (1982). On the "unexpected" termination of psychoanalytic therapy. *Psychoanalytic Inquiry, 2,* 419–440.

Lindon, J. A. (1994). Gratification and provision in psychoanalysis: Should we get rid of "the rule of abstinence"? *Psychoanalytic Dialogues, 4,* 549–582.

Little, M. I. (1990). *Psychotic anxieties and containment: A personal record of an analysis with Winnicott.* Northvale, NJ: Jason Aronson.

Loewald, H. W. (1960). On the therapeutic action of psycho-analysis. *International Journal of Psycho-Analysis, 41,* 16–33.

Loewald, H. W. (1980). *Papers on psychoanalysis.* New Haven, CT: Yale University Press.

Luborsky, L., Diguer, L., & Barber, J. P. (1994, May). *Changes in a transference measure in psychoanalysis.* Paper presented at the annual meeting of the American Psychiatric Association. Philadelphia, PA.

Mahler, M. S., Pine, F., & Bergman, A. (1975). *The psychological birth of the human infant: Symbiosis and individuation.* New York: Basic Books.

Mahony, P. J. (1987). *Psychoanalysis and discourse.* London: The New Library of Psychoanalysis.

Mahony, P. J. (1993). Freud's cases: Are they valuable today? *International Journal of Psycho-Analysis, 74,* 1027–1035.

Maltsberger, J. T. (1993, April 15). A career plundered. Presidential address of the American Association of Suicidology, San Francisco, CA.

Margolis, M. (1994, November 19–20). *Therapist–patient sexual involvement: Clinical experiences and institutional responses.* Paper presented at the conference, New Psychoanalytic Perspectives on the Treatment of Sexual

Trauma, sponsored by the Boston Psychoanalytic Society and Institute, Boston, MA.

Margolis, M. (in press). Therapist–patient sexual involvement: Clinical experiences and institutional responses. *Psychoanalytic Inquiry*.

Mayer, E. L. (1994a, December). A case of "severe boundary violations" between analyst and patient. Presented to the Panel on Enactments of Boundary Violations at the meeting of the American Psychoanalytic Association, New York, NY.

Mayer, E. L. (1994b). Some implications for psychoanalytic technique drawn from analysis of a dying patient. *Psychoanalytic Quarterly, 63*, 1–19.

McCarthy, B. (1994). *Nightmares and sleepwalking following child sexual abuse: Report of an adult in analysis.* Paper presented at the Ontario Psychiatric Association, Toronto.

McGuire, W. (Ed.). (1974). *The Freud/Jung letters: The correspondence between Sigmund Freud and C. G. Jung.* Princeton, NJ: Princeton University Press.

McLaughlin, J. T. (1991). Clinical and theoretical aspects of enactment. *Journal of the American Psychoanalytic Association, 39*, 595–614.

McLaughlin, J. T. (1995). Touching limits in the analytic dyad. *Psychoanalytic Quarterly, 64*, 433–465.

Meerloo, J. A. M. (1952). Free association, silence, and the multiple function of speech. *Psychiatric Quarterly, 26*, 21–32.

Meloy, J. R. (1988). *The psychopathic mind: Origins, dynamics, and treatment.* Northvale, NJ: Jason Aronson.

Meltzer, D. (1975). Adhesive identification. *Contemporary Psychoanalysis, 11*, 289–310.

Meltzoff, A. N., & Moore, M. K. (1992). Early imitation within a functional framework: The importance of person identity, movement, and development. *Infant Behavior and Development, 15*, 479–505.

Meng, H., & Freud, E. L. (Eds.). (1963). *Psychoanalysis and faith: The letters of Sigmund Freud and Oscar Pfister.* New York: Basic Books.

Meyers, H. C. (1991). Perversion in fantasy and furtive enactments. In E. I. Fogel & W. A. Myers (Eds.), *Perversions and near-perversions in clinical practice: New psychoanalytic perspectives* (pp. 93–108). New Haven, CT: Yale University Press.

Mitchell, S. A. (1993). *Hope and dread in psychoanalysis.* New York: Basic Books.

Norman, H. F., Blacker, K. H., Oremland, J. D., & Barrett, W. G. (1976). The fate of the transference neurosis after termination of a satisfactory analysis. *Journal of the American Psychoanalytic Association, 24*, 471–498.

Notman, M. T., & Nadelson, C. (1991). A review of gender differences in brain and behavior. In M. T. Notman & C. C. Notman (Eds.), *Women and men: New perspectives on gender differences* (pp. 23–35). Washington, DC: American Psychiatric Press.

Novey, R. (1991). The abstinence of the psychoanalyst. *Bulletin of the Menninger Clinic, 55,* 344–362.

Novick, J. (1982) Termination: Themes and issues. *Psychoanalytic Inquiry, 2,* 329–365.

Novick, J. (in press). Termination conceivable and inconceivable. *Psychoanalytic Psychology, 12.*

Ogden, T. H. (1979). On projective identification. *International Journal of Psycho-Analysis, 60,* 357–373.

Ogden, T. H. (1982). *Projective identification and psychotherapeutic technique.* New York: Jason Aronson.

Ogden, T. H. (1986). *The matrix of the mind: Object relations and the psychoanalytic dialogue.* Northvale, NJ: Jason Aronson.

Ogden, T. H. (1989). *The primitive edge of experience.* Northvale, NJ: Jason Aronson.

Ogden, T. H. (1994). *Subjects of analysis.* Northvale, NJ: Jason Aronson.

Oremland, J. D., Blacker, K. H., & Norman, H. F. (1975). Incompleteness in "successful" psychoanalyses: A follow-up study. *Journal of the American Psychoanalytic Association, 23,* 819–844.

Panel (1992). Enactments in psychoanalysis (Morton Johan, reporter). *Journal of the American Psychoanalytic Association, 40,* 827–841.

Paris, J., & Zweig-Frank, H. (1993). Parental bonding in borderline personality disorder. In J. Paris (Ed.), *Borderline personality disorder: Etiology and treatment* (pp. 141–159). Washington, DC: American Psychiatric Press.

Parker, S. (1976). The precultural basis of the incest taboo: Toward a biosocial theory. *American Anthropologist, 78,* 285–305.

Paskauskas, R. A. (Ed.). (1993). *The complete correspondence of Sigmund Freud and Ernest Jones, 1908–1939.* Cambridge, MA: The Belknap Press of Harvard University Press.

Pfeffer, A. Z. (1963). The meaning of the analyst after analysis: A contribution to the theory of therapeutic results. *Journal of the American Psychoanalytic Association, 11,* 229–244.

Pfeffer, A. Z. (1993). After the analysis: Analyst as both old and new object. *Journal of the American Psychoanalytic Association, 41,* 323–337.

Phillips, A. (1994). *On flirtation.* Cambridge, MA: Harvard University Press.

Pine, F. (1990). *Drive, ego, object, and self.* New York: Basic Books.

Polster, S. (1983). Ego boundary as process: A systematic contextual approach. *Psychiatry, 46,* 247–258.

Pope, K. S., & Bouhoutsos, J. (1986). *Sexual intimacy between therapists and patients.* New York: Praeger.

Pope, K. S., Levenson, H., & Schover, L. R. (1979). Sexual intimacy in psychological training: Results and implications of a national survey. *American Psychologist, 34,* 682–689.

Pope, K. S., & Vetter, V. A. (1991). Prior therapist–patient sexual involvement among patients seen by psychologists. *Psychotherapy, 28,* 429–438.

Pulver, S. E. (1992). Psychic change: Insight or relationship? *International Journal of Psycho-Analysis, 73,* 199–208.

Quinn, S. (1987). *A mind of her own: The life of Karen Horney.* New York: Summit Books.

Rangell, L. (in press). Review of *The complete correspondence of Sigmund Freud and Ernest Jones, 1908–1939.* R. A. Paskauskas (Ed.). *Journal of the American Psychoanalytic Association.*

Rapaport, D., & Gill, M. M. (1959). The points of view and assumptions of metapsychology. In M. M. Goldberg (Ed.), *The collected papers of David Rapaport* (pp. 795–811). New York: Basic Books.

Reich, W. (1949). *Character-analysis* (T. P. Wolfe, Trans.). New York: Orgone Institute Press.

Reiser, M. F. (1990). *Memory in mind and brain: What dream imagery reveals.* New York: Basic Books.

Renik, O. (1993). Analytic interaction: Conceptualizing technique in light of the analyst's irreducible subjectivity. *Psychoanalytic Quarterly, 62,* 553–571.

Richards, A. (1991, fall). Discussion presented to the panel, Toward a Definition of the Term and Concept of Interaction, at the meeting of the American Psychoanalytic Association, New York, NY.

Roazen, P. (1975). *Freud and his followers.* New York: Knopf.

Rockland, L. H. (1992). *Supportive psychotherapy for borderline patients: A psychodynamic approach.* New York: Guilford Press.

Rothstein, A. (1994, December). *The seduction of money.* Paper presented at the meeting of the American Psychoanalytic Association, New York, NY.

Roughton, R. E. (1993). Useful aspects of acting out: Repetition, enactment, and actualization. *Journal of the American Psychoanalytic Association, 41,* 443–472.

Royce, J. (1901). *The world and the individual.* New York: Macmillan.

Sabbadini, A. (1989). Boundaries of timelessness: Some thoughts about the temporary dimension of the psychoanalytic space. *International Journal of Psycho-Analysis, 70,* 305–313.

Sachs, D. M., & Shapiro, S. H. (1976). On parallel processes in therapy and teaching. *Psychoanalytic Quarterly, 45,* 394–415.

Sandler, J. (1976). Countertransference and role-responsiveness. *International Review of Psycho-Analysis, 3,* 43–47.

Sartre, J. P. (1956). *Being and nothingness: An essay on phenomenological ontology.* London: Methuen.

Schachter, J. (1990). Post-termination patient–analyst contact: I. Analysts' attitudes and experience; II. Impact on patients. *International Journal of Psycho-Analysis, 71*, 475–486.

Schachter, J. (1992). Concepts of termination and post-termination patient-analyst contact. *International Journal of Psycho-Analysis, 73*, 137–154.

Schafer, R. (1983). *The analytic attitude.* New York: Basic Books.

Schafer, R. (1992). *Retelling a life: Narration and dialogue in psychoanalysis.* New York: Basic Books.

Schafer, R. (1993). Five readings of Freud's "Observations on transference-love." In E. S. Person, A. Hagelin, & P. Fonagy (Eds.), *On Freud's observations on transference love* (pp. 75–95). New Haven, CT: Yale University Press.

Schlessinger, N., & Robbins, F. (1974). Assessment and follow-up in psychoanalysis. *Journal of the American Psychoanalytic Association, 22*, 542–567.

Schoener, G. R., Milgrom, J. H., Gonsiorek, J. C., Luepker, E. T., & Conroe, R. M. (1989). *Psychotherapists' sexual involvement with clients: Intervention and prevention.* Minneapolis, MN: Walk-In Counseling Center.

Searles, H. F. (1979). *Countertransference and related subjects: Selected papers.* Madison, CT: International Universities Press.

Segal, H. (1957). Notes on symbol formation. *International Journal of Psycho-Analysis, 38*, 391–397.

Segal, H. (1994). Phantasy and reality. *International Journal of Psycho-Analysis, 75*, 395–401.

Simon, R. I. (1992). Treatment boundary violations: Clinical, ethical, and legal considerations. *Bulletin of the American Academy of Psychiatry and the Law, 20*, 269–288.

Spillius, E. B. (1992). Clinical experiences of projective identification. In R. Anderson (Ed.), *Clinical lectures on Klein and Bion* (pp. 59–73). London and New York: Tavistock/Routledge.

Spruiell, V. (1983). The rules and frames of the psychoanalytic situation. *Psychoanalytic Quarterly, 52*, 1–33.

Stepansky, P. E. (Ed.). (1988). *The memoirs of Margaret S. Mahler.* New York: Free Press.

Sterba, R. (1934). The fate of the ego in analytic therapy. *International Journal of Psycho-Analysis, 15*, 117–126.

Stern, D. N. (1985). *The interpersonal world of the child: A view from psychoanalysis and developmental psychology.* New York: Basic Books.

Stoller, R. J. (1985). *Observing the erotic imagination.* New Haven: Yale University Press.

Stone, L. (1984). *Transference and its context: Selected papers on psychoanalysis*, New York: Jason Aronson.

Stone, M. H. (1989). Borderline personality disorder. In R. Michels, A. M. Cooper, S. B. Guze, L. L. Judd, G. L. Klerman, & A. J. Solnit (Eds.), *Psychiatry* (Vol. 1, pp. 1–18). New York: Basic Books.

Stone, M. H. (1993). Etiology of borderline personality disorder: Psychobiological factors contributing to an underlying irritability. In J. Paris (Ed.), *Borderline personality disorder* (pp. 87–101). Washington, DC: American Psychiatric Press.

Strasburger, L. H., Jorgenson, L., & Sutherland, P. (1992). The prevention of psychotherapist sexual misconduct: Avoiding the slippery slope. *American Journal of Psychotherapy, 46*, 544–555.

Strean, H. S. (1993). *Therapists who have sex with their patients: Treatment and recovery.* New York: Brunner/Mazel.

Sullivan, H. S. (1954). *The psychiatric interview.* New York: Norton.

Tausk, V. (1918/1933). On the origin of the "influencing machine" in schizophrenia. *Psychoanalytic Quarterly, 2*, 519–556.

Torras de Beà, E. (1992). Towards a "good enough" training analysis. *International Review of Psycho-Analysis, 19*, 159–167.

Treurniet, N. (1988). *Some vulnerabilities inherent to the training situation.* Paper presented at the Third EPF Conference of Training Analysts, Amsterdam, Holland.

Tustin, F. (1980). Autistic objects. *International Review of Psycho-Analysis, 7*, 27–39.

Tustin, F. (1981). *Autistic states in children.* London: Routledge & Kegan Paul.

Tustin, F. (1984). Autistic shapes. *International Review of Psycho-Analysis, 11*, 279–290.

Twemlow, S. W., & Gabbard, G. O. (Eds.). (1989). The lovesick therapist. In *Sexual exploitation in professional relationships* (pp. 71–87). Washington, DC: American Psychiatric Press.

Van der Waals, H. G. (1965). Problems of narcissism. *Bulletin of the Menninger Clinic, 29*, 293–311.

Viederman, M. (1991). The real person of the analyst and his role in the process of psychoanalytic cure. *Journal of the American Psychoanalytic Association, 39*, 451–489.

Viorst, J. (1982). Experiences in loss at end of analysis: The analyst's response to termination. *Psychoanalytic Inquiry, 2*, 399–418.

Waldinger, R. J. (1994). Boundary crossings and boundary violations: Thoughts on navigating a slippery slope. *Harvard Review of Psychiatry, 2*, 225–227.

Wallace, E., & Alonso, A. (1994). Privacy versus disclosure in psychotherapy supervision. In S. E. Greben & R. Ruskin (Eds.), *Clinical perspectives on psychotherapy supervision* (pp. 211–230). Washington, DC: American Psychiatric Press.

Wallerstein, R. S. (1986). *Forty-two lives in treatment: A study of psychoanalysis and psychotherapy.* New York: Guilford Press.

Warner, S. L. (1994). Freud's analysis of Horace Frink, M.D.: A previously unexplained therapeutic disaster. *Journal of the American Academy of Psychoanalysis, 22,* 137–152.

Weigert, E. (1955). Special problems in connection with termination of training analyses. *Journal of the American Psychoanalytic Association, 3,* 630–640.

Weinshel, E. M. (1990). Further observations on the psychoanalytic process. *Psychoanalytic Quarterly, 59,* 629–649.

Weiss, E. (1952). Introduction to *Ego psychology and the psychosis,* by P. Federn (pp. 1–21). New York: Basic Books.

Weiss, J., Sampson, H., & the Mount Zion Psychotherapy Research Group (1986). *The psychoanalytic process: Theory, clinical observation, and empirical research.* New York: Guilford Press.

Wilden, A. (1972). *System and structure: Essays in communication and exchange.* London: Tavistock.

Williams, M. H. (1992). Exploitation and inference: Mapping the damage from therapist–patient sexual involvement. *American Psychologist, 47,* 412–421.

Winer, R. (1994). *Close encounters: A relational view of the therapeutic process.* Northvale, NJ: Jason Aronson.

Winnicott, D. W. (1953). Transitional objects and transitional phenomena. *International Journal of Psycho-Analysis, 34,* 89–97.

Winnicott, D. W. (1960/1965). The theory of the parent–infant relationship. In *The maturational processes and the facilitating environment: Studies in the theory of emotional development* (pp. 37–55). New York: International Universities Press.

Winnicott, D. W. (1963/1965). Morals and education. In *The maturational processes and the facilitating environment: Studies in the theory of emotional development* (pp. 93–105). New York: International Universities Press.

Witelson, S. F. (1985). The brain connection: The corpus callosum is larger in left-handers. *Science, 229,* 665–668.

Wohlberg, J. (in press). What do victims want? *Psychoanalytic Inquiry.*

Wurmser, L. (1987). Flight from conscience: Experiences with the psychoanalytic treatment of compulsive drug abusers: Part Two. Dynamic and therapeutic conclusions from the experiences with psychoanalysis of drug users. *Journal of Substance Abuse Treatment, 4,* 169–179.

Yariv, G. (1989). Blurred edges: Some difficulties and paradoxes about forming boundaries. *British Journal of Psychotherapy, 6,* 103–111.

Young-Bruehl, E. (1988). *Anna Freud: A biography.* New York: Summit Books.

Zweibel, R. (1985). The dynamics of the countertransference dream. *International Review of Psycho-Analysis, 12,* 87–99.

Index